BASIC

ENGLISH GRAMMAR

Third Edition

RESOURCE DISC

TEACHER'S GUIDE

PEARSON Longman

Betty Schrampfer Azar
Stacy A. Hagen

Basic English Grammar, Third Edition
Teacher's Guide

Pearson Education, 10 Bank Street, White Plains, NY 10606

Staff credits: The people who made up the **Basic English Grammar
Teacher's Guide, Third Edition** team, representing editorial, production,
design, and manufacturing, are Nancy Flaggman, Margo Grant, Melissa
Leyva, Robert Ruvo, Ruth Voetmann, and Pat Wosczyk.

Azar Associates
Shelley Hartle, Editor
Susan Van Etten, Manager

Text design and composition: Carlisle Publishing Services
Text font: 10.5/12 Plantin

ISBN: 0-13-205215-6
      978-0-13-205215-3

Printed in the United States of America
1 2 3 4 5 6 7 8 9 10-BAH-11 10 09 08 07 06

Contents

PREFACE . . . . **ix**

INTRODUCTION . . . . **xi**

    General Aims of *Basic English Grammar* . . . . **xi**

    Suggestions for the Classroom . . . . **xi**
        Presenting the Grammar Charts xi
        Additional Suggestions for Using the Charts xii
            The Here-and-Now Classroom Context xii
            Demonstration Techniques xii
            Using the Board xii
            Oral Exercises with Chart Presentations xii
            The Role of Terminology xiii
        Balancing Teacher and Student Talk xiii
        Exercise Types xiii
            Preview Exercises xiii
            First Exercise after a Chart xiii
            Written Exercises: General Techniques xiii
                Open-Ended Exercises xv
                Paragraph Practice xv
                 Error-Analysis Exercises xvi
            "Let's Talk" Exercises xvi
                Pairwork Exercises xvii
                Small Group Exercises xvii
                Class Activity Exercises (teacher-led) xvii
            Listening Exercises xvii
            Pronunciation Exercises xviii
            Games and Activities xviii
        Monitoring Errors in Oral Work xviii
        Homework xix

    The *Workbook* As Independent Study . . . . **xix**

    Supplementary Resource Texts . . . . **xx**

    Notes on American vs. British English . . . . **xx**
        Differences in Grammar xx
        Differences in Spelling xx
        Differences in Vocabulary xxi

    Key to Pronunciation Symbols . . . . **xxii**
        The Phonetic Alphabet (Symbols for American English) xxii
            Consonants xxii
            Vowels xxii

Chapter 1   **USING *BE*** 1

    1-1   Noun + *is* + noun: singular 2
    1-2   Noun + *are* + noun: plural 4
    1-3   Pronoun + *be* + noun 5
    1-4   Contractions with *be* 6
    1-5   Negative with *be* 7
    1-6   *Be* + adjective 8
    1-7   *Be* + a place 10
    1-8   Summary: basic sentence patterns with *be* 11

Chapter 2   **USING *BE* AND *HAVE*** 12

    2-1   Yes/no questions with *be* 12
    2-2   Short answers to yes/no questions 12
    2-3   Questions with *be*: using *where* 13
    2-4   Using *have* and *has* 14
    2-5   Using *my, your, his, her, our, their* 15
    2-6   Using *this* and *that* 17
    2-7   Using *these* and *those* 17
    2-8   Asking questions with *what* and *who* + *be* 18

Chapter 3   **USING THE SIMPLE PRESENT** 22

    3-1   Form and basic meaning of the simple present tense 22
    3-2   Using frequency adverbs: *always, usually, often, sometimes, seldom, rarely, never* 23
    3-3   Other frequency expressions 24
    3-4   Using frequency adverbs with *be* 25
    3-5   Spelling and pronunciation of final *-es* 26
    3-6   Adding final *-s/-es* to words that end in *-y* 26
    3-7   Irregular singular verbs: *has, does, goes* 27
    3-8   Spelling and pronunciation of final *-s/-es* 28
    3-9   The simple present: negative 29
   3-10   The simple present: yes/no questions 30
   3-11   The simple present: asking information questions with *where* 31
   3-12   The simple present: asking information questions with *when* and *what time* 32
   3-13   Summary: information questions with *be* and *do* 33

Chapter 4   **USING THE PRESENT PROGRESSIVE** 36

    4-1   *Be* + *-ing*: the present progressive tense 36
    4-2   Spelling of *-ing* 38
    4-3   The present progressive: negatives 39
    4-4   The present progressive: questions 40
    4-5   The simple present vs. the present progressive 41
    4-6   Nonaction verbs not used in the present progressive 43
    4-7   *See, look at, watch, hear*, and *listen to* 43
    4-8   *Think about* and *think that* 44

Chapter 5   **TALKING ABOUT THE PRESENT** 46

    5-1   Using *it* to talk about time 46
    5-2   Prepositions of time 47
    5-3   Using *it* to talk about the weather 48
    5-4   *There* + *be* 49
    5-5   *There* + *be*: yes/no questions 50
    5-6   *There* + *be*: asking questions with *how many* 51
    5-7   Prepositions of place 52

5-8	Some prepositions of place: a list	52
5-9	*Need* and *want* + a noun or an infinitive	54
5-10	*Would like*	55
5-11	*Would like* vs. *like*	56

Chapter 6 NOUNS AND PRONOUNS **60**

6-1	Nouns: subjects and objects	60
6-2	Adjective + noun	62
6-3	Subject pronouns and object pronouns	64
6-4	Nouns: singular and plural	65
6-5	Nouns: irregular plural forms	67

Chapter 7 COUNT AND NONCOUNT NOUNS **69**

7-1	Nouns: count and noncount	69
7-2	Using *an* vs. *a*	70
7-3	Using *a/an* vs. *some*	71
7-4	Measurements with noncount nouns	73
7-5	Using *many, much, a few, a little*	74
7-6	Using *the*	76
7-7	Using Ø (no article) to make generalizations	78
7-8	Using *some* and *any*	79

Chapter 8 EXPRESSING PAST TIME, PART 1 .... **81**

8-1	Using *be:* past time	81
8-2	Past of *be:* negative	82
8-3	Past of *be:* questions	83
8-4	The simple past tense: using *-ed*	85
8-5	Past time words: *yesterday, last,* and *ago*	86
8-6	The simple past: irregular verbs (Group 1)	87
8-7	The simple past: negative	89
8-8	The simple past: yes/no questions	91
8-9	Irregular verbs (Group 2)	92
8-10	Irregular verbs (Group 3)	93
8-11	Irregular verbs (Group 4)	94

Chapter 9 EXPRESSING PAST TIME, PART 2 .... **97**

9-1	The simple past: using *where, when, what time,* and *why*	97
9-2	Questions with *what*	98
9-3	Questions with *who*	100
9-4	Irregular verbs (Group 5)	101
9-5	Irregular verbs (Group 6)	102
9-6	Irregular verbs (Group 7)	102
9-7	*Before* and *after* in time clauses	103
9-8	*When* in time clauses	104
9-9	The present progressive and the past progressive	105
9-10	Using *while* with the past progressive	106
9-11	*While* vs. *when* in past time clauses	107
9-12	Simple past vs. past progressive	107

Chapter 10 EXPRESSING FUTURE TIME, PART 1 .... **111**

10-1	Future time: using *be going to*	111
10-2	Using the present progressive to express future time	113
10-3	Words used for past time and future time	114
10-4	Using *a couple of* or *a few* with *ago* (past) and *in* (future)	115

10-5	Using *today, tonight,* and *this* + *morning, afternoon, evening, week, month, year* 116
10-6	Future time: using *will* 118
10-7	Asking questions with *will* 119
10-8	Verb summary: present, past, and future 120
10-9	Verb summary: forms of *be* 121

Chapter 11   EXPRESSING FUTURE TIME, PART 2 .... **124**

11-1	*May/Might* vs. *will* 124
11-2	*Maybe* (one word) vs. *may be* (two words) 125
11-3	Future time clauses with *before, after,* and *when* 126
11-4	Clauses with *if* 127
11-5	Expressing habitual present with time clauses and *if*-clauses 128
11-6	Using *what* + a form of *do* 129

Chapter 12   MODALS, PART 1: EXPRESSING ABILITY **133**

12-1	Using *can* 133
12-2	Pronunciation of *can* and *can't* 134
12-3	Using *can:* questions 135
12-4	Using *know how to* 136
12-5	Using *could:* past of *can* 137
12-6	Using *be able to* 138
12-7	Using *very* and *too* + adjective 139
12-8	Using *two, too,* and *to* 140
12-9	More about prepositions: *at* and *in* for place 141

Chapter 13   MODALS, PART 2: ADVICE, NECESSITY, REQUESTS, SUGGESTIONS **143**

13-1	Using *should* 143
13-2	Using *have* + infinitive *(have to/has to)* 144
13-3	Using *must* 145
13-4	Polite questions: *may I, could I,* and *can I* 147
13-5	Polite questions: *could you* and *would you* 147
13-6	Imperative sentences 148
13-7	Modal auxiliaries 149
13-8	Summary chart: modal auxiliaries and similar expressions 150
13-9	Using *let's* 150

Chapter 14   NOUNS AND MODIFIERS **152**

14-1	Modifying nouns with adjectives and nouns 152
14-2	Word order of adjectives 154
14-3	Expressions of quantity: *all of, most of, some of, almost all of* 156
14-4	Expressions of quantity: subject-verb agreement 156
14-5	Expressions of quantity: *one of, none of* 157
14-6	Indefinite pronouns: *nothing* and *no one* 159
14-7	Indefinite pronouns: *something, someone, anything, anyone* 159
14-8	Using *every* 160
14-9	Linking verbs + adjectives 160
14-10	Adjectives and adverbs 161

Chapter 15   POSSESSIVES **163**

15-1	Possessive nouns 163
15-2	Possessive: irregular plural nouns 164
15-3	Possessive pronouns: *mine, yours, his, hers, ours, theirs* 165
15-4	Questions with *whose* 166

Chapter 16   **MAKING COMPARISONS** **169**

16-1   Comparisons: using *the same (as)*, *similar (to)* and *different (from)* 169
16-2   Comparisons: using *like* and *alike* 171
16-3   The comparative: using *-er* and *more* 171
16-4   The superlative: using *-est* and *most* 173
16-5   Using *one of* + superlative + plural noun 175
16-6   Using *but* 176
16-7   Using verbs after *but* 177
16-8   Making comparisons with adverbs 178

MAP **180**

INDEX **182**

Preface

This *Teacher's Guide* is intended as a practical aid to teachers. In it, you will find notes on the content of each unit, suggestions for exercises and classroom activities, and answers to the exercises.

General teaching information can be found in the *Introduction.* It includes
- the rationale and general aims of *Basic English Grammar.*
- classroom techniques for presenting charts and using exercises.
- suggestions for using the *Workbook* in connection with the student book.
- supplementary resource texts.
- comments on differences between American and British English.
- a key to the pronunciation symbols used in this *Guide.*

The rest of the *Guide* contains notes on charts and exercises. The chart notes may include
- suggestions for presenting the information to students.
- points to emphasize.
- common problems to anticipate.
- assumptions underlying the contents.
- additional background notes on grammar and usage.

The exercise notes may include
- the focus of the exercise.
- suggested techniques.
- points to emphasize.
- expansion activities.
- answers.
- item notes on cultural content, vocabulary, and idiomatic usage. (Some of these item notes are specifically intended to aid teachers who are nonnative speakers of English.)

Introduction

General Aims of *Basic English Grammar*

Basic English Grammar is a beginning-level ESL/EFL developmental skills text. In the experience of many classroom teachers, adult language learners like to spend at least some time on grammar with a teacher to help them. The process of looking at and practicing grammar becomes a springboard for expanding the learners' abilities in speaking, writing, listening, and reading.

Most students find it helpful to have special time set aside in their English curriculum to focus on grammar. Students generally have many questions about English grammar and appreciate the opportunity to work with a text and a teacher to make some sense out of the bewildering array of forms and usages in this strange language. These understandings provide the basis for advances in usage ability in a relaxed, accepting classroom that encourages risk-taking as students experiment, both in speaking and writing, with ways to communicate their ideas in a new language.

Teaching grammar does not mean lecturing on grammatical patterns and terminology. It does not mean bestowing knowledge and being an arbiter of correctness. Teaching grammar is the art of helping students make sense, little by little, of a huge, puzzling construct, and of engaging them in various activities that enhance usage abilities in all skill areas and promote easy, confident communication.

The text depends upon a partnership with a teacher; it is the teacher who animates and directs the students' language-learning experiences. In practical terms, the aim of the text is to support you, the teacher, by providing a wealth and variety of material for you to adapt to your individual teaching situation. Using grammar as a base to promote overall English usage ability, teacher and text can engage students in interesting discourse, challenge their minds and skills, and intrigue them with the power of language as well as the need for accuracy to create understanding among people.

Suggestions for the Classroom

• Presenting the Grammar Charts

Each chart contains a concise visual presentation of the structures to be learned. Presentation techniques often depend upon the content of the chart, the level of the class, and students' learning styles. Not all students react to the charts in the same way. Some students need the security of thoroughly understanding a chart before trying to use the structure. Others like to experiment more freely with using new structures; they refer to the charts only incidentally, if at all.

Given these different learning strategies, you should vary your presentation techniques and not expect students to "learn" or memorize the charts. The charts are simply a starting point (and a point of reference) for class activities. Some charts may require particular methods of presentation, but generally any of the following techniques are viable.

Technique #1: Present the examples in the chart, perhaps highlighting them on the board. Add your own examples, relating them to your students' experience as much as possible. For example, when presenting simple present tense, talk about what students do every day: come to school, study English, and so on. Elicit other examples of the target structure from your students. Then proceed to the exercises.

Technique #2: Elicit target structures from students before they look at the chart in the *Student Book.* Ask leading questions that are designed so the answers will include the target structure. (For example, with present progressive, ask: "What are you doing right now?") You may want to write students' answers on the board and relate them to selected examples in the chart. Then proceed to the exercises.

Technique #3: Instead of beginning with a chart, begin with the first exercise after the chart. As you work through it with your students, present the information in the chart or refer to examples in the chart.

Technique #4: Assign a chart for homework; students bring questions to class. (You may even want to include an accompanying exercise.) With advanced students, you might not need to deal with every chart and exercise thoroughly in class. With intermediate students, it is generally advisable to clarify charts and do most of the exercises in each section.

Technique #5: Some charts have a preview exercise or pretest. Begin with these, and use them as a guide to decide what areas to focus on. When working through the chart, you can refer to the examples in these exercises.

With all of the above, the explanations on the right side of the chart are most effective when recast by the teacher, not read word for word. Keep the discussion focus on the examples. Students by and large learn from examples and lots of practice, not from explanations. In the charts, the explanations focus attention on what students should be noticing in the examples and the exercises.

• Additional Suggestions for Using the Charts

The Here-and-Now Classroom Context
For every chart, try to relate the target structure to an immediate classroom or real-life context. Make up or elicit examples that use the students' names, activities, and interests. For example, when introducing possessive adjectives (Chart 2-5) use yourself and your students to present all the sentences in the chart. Then have students refer to the chart. The here-and-now classroom context is, of course, one of the grammar teacher's best aids.

Demonstration Techniques
Demonstration can be very helpful to explain the meaning of a structure. You and your students can act out situations that demonstrate the target structure. For example, the present progressive can easily be demonstrated (e.g., "I *am writing* on the board right now"). Of course, not all grammar lends itself to this technique.

Using the Board
In discussing the target structure of a chart, use the classroom board whenever possible. Not all students have adequate listening skills for teacher talk, and not all students can visualize and understand the various relationships within, between, and among structures. Draw boxes, circles, and arrows to illustrate connections between the elements of a structure. A visual presentation helps many students.

Oral Exercises with Chart Presentations

Oral exercises usually follow a chart, but sometimes they precede it so that you can elicit student-generated examples of the target structure as a springboard to the discussion of the grammar. If you prefer to introduce a particular structure to your students orally, you can always use an oral exercise prior to the presentation of a chart and its written exercises, no matter what the given order in the text.

The Role of Terminology

Students need to understand the terminology, but don't require or expect detailed definitions of terms, either in class discussion or on tests. Terminology is just a tool, a useful label for the moment, so that you and your students can talk to each other about English grammar.

• Balancing Teacher and Student Talk

The goal of all language learning is to understand and communicate. The teacher's main task is to direct and facilitate that process. The learner is an active participant, not merely a passive receiver of rules to be memorized. Therefore, many of the exercises in the text are designed to promote interaction between learners as a bridge to real communication.

The teacher has a crucial leadership role, with teacher talk a valuable and necessary part of a grammar classroom. Sometimes you will need to spend time clarifying the information in a chart, leading an exercise, answering questions about exercise items, or explaining an assignment. These periods of teacher talk should, however, be balanced by longer periods of productive learning activity when the students are doing most of the talking. It is important for the teacher to know when to step back and let students lead. Interactive group and pairwork play an important role in the language classroom.

• Exercise Types

Preview Exercises (SEE Exercise 2, p. 2 and Exercise 1, p. 179.)

The purpose of these exercises is to let students discover what they know and don't know about the target structure in order to get them interested in a chart. Essentially, preview exercises illustrate a possible teaching technique: quiz students first as a springboard for presenting the grammar in a chart.

Any exercise can be used as a preview. You do not need to follow the order of material in the text. Adapt the material to your own needs and techniques.

First Exercise after a Chart (SEE Exercise 14, p. 33 and Exercise 16, p. 63.)

In most cases, this exercise includes an example of each item shown in the chart. Students can do the exercise together as a class, and the teacher can refer to chart examples where necessary. More advanced classes can complete it as homework. The teacher can use this exercise as a guide to see how well students understand the basics of the target structure(s).

Written Exercises: General Techniques

The written exercises range from those that are tightly controlled and manipulative to those that encourage free responses and require creative, independent language use. Following are some general techniques for the written exercises.

Technique A: A student can be asked to read an item aloud. You can say whether the student's answer is correct or not, or you can open up discussion by asking the rest of the class if the answer is correct. For example:

> TEACHER: Juan, would you please read item 3?
> STUDENT: Ali *speaks* Arabic.
> TEACHER (to the class): Do the rest of you agree with Juan's answer?

The slow-moving pace of this method is beneficial for discussion not only of grammar items, but also of vocabulary and content. Students have time to digest information and ask questions. You have the opportunity to judge how well they understand the grammar. However, this time-consuming technique doesn't always, or even usually, need to be used, especially with more advanced classes.

Technique B: The teacher reads the first part of the item, then pauses for students to call out the answer in unison. For example:

> ITEM entry: "Ali *(speak)* _____ Arabic."
> TEACHER (with the students looking at their texts): Ali . . . .
> STUDENTS (in unison): speaks (with possibly a few incorrect responses scattered about)
> TEACHER: . . . speaks Arabic. *Speaks.* Do you have any questions?

This technique saves a lot of time in class, but is also slow-paced enough to allow for questions and discussion of grammar, vocabulary, and content. It is essential that students have prepared the exercise by writing in their books, so it must be assigned ahead of time as homework.

Technique C: Students complete the exercise for homework, and you go over the answers with them. Students can take turns giving the answers, or you can supply them. Depending on the importance and length of the sentence, you may want to include the entire sentence or just the answer. Answers can be given one at a time while you take questions, or you can give the answers to the whole exercise before opening it up for questions. When a student supplies the answers, the other students can ask him/her questions if they disagree.

Technique D: Divide the class into groups (or pairs) and have each group prepare one set of answers that they all agree is correct prior to class discussion. The leader of each group can present its answers.

Another option is to have the groups (or pairs) hand in their sets of answers for correction and possibly a grade.

It's also possible to turn these exercises into games wherein the group with the best set of answers gets some sort of reward (perhaps applause from the rest of the class).

One option for correction of group work is to circle or mark the errors on one paper the group turns in, make photocopies of that paper for each member of the group, and then hand back the papers for students to rewrite individually. At that point, you can assign a grade if desired.

Of course, you can always mix Techniques A, B, C, and D — with students reading some aloud, with you prompting unison responses for some, with you simply giving the answers for others, or with students collaborating on the answers. Much depends on the level of the class, their familiarity and skill with the grammar at hand, their oral-aural skills in general, and the flexibility or limitations of class time.

Technique E: When an exercise item has a dialogue between two speakers, A and B (e.g., Exercise 32, p. 78), ask one student to be A and another B and have them read the entry aloud. Then, occasionally, say to A and B: "Without looking at your text, what did you just say to each other?" (If necessary, let them glance briefly at their texts before they repeat what they've just said in the exercise item.) Students may be pleasantly surprised by their own fluency.

Technique F: Some exercises ask students to change the form but not the substance, or to combine two sentences or ideas. Generally, these exercises are intended for class discussion of the form and meaning of a structure.

The initial stages of such exercises are a good opportunity to use the board to draw circles and arrows to illustrate the characteristics and relationships of a structure. Students can read their answers aloud to initiate class discussion, and you can write on the board as problems arise. Or, students can write their sentences on the board themselves. Another option is to have them work in small groups to agree upon their answers prior to class discussion.

- OPEN-ENDED EXERCISES

The term "open-ended" refers to those exercises in which students use their own words to complete the sentences, either orally or in writing.

Technique A: Exercises where students must supply their own words to complete a sentence (e.g., Exercise 23, p. 341) should usually be assigned for out-of-class preparation. Then in class, one, two, or several students can read their sentences aloud; the class can discuss the correctness and appropriateness of the completions. Perhaps you can suggest possible ways of rephrasing to make a sentence more idiomatic. Students who don't read their sentences aloud can revise their own completions based on what is being discussed in class. At the end of the exercise discussion, you can tell students to hand in their sentences for you to look at, or simply ask if anybody has questions about the exercise and not have them submit anything to you.

Technique B: If you wish to use a completion exercise in class without having previously assigned it, you can turn the exercise into a brainstorming session in which students try out several completions to see if they work. As another possibility, you may wish to divide the class into small groups and have each group come up with completions that they all agree are correct and appropriate. Then use only those completions for class discussion or as written work to be handed in.

Technique C: Some completion exercises are done on another piece of paper because not enough space has been left in the *Student Book* (e.g., Exercise 45, p. 155). It is often beneficial to use the following progression: (1) assign the exercise for out-of-class preparation; (2) discuss it in class the next day, having students make corrections on their own papers based on what they are learning from discussing other students' completions; (3) then ask students to submit their papers to you, either as a requirement or on a volunteer basis.

- PARAGRAPH PRACTICE (SEE Exercise 36, p. 82.)

Some writing exercises are designed to produce short, informal paragraphs. Generally, the topics concern aspects of the students' lives to encourage free and relatively effortless communication as they practice their writing skills. While a course in English rhetoric is beyond the scope of this text, many of the basic elements are included and may be developed and emphasized according to your needs.

For best results, whenever you give a writing assignment, let your students know what you expect: "This is what I suggest as content. This is how you might organize it. This is how long I expect it to be." If at all possible, give your students composition models, perhaps taken from good compositions written by previous classes, perhaps written by you, perhaps composed as a group activity by the class as a whole (e.g., you write on the board what students tell you to write, and then you and your students revise it together).

In general, writing exercises should be done outside of class. All of us need time to consider and revise when we write. And if we get a little help here and there, that's not unusual. The topics in the exercises are structured so that plagiarism should not be a problem. Use in-class writing if you want to appraise the students' unaided, spontaneous writing skills. Tell your students that these writing exercises are simply for practice and that — even though they should always try to do their best — mistakes that occur should be viewed simply as tools for learning.

Encourage students to use a basic dictionary whenever they write. Point out that you yourself never write seriously without a dictionary at hand. Discuss the use of margins, indentation of paragraphs, and other aspects of the format of a well-written paper.

• ERROR-ANALYSIS EXERCISES

For the most part, the sentences in this type of exercise have been adapted from actual student writing and contain typical errors. Error-analysis exercises focus on the target structures of a chapter but may also contain miscellaneous errors that are common in student writing at this level (e.g., final -s on plural nouns or capitalization of proper nouns). The purpose of including them is to sharpen the students' self-monitoring skills.

Error-analysis exercises are challenging, fun, and a good way to summarize the grammar in a unit. If you wish, tell students they are either newspaper editors or English teachers; their task is to locate all the mistakes and then write corrections. Point out that even native speakers — including you yourself — have to scrutinize, correct, and revise their own writing. This is a natural part of the writing process.

The recommended technique is to assign an error-analysis exercise for in-class discussion the next day. Students benefit most from having the opportunity to find the errors themselves prior to class discussion. These exercises can, of course, be handled in other ways: seatwork, written homework, group work, or pairwork.

"Let's Talk" Exercises

The third edition of *Basic English Grammar* has many more exercises explicitly set up for interactive work than the last edition had. Students work in pairs, in groups, or as a class. Interactive exercises may take more class time than they would if teacher-led, but it is time well spent, for there are many advantages to student-student practice.

When students are working in groups or pairs, their opportunities to use what they are learning are greatly increased. In interactive work, the time students have for using English is many times greater than in a teacher-centered activity. Obviously, students working in groups or pairs are often much more active and involved than in teacher-led exercises.

Groups and pairwork also expand student opportunities to practice many communication skills at the same time that they are practicing target structures. In peer interaction in the classroom, students have to agree, disagree, continue a conversation, make suggestions, promote cooperation, make requests, and be sensitive to each other's needs and personalities — the kinds of exchanges that are characteristic of any group communication, whether in the classroom or elsewhere.

Students will often help and explain things to each other during pairwork, in which case both students benefit greatly. Ideally, students in interactive activities are "partners in exploration." Together they go into new areas and discover things about English usage, supporting each other as they proceed.

Groups and pairwork help to produce a comfortable learning environment. In teacher-centered activities, students may sometimes feel shy and inhibited or may experience stress.

They may feel that they have to respond quickly and accurately and that *what* they say is not as important as *how* they say it. When you set up groups or pairs that are non-competitive and cooperative, students usually tend to help, encourage, and even joke with one another. This encourages them to experiment with the language and to speak more often.

- PAIRWORK EXERCISES

Tell the student whose book is open that s/he is the teacher and needs to listen carefully to the other's responses. Vary the ways in which students are paired up, ranging from having them choose their own partners, counting off, or drawing names or numbers from a hat. Walk around the room and answer questions as needed.

- SMALL GROUP EXERCISES

The role of group leader can be rotated for long exercises, or one student can lead the entire exercise if it is short. The group can answer individually or chorally, depending on the type of exercise. Vary the ways in which you divide the class into groups and choose leaders. If possible, groups of 3–5 students work best.

- CLASS ACTIVITY EXERCISES (teacher-led)

The teacher conducts the oral exercise. (You can also lead an oral exercise when the directions call for something else; exercise directions calling for pairwork or group work are suggestions, not ironclad instructions.) You don't have to read the items aloud as though reading a script word for word. Modify or add items spontaneously as they occur to you. Change the items in any way you can to make them more relevant to your students. (For example, if you know that some students plan to watch the World Cup soccer match on TV soon, include a sentence about that.) Omit irrelevant items.

   Sometimes an item will start a spontaneous discussion of, for example, local restaurants or current movies or certain experiences your students have had. These spur-of-the-moment dialogues are very beneficial to your class. Being able to create and encourage such interactions is one of the chief advantages of a teacher leading an oral exercise.

Listening Exercises

Two audio CDs can be found at the back of *Basic English Grammar*. There are 86 listening exercises in the text, all marked with a headphone icon. They reinforce the grammar being taught — some focusing on form, some on meaning, most on both.

   You will find an audio tracking script on p. 500 to help you locate a particular exercise on the CD. The scripts for all the exercises are also in the back of *Basic English Grammar*, beginning on p. 489.

   Depending on your students' listening proficiency, some of the exercises may prove to be easy and some more challenging. You will need to gauge how many times to replay a particular item. In general, unless the exercise consists of single sentences, you will want to play the dialogue or passage in its entirety to give your students the context. Then you can replay the audio to have your students complete the task.

   It is very important that grammar students be exposed to listening practice early on. Native speech can be daunting to new learners; many say that all they hear is a blur of words. Students need to understand that what they see in writing is not exactly what they may hear in normal, rapidly spoken English. If students can't hear a structure, there is little chance it will be reinforced through interactions with other speakers. The sooner your students practice grammar from a listening perspective, the more confidence they will develop and the better equipped they will be to interact in English.

Pronunciation Exercises

A few exercises focus on pronunciation of grammatical features, such as endings on nouns or verbs and contracted or reduced forms.

Some phonetic symbols are used in these exercises to point out sounds which should not be pronounced identically; for example, /s/, /əz/, and /z/ represent the three predictable pronunciations of the grammatical suffix which is spelled *-s* or *-es*. It is not necessary for students to learn a complete phonetic alphabet; they should merely associate each symbol in an exercise with a sound that is different from all others. The purpose is to help students become more aware of these final sounds in the English they hear to encourage proficiency in their own speaking and writing.

In the exercises on spoken contractions, the primary emphasis should be on students' hearing and becoming familiar with spoken forms rather than on their accurate pronunciation of these forms. The most important part of most of these exercises is for students to listen to the oral production and become familiar with the reduced forms. At a beginning level, it can sound strange for students to try to pronounce reduced forms because of their lack of experience with English.

Language learners know that their pronunciation is not like that of native English speakers; therefore, some of them are embarrassed or shy about speaking. In a pronunciation exercise, they may be more comfortable if you ask groups or the whole class to say a sentence in unison. After that, individuals may volunteer to speak the same sentence. Students' production does not need to be perfect, just understandable. You can encourage students to be less inhibited by having them teach you how to pronounce words in their languages (unless, of course, you're a native speaker of the students' language in a monolingual class). It's fun — and instructive — for students to teach the teacher.

Games and Activities

Games and activities are important parts of the grammar classroom. The study of grammar is (and should be) fun and engaging. Some exercises in the text and in this *Teacher's Guide* are designated "expansion" or "activity." They are meant to promote independent, active use of target structures.

If a game is suggested, the atmosphere should be relaxed and not necessarily competitive. The goal is clearly related to the chapter's content, and the reward is the students' satisfaction in using English to achieve that goal. (For additional games and activities, see *Fun with Grammar: Communicative Activities for the Azar Grammar Series* by Suzanne W. Woodward, available as a photocopiable book from Longman — 877-202-4572 — or as downloads from www.longman.com).

• Monitoring Errors in Oral Work

Students should be encouraged to monitor each other to some extent in interactive work, especially when monitoring activities are specifically assigned. (Perhaps you should remind them to give some *positive* as well as corrective comments to each other.) You shouldn't worry about losing control of students' language production; not every mistake needs to be corrected. Mistakes are a natural part of learning a new language. As students gain experience and familiarity with a structure, their mistakes will begin to diminish.

Students shouldn't worry that they will learn one another's mistakes. Being exposed to imperfect English in an interactive classroom is not going to impede their progress in the slightest. In today's world, with so many people using English as a second language, students will likely be exposed to all levels of English proficiency in people they meet —

from airline reservation clerks to new neighbors from a different country to a co-worker whose native language is not English. Encountering imperfect English is not going to diminish their own English language abilities, either now in the classroom or later in different English-speaking situations.

Make yourself available to answer questions about correct answers during group work and pairwork. If you wish, you can take some time at the end of an exercise to call attention to mistakes that you heard as you monitored the groups. Another possible way of correcting errors is to have students use the answer key in the back of the book to look up their own answers when they need to. If your edition of *BEG*, third edition, doesn't include the answer key, you can make student copies of the answers from the separate *Answer Key* booklet.

• **Homework**

The student book assumes that students will have the opportunity to prepare most of the written exercises by writing in their books prior to class discussion. Students should be assigned this homework as a matter of course.

Whether you have students write their answers on paper for you to collect is up to you. This generally depends upon such variables as class size, class level, available class time, your available paper-correcting time, not to mention your preferences in teaching techniques. Most of the exercises in the text can be handled through class discussion without the students' needing to hand in written homework. Most of the written homework that is suggested in the text and in the chapter notes in this *Teacher's Guide* consists of activities that will produce original, independent writing.

Although it's better to assign exercises for out-of-class preparation, it's sometimes necessary to cover an exercise in class. In "seatwork," you ask students to do an unassigned exercise in class immediately before discussing it. Seatwork may be done individually, in pairs, or in groups.

The *Workbook* As Independent Study

Earnest students can use the *Workbook* to teach themselves. It contains self-study exercises for independent study, with a perforated answer key located at the end of the book. Encourage your students to remove this answer key and put it in a folder. It's much easier for students to correct their own answers if they make their own booklet.

If you prefer that students not have the answers to the exercises, ask them to hand in the answer key at the beginning of the term (to be returned at the end of the term). Some teachers may prefer to use the *Workbook* for in-class teaching rather than independent study.

The *Workbook* mirrors the student book. Exercises are called "exercises" in the *Student Book* and "practices" in the *Workbook* to minimize confusion when you make assignments. Each practice in the *Workbook* has a content title and refers students to appropriate charts in the *Student Book* and in the *Workbook* itself.

Workbook practices can be assigned by you or, depending upon the level of maturity or sense of purpose of the class, simply left for students to use as they wish. They may be assigned to the entire class or only to those students who need further practice with a particular structure. They may be used as reinforcement after you have covered a chart and exercises in class or as introductory material prior to discussing a chart.

In addition, students can use the *Workbook* to acquaint themselves with the grammar of any units not covered in class.

Supplementary Resource Texts

Two teacher resource texts are available. One is *Fun with Grammar: Communicative Activities for the Azar Grammar Series* by Suzanne W. Woodward, available as a photocopiable book from Longman (877-202-4572) or as downloads from www.longman.com. The text contains games and other language-learning activities compiled by the author from her and other teachers' experience in using the Azar texts in their classrooms.

The other is *Test Bank for Basic English Grammar* by Janis van Zante. The tests are keyed to charts or chapters in the *Student Book*. They can be reproduced, or items can be excerpted for tests that teachers prepare themselves. The *Test Bank* will be available on CD in the fall of 2006.

As another resource, the Grammar Exchange at the Azar Web site (www.longman.com/grammarexchange) is a place to ask questions you might have about grammar (sometimes our students ask real stumpers). It is also a place to communicate with the authors about the text and to offer teaching/exercise suggestions.

Notes on American vs. British English

Students are often curious about differences between American and British English. They should know that the differences are minor. Any students who have studied British English (BrE) should have no trouble adapting to American English (AmE), and vice-versa.

Teachers need to be careful not to inadvertently mark differences between AmE and BrE as errors; rather, they should simply point out to students that a difference in usage exists.

• Differences in Grammar

Differences in article and preposition usage in certain common expressions follow. These differences are not noted in the text; they are given here for the teacher's information.

AmE	BrE
be in the hospital	*be in Ø hospital*
be at the university (be in college)	*be at Ø university*
go to a university (go to college)	*go to Ø university*
go to Ø class/be in Ø class	*go to a class/be in a class*
in the future	*in Ø future* (OR *in the future*)
did it the next day	*did it Ø next day* (OR *the next day*)
haven't done something for/in weeks	*haven't done something for weeks*
ten minutes past/after six o'clock	*ten minutes past six o'clock*
five minutes to/of/till seven o'clock	*five minutes to seven o'clock*

• Differences in Spelling

Variant spellings can be noted but should not be marked as incorrect in student writing. Spelling differences in some common words follow.

AmE	BrE
jewelry, traveler, woolen	*jewellry, traveller, woollen*
skillful, fulfill, installment	*skilful, fulfil, instalment*
color, honor, labor, odor	*colour, honour, labour, odour*
-ize (realize, apologize)	*-ise/ize (realise/realize, apologise/apologize)*
analyze	*analyse*

defense, offense, license	defence, offence, licence (n.)
theater, center, liter	theatre, centre, litre
check	cheque (bank note)
curb	kerb
forever	for ever/forever
focused	focused/focussed
fueled	fuelled/fueled
jail	gaol
practice (n. and v.)	practise (v.); practice (n. only)
program	programme
specialty	speciality
story	storey (of a building)
tire	tyre

• Differences in Vocabulary

Differences in vocabulary usage between AmE and BrE usually do not significantly interfere with communication, but some misunderstandings may develop. For example, a BrE speaker is referring to underpants or panties when using the word "pants," whereas an AmE speaker is referring to slacks or trousers. Students should know that when American and British speakers read each other's literature, they encounter very few differences in vocabulary usage. Similarly, in the United States, Southerners and New Englanders use different vocabulary but not so much as to interfere with communication. Some differences between AmE and BrE follow.

AmE	**BrE**
attorney, lawyer	barrister, solicitor
bathrobe	dressing gown
can (of beans)	tin (of beans)
cookie, cracker	biscuit
corn	maize
diaper	nappy
driver's license	driving licence
drug store	chemist's
elevator	lift
eraser	rubber
flashlight	torch
gas, gasoline	petrol
hood of a car	bonnet of a car
living room	sitting room, drawing room
math	maths (e.g., a maths teacher)
raise in salary	rise in salary
rest room	public toilet, WC (water closet)
schedule	timetable
sidewalk	pavement, footpath
sink	basin
soccer	football
stove	cooker
truck	lorry, van
trunk (of a car)	boot (of a car)
be on vacation	be on holiday

Key to Pronunciation Symbols

• The Phonetic Alphabet (Symbols for American English)

CONSONANTS

Phonetic symbols for most consonants use the same letters as in conventional English spelling: /b, d, f, g, h, k, l, m, n, o, p, r, s, t, v, w, y, z/.*

Spelling consonants that are <u>not</u> used phonetically in English: c, q, x.

A few additional symbols are needed for other consonant sounds.

/ θ / (Greek theta) = voiceless *th* as in ***th**in,* ***th**ank*
/ ð / (Greek delta) = voiced *th* as in ***th**en,* ***th**ose*
/ ŋ / = *ng* as in *si**ng**, thi**nk*** (but not in *danger*)
/ š / = *sh* as in ***sh**irt, mi**ss**ion, na**t**ion*
/ ž / = *s* or *z* in a few words like *plea**s**ure, a**z**ure*
/ č / = *ch* or *tch* as in *wa**tch**, **ch**urch*
/ ǰ / = *j* or *dge* as in ***j**ump, le**dge***

VOWELS

The five vowels in the spelling alphabet are inadequate to represent the 12–15 vowel sounds of American speech. Therefore, new symbols and new sound associations for familiar letters must be adopted.

Front	**Central**	**Back** (lips rounded)
/i/ or /iy/ as in *beat*		/u/, /u:/, or /uw/ as in *boot*
/ɪ/ as in *bit*		/ʊ/ as in *book*
/e/ or /ey/ as in *bait*		/o/ or /ow/ as in *boat*
		/ɔ/ as in *bought*
/ɛ/ as in *bet*	/ə/ as in *but*	
/æ/ as in *bat*	/a/ as in *bother*	

Glides: /ai/ or /ay/ as in *bite*
/ɔi/ or /ɔy/ as in *boy*
/au/ or /aw/ as in *about*

British English has a somewhat different set of vowel sounds and symbols. You might want to consult a standard pronunciation text or BrE dictionary for that system.

---

*Slanted lines indicate phonetic symbols.

CHAPTER 1
Using *Be*

Overview

This chapter presents very simple sentences for near-beginners. The assumption is that all students of this textbook can read words in English and that the teacher can both model and monitor good spoken and written English.

The purpose of the lessons in Chapter 1 is to give learners basic phrases for exchanging information with other speakers of English. Thus, they begin by getting acquainted with each other. Then the text presents simple statements of definition and description and introduces a basic vocabulary of nouns and adjectives. Negative verb phrases and contractions are also presented early so that learners get plenty of practice with them throughout the course. A few prepositions of place are also illustrated and practiced.

For general teaching suggestions and techniques, see the *Introduction* to this *Teacher's Guide*.

☐ **EXERCISE 1, p. 1. Let's talk: class activity.**

This introductory exercise is designed as an ice-breaker for the first day of class. It shows learners how *be* is used in simple questions and answers while giving them an opportunity to get acquainted with classmates.

TEACHING SUGGESTIONS: Model the activity by choosing one student as your partner. Ask the two questions in the illustration on page 1 of the text; then, have the student ask you those two questions.

Introduce the student to the class, saying, "This is (. . .)" or "I would like you to meet (. . .)." Write the student's name and country on the board. Ask that student to do the same, introducing you to the class and writing your name and country on the board. Choose another student and model the pattern again, if necessary, until you are sure the class understands what they are supposed to do.

Divide the students into pairs and ask them to find out his/her partner's name and country of origin. The students should write this information down. Ask the students in turn to write their partner's name and country on the board as they orally introduce this person to the class.

If you are teaching a multicultural class, mix nationalities in the pairs. If you are teaching a monolingual class, ask one student in each pair to find out the other student's hometown or address instead of country of origin.

Encourage incidental communication and interaction; brief conversations may arise in their interviews. Spell names aloud to review the spoken alphabet.

CHART 1-1: NOUN + *IS* + NOUN: SINGULAR

• Chart 1-1 introduces some basic vocabulary for discussing grammar: *singular, noun, verb, article, consonant, vowel.* These terms are used frequently throughout the text, and students will become familiar with them very quickly. Give these terms attention when you discuss the chart with your students. See p. xi of this *Teacher's Guide* for suggestions on different ways of presenting charts in class.

• To convey the concept of what a noun is, you may ask students to name things and people in the classroom: *floor, door, desk, man, woman,* etc.

• In this lesson, names such as *Canada* and *Mexico* are called singular nouns because they require singular verb forms. Perhaps point out in Exercises 3 and 4 that names of people, places, and languages (i.e., proper nouns) are capitalized.

• Many languages do not use a verb where English requires a form of *be,* so a common error in spontaneous student usage of the grammar in the first eight charts of this chapter is omission of *be* (e.g., **I a student.* or **She not in class today.*).

• WORKBOOK: For additional exercises based on Chart 1-1, see *Workbook* Practices 1–3.

□ EXERCISE 2, p. 2. Preview: listening.

See p. xvii of this *Teacher's Guide* for suggestions on how to best use the listening exercises and audio CDs in the back of the student book.

This exercise has been designed as a diagnostic tool to see how advanced your class is. Beginning students sometimes feel they have been placed too low, and this exercise is meant to challenge those students.

ANSWERS: **2.** is a   **3.** They're in   **4.** is an   **5.** It's   **6.** aren't
7. They're happy   **8.** is   **9.** isn't   **10.** She's

□ EXERCISE 3, p. 2. Sentence practice. (Chart 1-1)

Students practice indefinite articles as a step along the way to producing the sentence pattern in Chart 1-1. The main focus of the first half of this chapter is sentence patterns with *be.*

TEACHING SUGGESTIONS: After you discuss the chart with the class, give your students a few minutes to complete the exercise by themselves. Students can read their answers aloud while you point out the sentence structure as you go through the exercise.

Or, since the sentences are short, they could be written on the board by students. That would give you nine sentences to use as additional examples of the pattern in Chart 1-1. You could go through each one, pointing out nouns and articles and the position of *is.*

Alternatively, students may be more comfortable if they answer together rather than as individuals. You might proceed like this:

TEACHER: Look at the example. *(pause)* We use *a* with *horse,* not *an.*
What letter does *horse* begin with?
CLASS: "H."
TEACHER: Is "h" a vowel or a consonant?
CLASS: A consonant.
TEACHER: Why do we use *a,* not *an,* in front of *horse?*
CLASS: "H" is a consonant.

TEACHER: Yes, we use *a* in front of *horse* because *a* is used in front of a consonant. Then we say **an** animal. Why?

CLASS: *Animal* begins with a vowel.

TEACHER: Right! Now, look at sentence number 2. *(pause)* Everybody, say this sentence now.

CLASS: English is a language.

TEACHER: Yes—*a* language. English is *a* language. Great!

Etc.

You may have to spend some time reviewing the alphabet and distinguishing between vowels and consonants.

Try to help learners understand new vocabulary words without the use of a dictionary. Some of the difficult vocabulary is illustrated *(bee, bear, ant)*. This vocabulary is recycled in subsequent exercises. You may have to explain some of the other vocabulary in this exercise (for example, by drawing a horse, or by using or drawing maps).

A large map of the world would be helpful for this and following exercises. There is a map of the world at the back of this *Teacher's Guide*, pp. 180-181, that you can photocopy if a wall map is not readily available. Also, there is a picture of a horse on p. 93 of the student book. Note that giving students page numbers to look at is a way of reviewing and practicing numbers.

EXPANSION: After you finish going through the exercise, have students close their books. Then, using a few of the items in this exercise, write sentences on the board that contain errors and ask the class to correct them; e.g., write *★English is language.* or *★A bee is a insect.* or *★Korea a country is.* You may want to include errors in capitalization.

ANSWERS: **2.** English is a language. **3.** Tokyo is a city. **4.** Australia is a country. **5.** Red is a color. **6.** A dictionary is a book. **7.** A hotel is a building. **8.** A bear is an animal. **9.** A bee is an insect. **10.** An ant is an insect.

☐ **EXERCISE 4, p. 3. Sentence practice. (Chart 1-1)**

Again, a map would be helpful for this exercise.

TEACHING SUGGESTION: Pronounce the words in the box and have the class repeat them. Everyone can read the first three sentences in chorus; then, either the whole class or individuals can call out the rest.

It's not necessary for students to write every answer in their books; some students will put their pens aside and simply join in orally, but others will insist on writing every answer completely and correctly. Learning styles differ.

ANSWERS: **4.** Tennis is a sport. **5.** Chicago is a city. **6.** Spanish is a language. **7.** Mexico is a country. **8.** A cow is an animal. **9.** A fly is an insect. **10.** Baseball is a sport. **11.** China is a country. **12.** Russian is a language.

☐ **EXERCISE 5, p. 4. Let's talk: small groups. (Chart 1-1)**

This exercise gives students a chance to use their own knowledge to complete the sentences. Help them with pronunciation, and congratulate them on their answers.

TEACHING SUGGESTION: Divide the students into small groups. Choose one group and have them model the example. After students finish the exercise, ask for different completions from a number of students. This is an exercise that allows the more advanced students to display their abilities and vocabularies. If a student uses a word that most of the rest of the class is unfamiliar with, ask that student to locate the place on a map or draw the animal or insect.

EXPANSION: If your class is more advanced, you may want to take some of the more common languages and have students come up with the names of the countries (Spanish–Spain; Japanese–Japan, etc.). You can put the answers in two columns on the board: one for language and one for country.

CHART 1-2: NOUN + *ARE* + NOUN: PLURAL

• This chart introduces the grammatical term "plural." You can write sentence (c) from Chart 1-1 and sentence (a) from Chart 1-2 to show the differences. Allow students to discover all the differences between the two; then, lead them through the rest of the points in Chart 1-2.

• Note the spelling variations of the plural *-s* ending. Model pronunciation of final *-s* and have the class repeat after you. (Focused work on pronunciation of final *-s/-es* follows in Chapter 3.)

• WORKBOOK: For additional exercises based on Chart 1-2, see *Workbook* Practices 4–8.

□ EXERCISE 6, p. 4. Sentence practice. (Charts 1-1 and 1-2)

This exercise can be done in class or assigned as homework. These sentences are simple definitions and introduce vocabulary. Some of these words are illustrated in the drawing: *a rose, a rabbit, a carrot, a chicken.*

Model pronunciation of final *-s* and have the class repeat after you.

ANSWERS: **2.** Computers are machines. **3.** Dictionaries are books. **4.** Chickens are birds. **5.** Roses are flowers. **6.** Carrots are vegetables. **7.** Rabbits are animals. **8.** Egypt and Indonesia are countries. **9.** Winter and summer are seasons.

□ EXERCISE 7, p. 5. Game. (Charts 1-1 and 1-2)

TEACHING SUGGESTION: Divide students into small groups. Each group chooses a leader who writes the group's sentence. Encourage all members of the group to contribute.

When you have finished all the sentences, give the groups time to check their sentences. If you have time, check each group's answers immediately. Because this is a game, students are generally excited to know who won. Whether you correct the sentences in class or later, you can choose some of the sentences for error correction the next day.

EXPANSION: For more advanced groups, this can turn into a fast-paced competition by asking the group leader to raise his/her hand as soon as the group decides it has the correct answer. The points will add up as the exercise continues.

ANSWERS: **1.** A bear is an animal. **2.** An ant is an insect. **3.** London is a city. **4.** Spring is a season. **5.** A carrot is a vegetable. **6.** September and October are months. **7.** Mexico and Canada are countries. **8.** A dictionary is a book. **9.** Chickens are birds. **10.** China is a country. **11.** Winter and summer are seasons. **12.** Arabic is a language. **13.** A computer is a machine. **14.** A fly is an insect.

□ EXERCISE 8, p. 6. Listening. (Charts 1-1 and 1-2)

Play the audio. Students can give choral responses for the examples. When you are sure they understand the task, play the remaining sentences. You may need to stop the audio if students need more time to figure out the answers.

ANSWERS: **1.** yes **2.** no **3.** yes **4.** no **5.** no **6.** yes **7.** no
8. yes **9.** yes

☐ EXERCISE 9, p. 6.   Let's talk: pairwork. (Charts 1-1 and 1-2)

>   *TEACHING SUGGESTION:* Choose a student to help you model the example so that the class understands the task.

>   Walk around the room ready to answer questions and to be sure partners are looking at each other as much as possible when they speak.

>   When the pairs are finished, ask for answers from a number of students. Pairs that finish early can write their answers.

CHART 1-3:   PRONOUN + *BE* + NOUN

• Languages of the world construct these simple sentences very differently. Some do not require *be;* others do not require articles; and others have the same pronoun for *he* and *she* (just as English has only the pronoun *they* for the plural). These differences may cause many mistakes as students try to learn the system of English. Encourage them to keep experimenting, and don't expect perfection.

• Some alert learners may ask about *my,* a possessive adjective in sentences (i)–(k). You might then point out that either an article or a possessive adjective — not both — may be used in front of a singular noun. (INCORRECT: *She is a my teacher.*) Possessive adjectives are introduced in Chart 2-5.

• Another possible problem is the pronoun *you,* which can be either singular or plural in meaning but always requires the plural form of *be.* This is an accident of English history.

• In discussing Chart 1-3 and Exercise 10, use yourself and students as props to demonstrate the meanings of the pronouns. For example, for *she,* point to a woman; for *we,* group yourself with another student or other students.

• WORKBOOK: For additional exercises based on Chart 1-3, see *Workbook* Practices 9–11.

☐ EXERCISE 10, p. 7.   Sentence practice. (Chart 1-3)

>   This exercise is a quick way of ascertaining whether or not your students have understood the core grammar in the preceding chart. You may want to do it in class.

>   Chapter 1 presents grammar and vocabulary slowly and deliberately, giving beginners no more than they can handle comfortably. If your class is more advanced, much of the material in this and the next chapter can be handled quickly and exercises can be shortened or deleted.

ANSWERS: **2.** I am a student. **3.** Rita is a student. **4.** Rita and Tom are students. **5.** You are a student. **6.** You are students.

☐ EXERCISE 11, p. 7.   Let's talk: class activity.   (Charts 1-1 → 1-3)

This is a teacher-led exercise.

Much of the emphasis in this exercise should be on the students' knowing one another; it's a follow-up, getting-to-know-each-other exercise, so include as many names as is practical in the course of the exercise to encourage the students' familiarity with one another's names. The grammar is secondary here.

Some beginners may have difficulty using all the correct singular and plural forms, but with patient encouragement they will improve.

CHART 1-4:   CONTRACTIONS WITH *BE*

• Some learners — and even some teachers — are not comfortable with contractions. But these are the most natural forms in spoken English, so they are introduced early in this chapter. You should encourage students to use contractions when they speak answers to the lessons in this book, but don't insist.

• NOTE: Contractions are not used in formal written English, but you should encourage them in written answers to exercises in this book.

• Start familiarizing the students with the term "apostrophe." They will meet it again whenever you discuss contractions and in the unit on possessive nouns.

• WORKBOOK: For additional exercises based on Chart 1-4, see *Workbook* Practice 12.

☐ EXERCISE 12, p. 8.   Sentence practice.   (Chart 1-4)

This exercise reviews pronouns while practicing contractions of *be*.

TEACHING SUGGESTIONS: Some students may not know whether certain names are masculine or feminine, so you may need to supply that information. The names the students encounter here will be encountered again as the text uses many common names.

You might have students work in pairs for this exercise. One speaks while the other listens carefully and helps with correct answers and pronunciation. They can change roles after every item, after every four items, or halfway through.

> *ANSWERS:* **2.** He's in my class. **3.** He's twenty years old. **4.** They're students. **5.** It's on my desk. **6.** They're friendly. **7.** They're on my desk. **8.** He's married. **9.** She's single. **10.** They're in my class. **11.** They're interesting. **12.** It's easy. **13.** We're roommates. [In American English, "we're" has the same pronunciation as "were."] **14.** It's on Pine Street. **15.** I'm a student. **16.** You're in my English class. [In American English, "You're" has the same pronunciation as "your."]

☐ EXERCISE 13, p. 9.   Listening.   (Chart 1-4)

Play the audio. Make sure students understand from the example that they will hear the first sentence but will see only the second sentence on their page. It may help to write the second sentence on the board, and write the answer in the blank after listening to the audio.

TEACHING SUGGESTION: If your class is having trouble with the apostrophe, tell them to write the words they hear in the blanks; then, go back after the audio is finished and add the apostrophes in the correct places.

□ EXERCISE 14, p. 9. Listening. (Chart 1-4)

This exercise adds a new level of difficulty by asking students to recognize contractions in
extended discourse. Remind students to add apostrophes to the contracted words.

   EXPANSION: For homework, more advanced students might like to make up a short
dialogue containing some contractions and present it to the class the next day.

CHART 1-5: NEGATIVE WITH *BE*

• The form and meaning of *be* + *not* are the focus of this chart. "Negative" is a grammar term
the students will find useful.

• A common mistake of beginners from some language groups is the use of *no* instead of *not*:
e.g., *★Tom is no a teacher.* Another common mistake is the omission of *be*: e.g., *★I not a teacher.*

• In example (c), you can point out that the only contracted form of *I am not* is *I'm not.*

• WORKBOOK: For additional exercises based on Chart 1-5, see *Workbook* Practices 13–16.

□ EXERCISE 15, p. 10. Sentence practice. (Chart 1-5)

Give students time to complete this exercise prior to class discussion. Students could work
alone or in pairs. The exercise looks easy, but it is a little tricky; students need to think
about meaning as they complete the sentences.

   You may want to review the plural spellings for *country* and *city.*

□ EXERCISE 16, p. 11. Sentence practice. (Chart 1-5)

Vocabulary from earlier exercises is used again here, and the drawings should help learners
understand the new vocabulary: *artist, photographer, gardener, bus driver, doctor,* and *police
officer.* If your class is interested, discuss other vocabulary suggested by the illustrations:
steering wheel, paintbrush, uniform, gloves, binoculars, stethoscope, etc.

   You may want to point out that *Ms.* is used for both married and single women, and
Mr. is for men. *Mrs.,* first seen in Exercise 2, is only for married women. While some
married women prefer *Ms.,* others prefer being called *Mrs.*

   EXPANSION: Bring to class pictures of people with different occupations. Have
students make sentences with *is / isn't / am / am not.* If students have jobs, use their
occupations. If not, their occupation is "student."

CHART 1-6: *BE* + ADJECTIVE

• The term "adjective" might need more explanation, either from examples you make up or from the examples of adjective usage in the exercises that follow. The eight exercises that follow this chart are designed to help students understand what an adjective is and to learn some common ones.

• Again, in this type of sentence many languages do not use a form of *be,* but *be* is required in English. You might want to point out that adjectives in English do NOT add *-s* when the noun is plural, as in example (b) — contrary to the use of adjectives in some other languages.
INCORRECT: *★Balls are rounds.*

• SUGGESTION: Bring to class several balls to illustrate the meaning of *round.* You may also want to use a box to compare *round* and *square.*

• WORKBOOK: For additional exercises based on Chart 1-6, see *Workbook* Practices 17 and 18.

☐ EXERCISE 17, p. 12.   Sentence practice. (Chart 1-6)

TEACHING SUGGESTIONS: Explain the word "opposite" in the directions. This exercise builds a vocabulary of basic adjectives by using opposites *(sad-happy, hot-cold,* etc.).

Encourage learners to figure out the meanings of new words without using a dictionary. Help them with pronunciation, including the use of contractions in their answers.

EXPANSION: Write pairs of adjectives on the board *(happy/sad,* etc.) Ask students to make sentences (e.g., _____ *(name of city) isn't cheap. It's expensive.).* This can be done in groups or pairs.

☐ EXERCISE 18, p. 13.   Sentence practice. (Chart 1-6)

TEACHING SUGGESTION: You may want to go over the words in the vocabulary list first to be sure the students know their meanings. Make sure the definitions you have chosen won't give away the answers to the sentences.

2. Ice and snow are cold.   **3.** A box is square.   **4.** Balls and oranges are round.   **5.** Sugar is sweet.   **6.** An elephant is large/big, but a mouse is small/little.   **7.** A rain forest is wet, but a desert is dry.   **8.** A joke is funny.   **9.** Good health is important.   **10.** They are/They're dangerous.   **11.** A coin is small, round, and flat.   **12.** A lemon is sour.

☐ **EXERCISE 19, p. 14.   Let's talk: pairwork. (Chart 1-6)**

This is a quick exercise that encourages spontaneous production of the target structure.

TEACHING SUGGESTION: Demonstrate what students are supposed to do by drawing faces on the board.

☐ **EXERCISE 20, p. 14.   Sentence practice. (Chart 1-6)**

Students again work with meaning in this exercise; they need to write true sentences.

ANSWERS: **3.** Lemons are yellow.   **4.** Ripe bananas are yellow too.   **5.** A lemon isn't sweet. It is/It's sour.   **6.** My pen isn't heavy. It is/It's light.   **7.** This room isn't dark. It is/It's light.   **8.** My classmates are friendly.   **9.** A turtle is slow.   **10.** Airplanes aren't slow. They are/They're fast.   **11.** The floor in the classroom is/isn't clean. It isn't/is dirty.   **12.** The weather is/isn't cold today.   **13.** The sun is/isn't bright today.   **14.** My shoes are/aren't comfortable.

☐ **EXERCISE 21, p. 15.   Let's talk: pairwork. (Chart 1-6)**

TEACHING SUGGESTIONS: Choose a student to help you model the example so that the class understands the task.

Walk around the room ready to answer questions and to be sure partners are looking at each other as much as possible when they speak.

After most of the pairs have finished this exercise, you may want to go over the answers with the class.

PARTNER A SENTENCES: **1.** The table isn't clean. It's dirty.   **2.** The little boy is sick. He isn't well.   **3.** The algebra problem isn't easy. It's difficult.   **4.** The cars are old. They aren't new.

PARTNER B SENTENCES: **1.** The man is friendly. He isn't unfriendly.   **2.** The coffee isn't cold. It's hot.   **3.** The woman is tall. She isn't short.   **4.** Ken's sister isn't old. She's young.

☐ **EXERCISE 22, p. 16.   Let's talk: game. (Chart 1-6)**

TEACHING SUGGESTION: Help the class with vocabulary as necessary.

If you have a large class, you may want to divide it into two groups. You can walk around the room and monitor both groups.

Students whose turn comes toward the end may become nervous because they have so many sentences to remember. The goal of this game is practice with the target structures, not memorization. If students are having trouble remembering the preceding sentences, encourage other students to help them.

□ **EXERCISE 23, p. 17. Let's talk: pairwork. (Chart 1-6)**

Use this exercise as an opportunity for general class discussion of your city. Encourage students to express their opinions and perhaps relate their experiences in this city.

□ **EXERCISE 24, p. 17. Let's talk: game. (Chart 1-6)**

This exercise encourages students to use their own knowledge and imaginations to answer your cue. Depending on how long it takes groups to make lists, you may want to limit the number of adjectives to ten or fewer.

CHART 1-7: *BE* + A PLACE

• Some students may ask about prepositions with similar meanings, e.g., *above/over, under/below/beneath, behind/in back of*. You may not wish to discuss those now because some learners might be confused. If you decide to explain the differences, be prepared with clear examples, perhaps from a dictionary for ESL/EFL students.

• The preposition *at* is usually difficult to explain and understand. Uses of *at* and *in* are emphasized and differentiated in Chart 12-9, p. 374, of the *BEG* student book.

• Note the new grammar terms "preposition" and "prepositional phrase." It is suggested that you not attempt to define a preposition but rather allow students' understanding to come from the examples. If students press you for a definition, you might say a preposition is a word that shows a particular relationship between nouns. For example, in the illustration, *on* shows the relationship between the ball and the box. A humorous definition of prepositions is "little words that cause learners big problems." Some simple definitions of the term "phrase" are "a group of related words that do not have a subject and a verb" (to contrast a phrase and a clause), or "a group of words that form a unit." These definitions are probably too confusing for students at this level. Perhaps easier is to define a phrase as "a short group of words." Easier still is not to attempt definitions at all at this point and to let the understandings emerge from the examples.

• Lead the students through an examination of the illustration. Use other objects in the classroom (e.g., an eraser and a book) to similarly demonstrate the meanings of the prepositions.

• WORKBOOK: For additional exercises based on Chart 1-7, see *Workbook* Practices 19 and 20.

□ **EXERCISE 25, p. 19. Sentence practice. (Chart 1-7)**

This exercise is simply another series of illustrations of the meanings of prepositions. Students can call out the answers and write them in later.

> *ANSWERS:* **2.** under **3.** on **4.** next to **5.** above **6.** behind
> **7.** between

□ **EXERCISE 26, p. 20. Let's talk: class activity. (Chart 1-7)**

This is a teacher-led activity.

The symbol "(. . .)" throughout the text means that you should supply the name of a student.

EXPANSION: If your class is advanced, let students assume the role of teacher, and have them take turns giving simple commands.

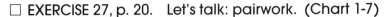

☐ EXERCISE 27, p. 20.   Let's talk: pairwork. (Chart 1-7)

    Students draw what their partner describes. When the class is finished, ask for volunteers to show their pictures.

        If some pairs finish early, have them think of additional objects to draw. Partners can give each other their new instructions.

CHART 1-8:   SUMMARY: BASIC SENTENCE PATTERNS WITH *BE*

  • This chart (1) summarizes the three completions for sentences with the main verb *be,* and (2) introduces the two very important grammar terms "subject" and "verb."

  • For review, ask students to make the example sentences negative. You could also preview the next chart by asking them to change the example sentences to questions (even though you would end up with the somewhat unnatural question "Am I a student?").

  • If structure recognition and identification are not important to your goals and purposes, skip class discussion of Chart 1-8 and omit Exercise 28.

  • WORKBOOK: For additional exercises based on Chart 1-8, see *Workbook* Practices 21–23.

☐ EXERCISE 28, p. 21.   Sentence practice. (Chart 1-8)

    This exercise can be done in class or assigned as homework.

> *ANSWERS:* **4.** are + a noun   **5.** is + a place   **6.** is + an adjective   **7.** are + a noun   **8.** am + a place   **9.** is + a place   **10.** are + an adjective

☐ EXERCISE 29, p. 22.   Listening. (Chart 1-8)

    The purpose of the exercise is to expose students to contractions that follow nouns. Pronunciation can help reinforce the listening, so the suggestion to practice saying the sentences is included in the directions; however, pronunciation is not a primary goal. The emphasis here should be on listening.

☐ EXERCISE 30, p. 22.   Listening. (Chart 1-8)

    The symbol "Ø" is included because many students don't hear the verb, and think that not having one is a possible option here. It's important for them to know that a missing verb is NOT an option. Even if they don't hear a verb in a sentence, they need to assume that one is there. This exercise helps them develop a better awareness of that.

> *ANSWERS:* **1.** B   **2.** A   **3.** A   **4.** B   **5.** A   **6.** B   **7.** B   **8.** A   **9.** A   **10.** B

☐ EXERCISE 31, p. 23.   Sentence review. (Chapter 1)

    From time to time, it's useful for students to edit another student's work. It gives them the opportunity to identify errors other than their own and to help one another learn. Some students enjoy being the "teacher" whereas others may resist. Explain to those students that they are learning to edit, an important part of learning how to write well in English.

CHAPTER 2
Using *Be* and *Have*

Overview

This chapter continues the study of forms of the verb *be*. Short questions and answers are introduced, followed by the use of *have* and *has*. Possessive adjectives build on the discussion of subject pronouns in Chapter 1. Demonstrative pronouns *(this, that, these, those)* complete the chapter.

☐ EXERCISE 1, p. 24.   Preview: listening.

This exercise introduces students to questions before they have been taught the correct word order. It will help you find out how much your students already know about asking simple questions.

ANSWERS: **1.** no   **2.** yes   **3.** no   **4.** yes/no   **5.** no   **6.** no   **7.** no
8. yes   **9.** no

CHARTS 2-1 AND 2-2:   YES/NO QUESTIONS AND SHORT ANSWERS WITH *BE*

• Two important structures are presented here: (1) word order in questions with *be*, and (2) verb use in short answers. Point out that contractions are not used in affirmative short answers.

• WORKBOOK: For additional exercises based on Charts 2-1 and 2-2, see *Workbook* Practices 1–6.

☐ EXERCISE 2, p. 24.   Question practice. (Chart 2-1)

Students must understand basic question structure before they can complete this exercise. Lead the class carefully through the example and the first few items. Students should be able to complete the rest on their own. Make sure they understand the correct use of the question mark.

ANSWERS: **2.** Is the sun a ball of fire?   **3.** Are carrots vegetables?   **4.** Are chickens birds?   **5.** Is Mr. Wu here today?   **6.** Are Sue and Mike here today?
7. Is English grammar fun?   **8.** Are you ready for the next grammar chart?

□ **EXERCISE 3, p. 25.   Question practice. (Charts 2-1 and 2-2)**

Students can work alone or in pairs. Make sure students know that the words in parentheses are long answers and that they are to supply short answers only.

> *ANSWERS:*
>
> **3.** A: Are you homesick?
>   B: No, I'm not.
> **4.** A: Is Bob homesick?
>   B: Yes, he is.
> **5.** A: Is Sue here today?
>   B: No, she isn't.
> **6.** A: Are the students in
>   this class intelligent?
>   B: Yes, they are.
>
> **7.** A: Are the chairs in this
>   room comfortable?
>   B: No, they aren't.
> **8.** A: Are you married?
>   B: No, I'm not.
> **9.** A: Are Tom and you roommates?
>   B: Yes, we are.
> **10.** A: Is a butterfly a bird?
>   B: No, it isn't.

□ **EXERCISE 4, p. 26.   Let's talk: find someone who . . . . (Charts 2-1 and 2-2)**

This interactive exercise gives students the opportunity to learn more about their classmates while engaging in real-world conversations.

NOTE: Students use their own words for phrases in parentheses in the box.

□ **EXERCISE 5, p. 27.   Let's talk: pairwork. (Charts 2-1 and 2-2)**

Tell students to help one another with word meanings or to ask you for help. (Not using a dictionary keeps the focus on oral interaction.)

□ **EXERCISE 6, p. 27.   Question practice. (Charts 2-1 and 2-2)**

If your class is advanced, this exercise can be done orally in pairs. Students can then write the answers for homework.

CHART 2-3:   QUESTIONS WITH *BE:* USING *WHERE*

- The forms of two types of questions are compared:
  (1) a yes/no question (i.e., a question that is answered by "Yes." or "No.")
  (2) an information question (a question that begins with a question word, also called a Q-word or WH-word, such as *where, when, why, who*)

- You might write the examples on the board, aligning them as they are in the chart to show the positions of the sentence parts. The similiarity in form between yes/no and information questions is emphasized throughout the text — whether the question uses *am/is/are, do/does, did, was/were, have/has,* or modal auxiliaries.

- WORKBOOK: For additional exercises based on Chart 2-3, see *Workbook* Practices 7 and 8.

□ **EXERCISE 7, p. 28.   Question practice. (Chart 2-3)**

Students must decide which type of question is necessary in each short conversation. The words in parentheses are not part of the conversation, just part of the meaning; they give the full meaning of the short answer.

☐ EXERCISE 8, p. 29.   Let's talk: pairwork. (Chart 2-3)

Where-questions are the target structure here, but the response part of this exercise is just as important and far more challenging.

CHART 2-4: USING *HAVE* AND *HAS*

• Students are now moving from the use of main verb *be* to the use of main verb *have*. The principal difficulty students have with this grammar is using *has* with third-person singular subjects (the pronouns *she/he/it* or singular noun subjects). A common mistake would be: *★My teacher have a blue pen.* You might point out that the final *-s* is consistent in the forms *is* and *has*.

• WORKBOOK: For additional exercises based on Chart 2-4, see *Workbook* Practices 9–12.

☐ EXERCISE 9, p. 30.   Sentence practice. (Chart 2-4)

This exercise can be done in class or assigned as homework. Learners must decide whether each item requires the basic form of *have* or the *-s* form, *has*.

ANSWERS: 2. have   3. has . . . has   4. have   5. has   6. have . . . have
7. has   8. have . . . has   9. have   10. has . . . has   11. has   12. have
13. have   14. has

☐ EXERCISE 10, p. 31.   Sentence practice. (Chart 2-4)

Students learn about common ailments while practicing *have* and *has*.

ANSWERS: 1. has a headache   2. have toothaches   3. have a fever   4. has a sore throat   5. have a cold   6. have backaches   7. has a stomachache

☐ EXERCISE 11, p. 31.   Let's talk: pairwork. (Chart 2-4)

Remind students that this is a speaking, not a reading, exercise. They can look at their books when preparing to speak, but they must look at their partners while speaking.

NOTE: Toothache and *sore tooth* have essentially the same meaning, as do *backache* and *sore back.*

EXPANSION: Students often have questions about other ailments. You may want to give them the chance to ask questions, and then write important vocabulary on the board.

ANSWERS: 1. A: How are you?   B: I have a headache.   2. A: How are you? B: I have a sore tooth.   3. A: How is/How's your mother?   B: She has a sore back.   4. A: How is/How's Mr. Lee?   B: He has a backache.   5. A: How are your parents?   B: They have colds.   6. A: How are the patients?   B: They have stomachaches.   7. A: How is/How's your little brother?   B: He has a sore throat. 8. A: How is/How's Mrs. Wood?   B: She has a fever.

□ **EXERCISE 12, p. 32.   Listening. (Chart 2-4)**

   Go over the vocabulary in the picture first.

   EXPANSION: Ask for volunteers to show the class that they are wearing an item similar to one in the picture.

   ANSWERS: **1.** have   **2.** has   **3.** has   **4.** has   **5.** has   **6.** have
   7. have   **8.** have

□ **EXERCISE 13, p. 32.   Let's talk: find someone who . . . . (Chart 2-4)**

   Students practice the common question "Do you have . . . ?" *Do* and *does* in questions will be formally taught in Chapter 3, but by now students will have heard this question frequently. They do not need to understand how *do* and *does* work with verbs in order to practice this question and short answers.

CHART 2-5:   USING *MY, YOUR, HIS, HER, OUR, THEIR*

• This chart builds upon the known (subject pronouns) to introduce the new forms (possessive adjectives).

• The terms "possessive adjective" and "possessive pronoun" can be confusing. *My, your, her,* etc., are pronouns in that they are noun substitutes, but they can also function as adjectives (i.e., they modify nouns); hence the term "possessive adjectives," to distinguish them from "possessive pronouns" (*mine, yours, hers,* etc.). See Chart 15-3 for possessive pronouns.

• WORKBOOK: For additional exercises based on Chart 2-5, see *Workbook* Practices 13–15.

□ **EXERCISE 14, p. 33.   Sentence practice. (Chart 2-5)**

   Students have been practicing "It's your turn" in pairwork, so they should be familiar with the meaning by now. You may want to practice "You're next" by having students line up for a task (e.g., writing their name on the board) and then saying "You're next" as each one takes a turn. (If you need to review "It's your turn," you can alternate between "It's your turn" and "You're next.")

   ANSWERS: **1.** your   **2.** her   **3.** their   **4.** her   **5.** my   **6.** their
   7. your   **8.** our   **9.** his   **10.** her

□ **EXERCISE 15, p. 33.   Sentence practice. (Chart 2-5)**

   Students learn important life-skill information including first name, middle initial, area code, etc. while practicing possessive adjectives.

   NOTE: Birthday = the month and day a person celebrates a birthday: April 12. *Birthdate* refers to the month, day, and year a person was born: 4/12/02. In American English, the month is written first, followed by the day and year. For dates beginning in 2000, usually just the last two numbers are written: 4/12/02. For dates in the 1900s, all four numbers are included: 8/15/1998.

   EXPANSION: Have students interview one another to get the following information: last name, middle name, middle initial, zip code, area code. Ask students to talk about other students in the class based on the information they received (e.g., *His middle initial is C. Her area code is 555.*).

Not all countries have zip codes or area codes. Ask students how phone numbers and addresses are written in their countries.

> ANSWERS: **1.** His . . . Palmer   **2.** His . . . John   **3.** His . . . B.   **4.** Their . . . 98301   **5.** Their . . . (888)   **6.** Her . . . 4/12/1970   **7.** Her . . . April 12   **8.** Her . . . Ellen   **9.–15.** My . . . (free response)

☐ EXERCISE 16, p. 35.   Let's talk: pairwork. (Chart 2-5)

Have students ask you questions about words they don't understand or would like you to pronounce. There are four illustrations to help explain the meaning of new vocabulary terms. Use items and colors in the classroom to broaden students' understanding of the vocabulary.

☐ EXERCISE 17, p. 36.   Sentence practice. (Chart 2-5)

This exercise can be done in class or assigned as homework.

One purpose of this practice is to familiarize students with the vocabulary for clothing and colors. Another is to provide a context for a passive understanding of the present progressive (e.g., *is wearing*). The first sentence in each item uses the present progressive, which is not explained until Chapter 4. The meaning of the verb form is "at this moment in time, right now" if students ask about it. It is not necessary to explain more about this until Chapter 4.

> ANSWERS: **2.** His   **3.** My   **4.** Their   **5.** Your   **6.** Our   **7.** Your   **8.** Her   **9.** His   **10.** Their   **11.** His   **12.** My

☐ EXERCISE 18, p. 37.   Let's talk: class activity. (Chart 2-5)

This exercise gives learners an opportunity to use the grammar they have been studying while practicing vocabulary. Encourage students to use complete sentences.

TEACHING SUGGESTION: Using the formats suggested in the examples, lead students through all or most of the colors and clothing types represented in the classroom. The method is for you to have a series of short conversations with individual students, using the true and present classroom context; the goal is for students to engage in effortless and clear communication using familiar structures and vocabulary — a real coup for a beginning student.

☐ EXERCISE 19, p. 37.   Sentence practice. (Charts 2-4 and 2-5)

This combines the lessons from Charts 2-4 and 2-5. If that grammar is a review for your students, not new, this exercise can be finished very quickly, assigned for homework, or skipped.

> ANSWERS: **2.** has . . . His   **3.** have . . . Your   **4.** has . . . Her   **5.** have . . . Their   **6.** have . . . Their   **7.** have . . . Our   **8.** have . . . My   **9.** have . . . Our   **10.** have . . . Your   **11.** has . . . Her   **12.** has . . . His

• Some languages have very different systems for indicating near and far objects. Demonstrate the English system by putting a book near you *(this book)* and one away from you *(that book)*. Use other objects in the classroom for additional contextualized examples.

• Chart 2-6 gives the singular English forms *this* and *that;* Chart 2-7 gives the plural forms *these* and *those.* These words are often called "demonstratives."

• Learners often have difficulty differentiating the pronunciation of *this* and *these.* It may help to tell them that the vowel in *these* is spoken a bit longer, and the *-s* in *these* is pronounced /z/. The *-ese* in *these* should sound exactly like the *-ease* in *please.* The *-is* in *this* should sound exactly like the *-iss* in *kiss.*

• While you may wish to emphasize good pronunciation of the *th*-sound /ð/, it may be too early for some learners; it's too difficult to think about correct forms and good pronunciation at the same time. Students can quickly slip into old pronunciation habits when they're concentrating on form and meaning. It will all come together eventually as they gain experience.

• *This, that, these,* and *those* can be used both as adjectives and as pronouns. In Chart 2-6, (a) and (b) illustrate their use as adjectives; (c) and (d) illustrate their use as pronouns. This information is not crucial and does not need to be given to students at this time.

• WORKBOOK: For additional exercises based on Charts 2-6 and 2-7, see *Workbook* Practices 16–18.

☐ EXERCISE 20, p. 38. Sentence completion. (Chart 2-6)

Students can complete this exercise in class, either individually or in pairs.

EXPANSION: Point to things in the classroom and ask "What is this/that?" Keep all the items singular at this point. Students must think about *this* vs. *that* as well as the possessive adjectives in their answers. Give students time to think of good answers.

Some students might naturally slip into use of possessive pronouns (*mine, hers,* etc.). For example, they might say *This book is mine. That book is yours.* If they already know how to use possessive pronouns, that's great. Don't discourage them simply because they didn't follow the exact pattern of the exercise. Keep the focus on *this* and *that.*

> *ANSWERS:* **3.** This **4.** That **5.** That **6.** This **7.** This **8.** That
> **9.** That **10.** This

☐ EXERCISE 21, p. 39. Let's talk: pairwork. (Chart 2-6)

This is a review of colors while the target structure is being practiced. Continue to model the pronunciation of the *th*-sound /ð/.

☐ EXERCISE 22, p. 39. Listening. (Chart 2-6)

The purpose of this exercise is to expose students to the spoken forms of *this* and *that.* Some students have trouble hearing the difference between the two, especially in questions. The contracted forms "that's" and "this's" are very common in spoken English. *That's* can also be used in writing, but not *this's.*

> *ANSWERS:* **1.** This **2.** That **3.** That **4.** This **5.** that **6.** This
> **7.** this **8.** that **9.** This **10.** That

☐ **EXERCISE 23, p. 40. Sentence practice. (Chart 2-7)**

This exercise type is identical to Exercise 20, except that it practices the plural forms.

EXPANSION: Point to things in the classroom and ask, "What are these/those?" Keep all the items plural. Students must think about *these* vs. *those* as well as the possessive adjectives in their answers. Give them time to think of a good answer. If this becomes easy for your students, you might want to add *this* and *that*.

> *ANSWERS:*   **1.** These   **2.** Those   **3.** Those   **4.** These   **5.** Those
> **6.** These

☐ **EXERCISE 24, p. 40. Sentence practice. (Charts 2-6 and 2-7)**

Errors in singular-plural usage of *this, that, these,* and *those* are common. This exercise encourages students to pay careful attention to singular and plural.

Emphasize the pronunciation differences between *this* and *these*, with *this* ending in an /s/ sound and *these* ending in a /z/ sound. The vowel sounds are also different *(these* is longer).

> *ANSWERS:*   **2.** This ... Those   **3.** These ... Those   **4.** This ... That
> **5.** These ... Those   **6.** This ... Those   **7.** these ... those   **8.** This ... Those

☐ **EXERCISE 25, p. 41. Let's talk: pairwork. (Charts 2-6 and 2-7)**

Students practice *this, that, these,* and *those* while using possessive adjectives.

CHART 2-8: ASKING QUESTIONS WITH *WHAT* AND *WHO* + *BE*

• The words in parentheses are usually omitted in conversations because both speaker and listener can see the same thing or person.

• NOTE: In singular questions with *who*, the demonstrative pronoun *that* (or possibly *this)* is used to ask about a person *(Who is that?/Who is this?)*, but in the plural, *these* and *those* are not used as pronouns. (INCORRECT: **Who are those?)* Correct plural questions are *Who are they?* or *Who are those people?* Students don't need this information, but an unusually alert student might have a query about it.

• WORKBOOK: For additional exercises based on Chart 2-8, see *Workbook* Practices 19 and 20.

☐ **EXERCISE 26, p. 42. Sentence practice. (Chart 2-8)**

Students can work in pairs, but they should exchange roles so that everyone has a chance to supply answers. They have to think about the differences between singular and plural as well as between people and things.

> *ANSWERS:*   **2.** What are   **3.** Who is   **4.** What is   **5.** Who are   **6.** What is
> **7.** Who is   **8.** Who are   **9.** What is   **10.** What are

□ EXERCISE 27, p. 43.   Let's talk: pairwork. (Charts 2-6 → 2-8)

This is intended as a short exercise that gives students a little practice with these very common questions.

□ EXERCISE 28, p. 44.   Let's talk: pairwork. (Charts 2-6 → 2-8)

Part I of this exercise is designed to familiarize students with the vocabulary they will need to use in Part II. Be sure to go over Part I answers before proceeding with Part II.

□ EXERCISE 29, p. 45.   Let's talk: class activity. (Charts 2-6 → 2-8)

This is a teacher-led activity. After students have learned the vocabulary in Exercise 28, they close their books and use that vocabulary while they practice using *this, that, these,* and *those.*

□ EXERCISE 30, p. 45.   Let's talk: pairwork. (Charts 2-6 → 2-8)

This is a very natural way to exchange information. Students should work in pairs, helping each other learn the vocabulary that is illustrated in the drawing on p. 46 of the student book. Supply vocabulary meanings only if asked.

TEACHING SUGGESTION: It's very tempting to use this illustration as a preview of the present progressive (after the class is done with the exercise as pairwork). If you think your class is ready and will enjoy the challenge rather than feel frustrated, ask them leading questions using the present progressive (e.g., "What is the cow doing?"), but be prepared to supply the answer yourself, as well as spend some time explaining new vocabulary. Some examples: "The cow is eating grass. The bat is hanging from a branch in the tree. The bat is sleeping. The bird is flapping/moving its wings. The dog is sitting. The horse is facing us. The bees are flying."

□ EXERCISE 31, p. 47.   Chapter review: error analysis. (Chapter 2)

These sentences contain typical errors. This kind of exercise encourages students to pay attention to important details as they develop self-monitoring skills. See p. xvi of this *Teacher's Guide* for more information about error-analysis exercises.

At this point, learners should be able to correct each error and understand the underlying grammar. If they can do this exercise easily and well, you and they have done a really good job in Chapters 1 and 2! Congratulate them lavishly and don't forget to congratulate yourself too.

> *ANSWERS:* **2.** I am not/I'm not hungry.   **3.** I am/I'm a student. He is a teacher.
> **4.** Yoko is not here. She is at school.   **5.** I'm from Mexico. Where are you from?
> **6.** Is Roberto he a student in your class?   **7.** Those pictures are beautiful.
> **8.** This is your dictionary. It is/It's not my dictionary.   **9.** Mr. Lee has a brown coat.
> **10.** They aren't here today.   **11.** These books are expensive. OR This book is
> expensive.   **12.** Cuba is an island.

□ EXERCISE 32, p. 47.   Chapter review. (Chapter 2)

This is a multiple-choice exercise, similar to parts of international English tests. Some students may not be familiar with this type of test.

EXPANSION: You may ask your students to do this exercise individually in class as though they were actually taking a test. The usual amount of time allotted per item in a multiple-choice test is 30 seconds, so you would give students six minutes to complete this exercise. Since this is a beginning class, however, be flexible. If some students don't finish in six minutes, give them some more time.

This is not a tricky or difficult exercise. The expectation is that students will easily mark the correct answers and gain self-confidence.

ANSWERS: **1.** C   **2.** C   **3.** B   **4.** B   **5.** B   **6.** C   **7.** C   **8.** C   **9.** A   **10.** A   **11.** C   **12.** B

☐ EXERCISE 33, p. 48.   Chapter review. (Chapter 2)

Again, this is a simple exercise. Students have to supply truthful answers using correct grammar. They should be able to do this confidently and effortlessly.

ANSWERS: **1.** are not/aren't   **2.** is   **3.** am/am not   **4.** are   **5.** are
6. are . . . are not/aren't   **7.** is not/isn't . . . is   **8.** is   **9.** are
10. is not/isn't . . . is

☐ EXERCISE 34, p. 49.   Chapter review. (Chapter 2)

This exercise is more complicated than it may look. Students must have control of a number of basic structures to complete these dialogues. If learners find this exercise easy, they should be pleased by their progress and proud of themselves.

ANSWERS:

1. A: is
   B: has
   A: are
   B: have
2. A: What is/What's
   B: is a
   A: Who is/Who's
   B: my
   A: Who are

3. A: this/that . . . this/that
   B: (free response)
4. (free response)
5. (free response)
6. A: What is/What's a . . . What is/What's a
   B: It is/It's an
   A: Is a
   B: They are/They're

☐ EXERCISE 35, p. 50.   Review: pairwork. (Chapter 1)

This is a review of the prepositions of place in Chapter 1. One of its main purposes is for students to have fun while interacting with each other. Give them entertaining examples and set a jovial mood by making up funny directions such as "Put your foot on your desk" or "Put your pen in Ali's pocket." Students will take their cue from you. In some classes, students will vie with each other to give the funniest or most outrageous directions.

☐ EXERCISE 36, p. 51.   Activity: let's talk. (Chapter 2)

This exercise contains four interactive activities for review. You may choose to intersperse them among the other chapter review exercises as you complete this chapter.

☐ EXERCISE 37, p. 51.   Chapter review. (Chapter 2)

This exercise is most effective when students copy the whole thing so that it looks like an essay. Tell them to indent the beginning of each paragraph. This exercise is good preparation for Exercise 38, which follows.

☐ EXERCISE 38, p. 52.   Review. (Chapters 1 and 2)

As in Exercise 37, students should copy the entire exercise. The blanks in the book are purposefully not long enough for the necessary information. What students should end up with is an essay about themselves using the structures they practiced in Chapters 1 and 2.

CHAPTER 3
Using the Simple Present

Overview

This chapter focuses on the simple present tense. Many languages do not have the variety of verb tenses that English employs, so learners must adjust their assumptions about the relationships between real time and the meanings of verb tenses. The simple present tense, the subject of Chapter 3, is used in talking or writing about repeated, habitual activities. Its main complication is the addition of *-s* to a verb whose subject is a singular noun or *she/he/it*. Final *-s* has variations in spelling and pronunciation which are presented in this chapter. Negative and question forms of the simple present tense (including questions with *where*, *when*, and *what time*) are also introduced. The chapter concludes with a summary of information questions with *be* and *do*.

CHART 3-1: FORM AND BASIC MEANING OF THE SIMPLE PRESENT TENSE

- This chapter and chart focus on the most common use of the simple present tense: expressing habits, routine activities, and customary situations. Of course, there are other uses for this tense, but this is a good place to start.

- Help students recall the use of *-s* on a verb with a third-person singular subject (*she/he/it* or a singular noun). In Chapter 2, they learned to use *is* and *has;* now they see *-s* added to many verbs.

- WORKBOOK: For additional exercises based on Chart 3-1, see *Workbook* Practices 1–4.

☐ EXERCISE 1, p. 54.   Let's talk: pairwork.   (Chart 3-1)

The purpose of this exercise is to provide vocabulary and phrases students can use to express their own habitual activities in the morning.

TEACHING SUGGESTION: First answer any questions about vocabulary in the left column. Then have students complete the sentences in the right column. Students choose the order of their morning activities and add the pronoun "*I.*" Remind them to end the sentence with a period.

EXPANSION: When students have finished writing, ask them to describe their mornings orally, books closed (or open if they wish). This oral work can be teacher-led, or students can be divided into pairs. Follow the oral part by having students describe their mornings in a written paragraph.

Note that *turn off the alarm clock* is checked because it was used for item 2. Checking off an item helps students keep track of which ones they have used in their lists. When an item contains a slash (/), the student can choose between the words before and after the slash. *Brush* and other verbs may need to be demonstrated.

Notice that the exercise introduces some common phrasal verbs. *Put on, pick up,* and *turn off* are separable phrasal verbs. In other words, they can be separated by a noun phrase (e.g., ***put on*** *my clothes* OR ***put*** *my clothes* ***on.***) *On, up,* and *off* can function as prepositions, but here they function as particles. ("Particles" are connected to the verbs they follow; "prepositions" are linked with the nouns that follow them. Students don't need to know the distinction between prepositions and particles at this stage of their language study.)

☐ EXERCISE 2, p. 55. Listening. (Chart 3-1)

You may want to read the first item from the listening script and discuss the correct answer *(wake)*. Then play the rest of the audio.

Final *-s* can be difficult for beginning students to hear. Sentences may need to be played more than once.

> *ANSWERS:* **1.** wake **2.** wakes **3.** gets **4.** go **5.** does **6.** watches
> **7.** take **8.** takes **9.** take **10.** talk

☐ EXERCISE 3, p. 55. Sentence practice. (Chart 3-1)

This exercise can be done in class or assigned as homework.

> *ANSWERS:* **2.** drinks **3.** take **4.** takes **5.** study **6.** walk **7.** begins
> **8.** stops **9.** eat **10.** go

CHART 3-2: USING FREQUENCY ADVERBS: *ALWAYS, USUALLY, OFTEN, SOMETIMES, SELDOM, RARELY, NEVER*

• Two points to learn here are the meaning of each adverb and its location in a sentence. Point out that the word *frequency* is used when talking about habits; therefore, frequency adverbs are frequently used with the simple present tense. (Frequency adverbs are also used with other tenses.)

• NOTE: *Often* may be pronounced with the /t/ sound, but it is usually pronounced without it.

• WORKBOOK: For additional exercises based on Chart 3-2, see *Workbook* Practices 5–8.

☐ EXERCISE 4, p. 56. Sentence practice. (Chart 3-2)

Do this exercise in class with your students. The illustration with cups of tea shows that the percentages of frequency are not precise; learners should see them as generalizations, not as absolute quantities.

> *ANSWERS:* **2.** usually **3.** often **4.** sometimes **5.** seldom **6.** rarely
> **7.** never

☐ EXERCISE 5, p. 57. Sentence practice. (Chart 3-2)

This exercise can be done in class or assigned as homework.

> *EXPANSION:* After going over the answers with your class, ask students to make sentences about themselves: "I sometimes eat breakfast in the morning," "I always eat lunch in the cafeteria," etc.

ANSWERS:

	S	V	
2.	I	eat	I <u>never</u> eat carrots
3.	I	watch	I <u>seldom</u> watch TV
4.	I	have	I <u>sometimes</u> have tea
5.	Sonya	eats	Sonya <u>usually</u> eats lunch
6.	Joe	drinks	Joe <u>rarely</u> drinks tea.
7.	We	listen	We <u>often</u> listen to music
8.	The students	speak	The students <u>always</u> speak English

☐ EXERCISE 6, p. 57.   Let's talk: class activity. (Chart 3-2)

This is a teacher-led exercise. It gives students an opportunity to practice their verbal skills without relying on the text, and it tells you which grammar structures need more work.

EXPANSION: After one student gives an answer, you can ask another student to tell you what that student does. For example:

TEACHER: Ricardo, tell me something you always do in the morning.
RICARDO: I always brush my teeth.
TEACHER: Talal, what does Ricardo always do?
TALAL: He always brushes his teeth.
Etc.

CHART 3-3:   OTHER FREQUENCY EXPRESSIONS

• These frequency expressions let speakers be more specific about how often something happens.

• *Once* = one time; *twice* = two times.

• Point out that *a* is necessary in the phrases *a day, a week, a month,* and *a year.*

• WORKBOOK: For additional exercises based on Chart 3-3, see *Workbook* Practice 9.

☐ EXERCISE 7, p. 58.   Sentence practice. (Chart 3-3)

This exercise focuses on a specific activity in one week. Thus *once a week* in this context would mean "rarely" whereas in other contexts it could mean "often."

ANSWERS: **2.** once . . . rarely   **3.** twice . . . seldom   **4.** six times . . . usually   **5.** five times . . . often   **6.** never   **7.** three times . . . sometimes

☐ EXERCISE 8, p. 59.   Listening. (Chart 3-3)

The endings of words can be very hard for beginning students to hear. You may want to play each sentence more than once.

ANSWERS: **1.** morning.   **2.** year   **3.** years   **4.** day   **5.** days   **6.** times   **7.** night   **8.** month

• Ask students to locate the verb in each example in this chart. Then ask them where the frequency adverb is located in relation to the verb. They should see the difference between sentences with *be* and with other verbs. You might use the board to show this.

• WORKBOOK: For additional exercises based on Chart 3-4, see *Workbook* Practices 10 and 11.

☐ EXERCISE 9, p. 60.   Sentence practice. (Chart 3-4)

This exercise can be done in class or assigned as homework. Students rewrite each sentence, adding the frequency adverb in correct word order. This exercise is written instead of oral so students have a visual representation of the word order differences presented in Charts 3-2 through 3-4.

Items 1–4: *on time* is the opposite of *late;* the preposition *for* follows *on time* and *late.*

ANSWERS: **3.** Maria is <u>often</u> late for class.   **4.** Maria <u>often</u> comes to class late.
5. It <u>never</u> snows in my hometown.   **6.** It is <u>never</u> very cold in my hometown.
7. Bob is <u>usually</u> at home in the evening.   **8.** Bob <u>usually</u> stays at home in the evening.   **9.** Tom <u>seldom</u> studies at the library in the evening.   **10.** His classmates are <u>seldom</u> at the library in the evening.   **11.** I <u>sometimes</u> skip breakfast.
12. I <u>rarely</u> have time for a big breakfast.   **13.** I am <u>usually</u> very hungry by lunchtime.   **14.** Sue <u>never</u> drinks coffee.

☐ EXERCISE 10, p. 60.   Let's talk: class activity. (Chart 3-4)

Item 5: *spend time* = use a period of time for some purpose.
Item 11: *surf the Internet* = go to different Web sites for short periods of time.
Items 13 and 14: *be in bed* and *go to bed.* Note the absence of an article before *bed.* A fairly common error students make is to say, ★"I usually go to <u>the</u> bed at eleven."

☐ EXERCISE 11, p. 61.   Paragraph practice. (Chart 3-4)

Most learners can write a simple paragraph in a chronological (time) sequence. Perhaps assign this as homework. When you mark it, focus on the correct use of final *-s* and the location of frequency adverbs. Don't penalize students for other errors; praise their successes.

The use of *after that* to show a sequence of events can be problematic. For example, students may write:
    ★*I ate breakfast. After, I went back to my room.*

What they mean to say is:
    I ate breakfast. After that, I went back to my room.

After is used both as a preposition and as a subordinating conjunction:
    I went back to my room after breakfast. (preposition)
    I ate breakfast. After that, I went back to my room. (preposition)
    I went back to my room after I ate breakfast. (subordinating conjunction)

Sometimes students will punctuate an adverb clause incorrectly:
    ★*I went back to my room. After I ate breakfast.*

Students aren't introduced to adverb clauses of time until Chart 9-7. These difficulties with the use of *after* may occur in the students' writing, but it is probably too soon to try to explain the grammar.

CHART 3-5: SPELLING AND PRONUNCIATION OF FINAL -ES

• There are three different pronunciations of final -s. This section teaches the /əz/ pronunciation of the -s ending.

• /s/ and /z/ pronunciations are taught in Chart 3-8. Because the difference in these endings is so difficult for students to hear or produce, correct pronunciation is not emphasized at this level. For some students, just having an ending is success.

• WORKBOOK: For additional exercises based on Chart 3-5, see *Workbook* Practices 12 and 13.

☐ **EXERCISE 12, p. 61.   Sentence practice. (Chart 3-5)**

This exercise can be done in class or assigned as homework.

In item 10, you may want to demonstrate the meanings of the words *stretch* and *yawn*.

> *ANSWERS:* 2. teaches   3. fixes   4. drinks   5. watches   6. kisses
> 7. wears   8. washes   9. walks   10. stretches . . . yawns

☐ **EXERCISE 13, p. 62.   Listening. (Chart 3-5)**

This exercise focuses on hearing final -es, but it's also an important reminder of subject-verb agreement.

> *ANSWERS:* 1. teaches   2. teach   3. fixes   4. fixes   5. watch
> 6. watches   7. brush   8. brushes   9. wash   10. washes

☐ **EXERCISE 14, p. 62.   Verb form practice. (Chart 3-5)**

This exercise serves a dual purpose: a review of when to use -s vs. -es endings as well as practice with the pronunciation of these endings. You can assign the written work for homework, but the pronunciation practice should be done in class. Walk around the room and listen as the groups read the paragraph aloud. Encourage students to make a distinction between the -s/-es endings *(brush vs. brushes)*. It's more important that they have an ending than be able to correctly articulate a /z/ pronunciation at the end of *brushes*.

> *ANSWERS:* gets . . . cooks . . . sits . . . washes . . . turns . . . watches . . . takes . . . brushes
> . . . reads . . . falls

CHART 3-6: ADDING FINAL -S/-ES TO WORDS THAT END IN -Y

• The focus here is on spelling. All of these endings take the /z/ pronunciation.

• WORKBOOK: For additional exercises based on Chart 3-6, see *Workbook* Practices 14–16.

☐ EXERCISE 15, p. 63.   Spelling practice. (Chart 3-6)

TEACHING SUGGESTION: This very basic exercise can be done quickly as seatwork. After correcting it as a class, make two columns on the board, one labeled *Singular* and the other labeled *Plural*. Write a sample answer under each heading (e.g., *tries* = singular; *study* = plural). Ask students to spell the others for you to write in the correct columns.

> *ANSWERS:*   **1.** tries   **2.** studies   **3.** says   **4.** worries   **5.** flies   **6.** stays   **7.** enjoys   **8.** buys   **9.** pays   **10.** plays

☐ EXERCISE 16, p. 63.   Sentence practice. (Chart 3-6)

This exercise can be done in class or assigned as homework.

> *ANSWERS:*   **2.** seldom cries   **3.** studies   **4.** usually stays   **5.** flies   **6.** always carries   **7.** seldom buys   **8.** worries   **9.** enjoys

---

CHART 3-7:   IRREGULAR SINGULAR VERBS: *HAS, DOES, GOES*

• Irregular verbs in English have unusual pronunciations and spellings. Students must simply learn them.

• It is also true in English that some words that look like they ought to rhyme simply do not. *Do* and *go* do not rhyme. Similarly, *meat* and *great* do not rhyme. There are many other examples: *rough* and *cough; know* and *now; says* and *pays; heard* and *beard.* This feature of English can be quite frustrating for students.

• WORKBOOK: For additional exercises based on Chart 3-7, see *Workbook* Practices 17 and 18.

☐ EXERCISE 17, p. 64.   Sentence practice. (Chart 3-7)

This exercise can be done in class or assigned as homework. It's a quick check of students' understanding of the information in Chart 3-7.

> *ANSWERS:*   **3.** have   **4.** has   **5.** goes   **6.** has   **7.** does   **8.** do   **9.** goes . . . go   **10.** go

☐ EXERCISE 18, p. 65.   Listening. (Chart 3-7)

TEACHING SUGGESTION: First, play the audio one time through so students have some context for the overall meaning of the story. Then play/read it a second time and have students write the verbs they hear.

> *ANSWERS:*   **3.** is   **4.** has   **5.** has   **6.** goes   **7.** has   **8.** does   **9.** has   **10.** does   **11.** has   **12.** goes   **13.** is   **14.** is

CHART 3-8: SPELLING AND PRONUNCIATION OF FINAL -S/-ES

- Beginning learners usually have great difficulty hearing and saying these forms. You should not expect perfection now but continue to help students as they use these forms. Problems with correct use of final -s/-es continue well into the advanced stages of most learners' study of English, well beyond the point at which they understand the grammar. Use of final -s/-es needs teacher attention and student self-monitoring.

- In this chart and the following exercises, have students exaggerate the pronunciation of final -s. In actuality, final /s/ and /z/ are tiny, unstressed sounds; students have difficulty hearing them and, subsequently, often omit them in their speaking and writing.

- The vocabulary used to explain the information in this chart is difficult for learners. Take some time to make sure students understand the terms "voiced" and "voiceless." Perhaps start out with the vocabulary item *voice*. Then explain that *voiced* means "with the voice," and *voiceless* means "without the voice." (Explain that the suffix *-less* means "without.") Voiced means we use our voice boxes; model sounds for students to repeat, and have them feel their voice boxes. For voiceless sounds, we're simply pushing air out of our mouths with our lips, teeth, and/or tongue in particular formations. For example, for /f/, we put our upper front teeth on top of the bottom lip and blow air out.

- You may want to draw a bumble bee on the board saying, "bzzzzz," and a snake saying, "hsssss" to illustrate the difference between voiced and voiceless sounds.

- In example (b), point out that the -gh in *laugh* is pronounced /f/, a voiceless sound.

- This summarizes the pronunciation and spelling rules given in Charts 3-5 through 3-7.

- WORKBOOK: For additional exercises based on Chart 3-8, see *Workbook* Practices 19–22.

☐ EXERCISE 19, p. 66.   Let's talk: class activity. (Chart 3-8)

Students' books are closed. This exercise gives practice in using singular and plural verbs. Learners not only must think about those correct forms and the correct pronunciation of forms with final -s, but must also produce complete sentences from their own experience.

In item 13, *put on* is a separable two-word verb, so both *put on my clothes* and *put my clothes on* are correct. The verb phrases in items 7 and 11 cannot be separated in this way.

☐ EXERCISE 20, p. 67.   Sentence practice. (Chart 3-8)

This exercise can be done in class or assigned as homework.

TEACHING SUGGESTION: Students may work in pairs and help each other complete the sentences correctly. You may want to use item 12 as a test or ask students to write out the entire paragraph.

ANSWERS: 2. usually studies   3. bites   4. cashes   5. worry . . . never worries . . . studies   6. teach . . . teaches   7. fly . . . have   8. flies . . . has 9. always does . . . never goes   10. always says   11. always pays . . . answers . . . listens . . . asks   12. enjoys . . . often tries . . . likes . . . invites . . . go . . . watch . . . has . . . watches . . . makes . . . washes . . . cleans . . . never cook . . . is . . . loves

□ EXERCISE 21, p. 68.   Let's talk: pairwork. (Chart 3-8)

The frequencies of the activities listed are relative. For example, doing homework once a week can be *rarely* or *seldom* because the overall time frame is a week, but surfing the Internet once a week can be *sometimes* because the time frame is a day, a week, and a month. You may see some variation in your students' answers.

Encourage students to make sentences not just in the singular but also in the plural:
  Billy and Jenny sometimes watch TV.
  Billy, Jenny, and Peter often read for pleasure. (also possible: *usually*)

□ EXERCISE 22, p. 69.   Let's talk and write: pairwork. (Chart 3-8)

This exercise uses listening, speaking, writing, and grammatical knowledge. When students mark each other's papers, they should mark only the use of the verbs and frequency adverbs since that is the focus here.

CHART 3-9:   THE SIMPLE PRESENT: NEGATIVE

• Allow students time to look carefully at the examples. The grammar term "negative" was introduced in Chart 1-5. Students should notice that two words are necessary in a negative sentence: a helping verb (or auxiliary) and *not*. They should also notice that the *-s* ending is added only to the helping verb, not to the main verb. This will be difficult to learn and remember; you must expect it to be a recurring problem.

• Another recurring problem is that some learners may be tempted to place *no* before the main verb: ★*I no like.* You may want to put some incorrect examples of this on the board as you work through the chart.

• Students learned the formation of the negative with main verb *be* in Chart 1-5. Remind them of this when you discuss this chart and point out that when the main verb is *be,* you cannot add the helping verb *do* to form the negative. Only *not* is used with a form of *be.*

• WORKBOOK: For additional exercises based on Chart 3-9, see *Workbook* Practices 23–27.

□ EXERCISE 23, p. 69.   Sentence practice. (Chart 3-9)

If you do this exercise orally in class, allow students time to figure out the answers before you ask them to respond. When they respond, be sure they pay attention to the word order and the *-s* endings, and encourage them to use contractions when they speak.

NOTE: The verb is *be* in items 7, 10, 11, and 14, so the helping verb *do* cannot be added.

ANSWERS: **3.** doesn't know   **4.** don't need   **5.** doesn't snow   **6.** don't speak
7. 'm not   **8.** don't live   **9.** doesn't have   **10.** isn't   **11.** aren't
12. don't have   **13.** doesn't have   **14.** isn't   **15.** doesn't rain

□ EXERCISE 24, p. 70.   Let's talk: pairwork. (Chart 3-9)

Explain the use of the "strikethrough," which means "no." Do the first two items (the examples) with your students.

EXPANSION: After completing the exercise with a partner, students can write the answers for items 2–10 for homework.

☐ EXERCISE 25, p. 72.   Let's talk: game.   (Chart 3-9)

If your class is large, you may want to divide it into two groups. Eight to ten students is a good size for this exercise. Rather than joining your students in the circles, you would need to walk around the room and monitor the groups.

Students whose turn comes toward the end may become nervous because they have so many sentences to remember. The goal of this game is practice with the target structures, not memorization. If students are having trouble remembering the preceding sentences, encourage other students to help them.

☐ EXERCISE 26, p. 72.   Sentence practice.   (Chart 3-9)

This exercise can be done in class or assigned as homework. Students are asked to use the words in the list, but accept and discuss any correct completion.

> ANSWERS: **2.** don't speak   **3.** doesn't shave   **4.** don't go   **5.** doesn't smoke
> **6.** don't eat   **7.** don't do   **8.** doesn't drink   **9.** doesn't make   **10.** don't do
> **11.** doesn't put on

☐ EXERCISE 27, p. 73.   Let's talk: class activity.   (Chart 3-9)

This exercise is usually fun because students have to tell the truth, which sometimes depends on their opinions. Some of the vocabulary may be difficult, but you can help your students understand it.

As seen in the example, students can change the given vocabulary to make truthful sentences.

CHART 3-10:   THE SIMPLE PRESENT: YES/NO QUESTIONS

• These are called yes/no questions because they produce simple answers beginning with "Yes" or "No." English has two categories, depending on the main verb in a sentence. Examples (a)–(g) introduce the helping verb *do/does* in questions. Students should recall the similarity with the use of *do/does* in negative sentences (Chart 3-9). Example (h) shows the other category of yes/no questions: with *be* as the main verb. The verb *be* is the first word in these questions.

• It is not easy for learners to remember to use *do/does* in some questions and to put the words in correct order. You will have to help them with these structures throughout the course.

• WORKBOOK: For additional exercises based on Chart 3-10, see *Workbook* Practices 28–31.

☐ EXERCISE 28, p. 74.   Question practice.   (Chart 3-10)

This exercise can be done in class or assigned as homework. The words in parentheses don't need to be spoken. They just give information for the responses.

3. A: Do you speak Chinese?
B: No, I don't.
4. A: Does Ann speak Italian?
B: Yes, she does.
5. A: Do Ann and Tom speak Arabic?
B: No, they don't.
6. A: Do you exercise every morning?
B: Yes, I do.

7. A: Does Sue have a cold?
B: Yes, she does.
8. A: Does Jim do his homework every day?
B: No, he doesn't.
9. A: Does it rain a lot in April?
B: Yes, it does.
10. A: Do frogs have tails?
B: No, they don't.

☐ **EXERCISE 29, p. 75. Interview and question practice: pairwork. (Chart 3-10)**

This exercise provides practice with authentic questions as students learn more about one another.

EXPANSION: You might ask students to share one of their answers without revealing the name of the classmate they interviewed. The rest of the class can try to guess who the person is, based on what they already know about him/her.

☐ **EXERCISE 30, p. 76. Let's talk: pairwork. (Chart 3-10)**

Lead your class through the examples carefully so that they understand they are supposed to use their classmates' names. In the examples, substitute your students' names for *Ali* and *Yoko.*

☐ **EXERCISE 31, p. 77. Let's talk: pairwork. (Chart 3-10)**

TEACHING SUGGESTIONS: Before students begin the activity, use the pictures in this exercise to introduce or review vocabulary terms: *the newspaper, send e-mails, truck, boots.*

Go over the answers with a different pair performing each exchange.

CHART 3-11: THE SIMPLE PRESENT: ASKING INFORMATION QUESTIONS WITH *WHERE*

• This chart contrasts two types of questions: yes/no questions and information questions. You might want to write (a) and (b) on the board and ask students to point out all the similarities and differences between them. The key points are the use of the same word order and the use of final -*s* on the helping verb with a singular subject.

• WORKBOOK: For additional exercises based on Chart 3-11, see *Workbook* Practices 32–34.

☐ **EXERCISE 32, p. 78. Question practice. (Chart 3-11)**

Point out the similarity in sentence structure in the pairs of sentences in items 1 and 2; 3 and 4; and 5 and 6. Perhaps draw a grid on the board showing the placement of *do/does,* the subject, and the main verb.

☐ **EXERCISE 33, p. 79.   Let's talk: pairwork. (Chart 3-11)**

Encourage students to use each other's names. After most pairs have finished, ask for volunteers to perform some of the exchanges.

CHART 3-12:   THE SIMPLE PRESENT: ASKING INFORMATION QUESTIONS WITH *WHEN* AND *WHAT TIME*

• Questions with *when* and *what time* follow the same pattern as questions with *where* (see Chart 3-11). Ask students why examples (a) and (b) use the helping verb *do*, whereas (c) and (d) use *does*. They should see that *Anna* is a singular noun that requires *does*.

• A question with *what time* usually asks about time on a clock:
  A: What time do you have class?
  B: At eight-thirty.

A question with *when* can be answered by any time expression:
  A: When do you have class?
  B: At eight-thirty. / Every day. / Monday morning. / In the afternoon. / Etc.

This information is presented in Chart 9-1, but you may wish to mention it at this point.

• WORKBOOK: For additional exercises based on Chart 3-12, see *Workbook* Practices 35–37.

☐ **EXERCISE 34, p. 80.   Question practice. (Chart 3-12)**

TEACHING SUGGESTION: Two students can read one exchange as a short dialogue. If everyone is satisfied with the response, two more students can read the next one. As you listen to the students, remind them to look at each other when they talk. Encourage them to speak so everyone can hear. Be sure that they say *do* or *does* clearly in every question, but it's not necessary to correct every pronunciation mistake.

Review ways of saying the time as you go through the exercise in class. For example, *6:45* can be said, "six forty-five," "a quarter to seven," "fifteen (minutes) before seven," etc.

☐ **EXERCISE 35, p. 81.   Let's talk: class interview. (Chart 3-12)**

Students who finish early can write out their answers in complete sentences.

□ EXERCISE 36, p. 82.   Interview and paragraph practice. (Chart 3-12)

> *TEACHING SUGGESTION:* You may want to refer students to Exercise 14, p. 62, for a paragraph sample they can model in their writing.

CHART 3-13:   SUMMARY: INFORMATION QUESTIONS WITH *BE* AND *DO*

• Learners benefit greatly from a contrastive summary like this. You might write the grammatical categories (Q-WORD + *BE* + SUBJECT) on the board and point to each as you say one of the examples. Discuss singular and plural verb use. Proceed in a similar way with the examples that use the helping verb *do/does*.

• WORKBOOK: For additional exercises based on Chart 3-13, see *Workbook* Practices 38 and 39.

□ EXERCISE 37, p. 82.   Question practice. (Chart 3-13)

> *TEACHING SUGGESTION:* Divide the class into pairs. Give each pair time to read a complete dialogue and write a form of the verb *be* or the helping verb *do/does*. Then ask partners to practice the dialogue and to discuss any differences in their answers. After that, ask a pair to perform the dialogue for the rest of the class so that everyone can make sure they have the correct completions.

> *ANSWERS:* 2. Do   3. is   4. Are   5. are   6. do   7. Do   8. Are
> 9. Does   10. Do   11. Does   12. Is   13. does   14. Does   15. Are
> 16. Do

□ EXERCISE 38, p. 84.   Let's talk: small group activity. (Chart 3-13)

This is a challenging exercise. You may want to review *be* + **adjective**, *be* + **noun**, and *do/does* + **verb**. For example:

> ***Are*** *you* **cold**? / ***Is*** *the room* **cold**?
>
> ***Is*** *Tom* **a student**?
>
> ***Do*** *you* **want** *a coat?*
>
> ***Does*** *Tom* **like** *English?*

The answers to the questions shouldn't be given until the groups have had a chance to come up with their own answers. They'll enjoy seeing how many they get right.

> *REMEMBER:* The object of this exercise is not a lesson in astronomy but a test of *is, are, do,* and *does.* The facts given below are just for fun.

> *ANSWERS:*
>
> **2.** Does   (no)
> **3.** Do   (yes)
> **4.** Is   (no)   [It's a star.]
> **5.** Are   (no)
> **6.** Is   (yes)   [about 900 degrees Fahrenheit]
> **7.** Is   (no)   [You need a telescope.]
> **8.** Is   (yes)   [The winds are stronger than the earth's winds.]
> **9.** Do   (yes)
> **10.** Do   (yes)   [Saturn has at least 24; Uranus has at least 21.]

□ EXERCISE 39, p. 85.   Question practice. (Chart 3-13)

> *TEACHING SUGGESTIONS:* This exercise can be assigned as homework since students will need time to think of good questions and answers. Then in class you could elicit completions from several students for each item.
>
> Another possibility would be to ask students to write the dialogues on paper to hand in. You can decide how to mark their papers. To save time with a large class, you could choose to mark only the same three items on everyone's paper, probably one each with *be, do,* and *does*. Or, take some of the most common errors and write them on the board for students to correct.

□ EXERCISE 40, p. 85.   Chapter review. (Chapter 3)

> Exercises 40–47 give learners more complete contexts for using the structures in this chapter.
>
> *TEACHING SUGGESTIONS:* You might save one part of each exercise to use in a test but assign the rest as either seatwork or homework.
>
> Exercises 41, 44, and 45 require students to use their own words and ideas, so you should check their accuracy on these tasks before testing them.
>
> You could either mark written homework or walk around the classroom as students work in pairs to answer their questions or to comment on their responses. It's advisable to praise their successes more than criticize mistakes.

> *ANSWERS:*   (2) walks = walk + /s/   (3) catches = catch + /əz/   (4) shares = share + /z/   (5) comes = come + /z/   (6) *(no change)*   (7) *(no change)*   (8) speaks ... speaks = speak + /s/   (9) *(no change)*   (10) tries = try + /z/ ... gives = give + /z/ [Note: Do not add *-s* to an infinitive (e.g., *to teach, to speak*).]   (11) *(no change)*   (12) enjoys = enjoy /z/ ... misses = miss + /əz/

□ EXERCISE 41, p. 86.   Chapter review: pairwork. (Chapter 3)

> This exercise encourages authentic language use of the target structures in this chapter.

□ EXERCISE 42, p. 87.   Chapter review: question practice. (Chapter 3)

> *ANSWERS:*   1. Do you study   2. study   3. studies   4. Do you spend   5. spend   6. don't like   7. are you   8. want   9. don't want   10. think

□ EXERCISE 43, p. 88.   Chapter review. (Chapter 3)

> *ANSWERS:*   1. have   2. washes   3. Do you know   4. is   5. doesn't change   6. keeps   7. never washes   8. wears   9. is always   10. is always   11. says   12. takes

□ EXERCISE 44, p. 88.   Chapter review: let's talk. (Chapter 3)

> Divide students into pairs. Walk around the room to help partners get started and to answer questions.

□ EXERCISE 45, p. 89.   Chapter review. (Chapter 3)

In item 9, *south of the United States* = outside of its borders.
In the southern part of the United States or *in the South* = a region inside its borders.

□ EXERCISE 46, p. 90.   Chapter review: let's talk. (Chapter 3)

This information-gap exercise provides authentic contexts for asking *wh*-questions. Be sure to go over all the example answers before proceeding with the exercise.

   EXPANSION: With a more advanced class, discuss the advantages and disadvantages of each lifestyle. Ask students to describe a perfect lifestyle for themselves.

ANSWER GRID: (*Answers in parentheses are answers already given in the student book.*)

Name	Where does she/he live?	What does he/she do?	Where does she/he work?	What pets does he/she have?
Peter	(on a boat)	catches fish	on his boat	a turtle
Kathy	in a cabin in the mountains	(teaches skiing)	at a ski school	ten fish
Ron	in an apartment in the city	makes jewelry	(at a jewelry store)	three cats
Lisa	in a beach cabin on an island	surfs and swims	has no job	(a snake)
Jack	in a house in the country	designs web pages	at home	a horse

□ EXERCISE 47, p. 91.   Chapter review: error analysis. (Chapter 3)

See p. xvi of this *Teacher's Guide* for suggestions on how to handle error-analysis exercises.

ANSWERS: 2. Ann <u>usually comes</u> to class on time.   3. Peter <u>uses</u> his cell phone often.   4. Amy <u>carries</u> a <u>computer notebook</u> to work every day.   5. She <u>enjoys</u> her job.   6. I <u>don't</u> know Joe.   7. Mike <u>doesn't</u> like milk. He never <u>drinks</u> it.
8. Tina doesn't <u>speak</u> Chinese. She <u>speaks</u> Spanish.   9. <u>Are you</u> a student?
10. Does your roommate <u>sleep</u> with the window open?   11. A: Do you like strong coffee? B: Yes, I <u>do</u>.   12. Where <u>do</u> your parents live?   13. What time <u>does</u> your English class <u>begin</u>?   14. Olga <u>doesn't</u> need a car. She <u>has</u> a bicycle.   15. <u>Does</u> Pablo <u>do</u> his homework every day?

CHAPTER 4
Using the Present Progressive

Overview

Chapter 4 introduces the present progressive (or present continuous). This verb form is used mainly to describe temporary situations at the moment of speaking. Because it adds *-ing* to the verb, some attention is given to spelling. Questions and negative forms are introduced, and the difference between the meanings and uses of simple and progressive present verbs is pointed out and practiced. Next, students are introduced to common uses of the simple present to express needs, wants, likes, and thoughts.

CHART 4-1: *BE* + *-ING:* THE PRESENT PROGRESSIVE TENSE

• The progressive tense (or aspect) expresses an activity that is in progress at the moment of speaking. This activity is usually of short duration: it began in the recent past, is continuing at present, and will probably end at some point in the near future.

   COMPARE: *Mr. Jones usually wears a jacket, but today he's wearing a sweater.* The best way to make this meaning clear to students is through a lot of practice that makes use of meaningful contexts. Use yourself to demonstrate the meaning by performing actions and describing them at the same time: "I am standing. I am sitting. I am walking. I am talking. I am writing on the board. I am opening the door. I am looking at the ceiling." Perhaps have students perform the same actions and say the same sentences. You stand and say, "I am standing." Then the class mimics you by standing and saying, "I am standing."

• Suggest to students that they describe their own actions silently to themselves as they go through their days: *I'm walking to class. I'm opening the door. I'm sitting down. I'm eating lunch. I'm listening to music.* Etc.

• WORKBOOK: For additional exercises based on Chart 4-1, see *Workbook* Practice 1.

☐ EXERCISE 1, p. 92. Let's talk: class activity. (Chart 4-1)

It's important that you model the present progressive for students: perform the action <u>while</u> you explain that action to them.

☐ EXERCISE 2, p. 92. Let's talk: pairwork. (Chart 4-1)

One use of the present progressive is to describe activities in progress in pictures. This exercise shows some typical activities. Some of the vocabulary may be unfamiliar. Write new words on the board.

EXPANSION: Write the activities shown in this exercise on 3″ × 5″ cards or slips of paper: *eat a carrot, paint a picture, read a newspaper,* etc. Pass out the cards. Then ask students, in turn, to pantomime the activities on their cards so that other students can describe the activity in progress.

ANSWERS: **1.** The rabbit is eating a carrot. **2.** The monkey is painting a picture (of a clown). **3.** The elephant is reading a newspaper/wearing glasses. **4.** The tiger is talking on the telephone/making a telephone call. **5.** The horse is sleeping/snoring. **6.** The cat is drinking a cup of coffee/tea. **7.** The dog is playing the piano. The mouse is singing. **8.** The bird is taking a bath. **9.** The giraffe is driving a car.

☐ EXERCISE 3, p. 94. Let's talk: class activity. (Chart 4-1)

This exercise uses the verb *wear* and familiar vocabulary to practice the basic form and meaning of the present progressive. Lead students through the questions. Keep the pace lively, but be patient as your learners struggle to understand your questions and formulate their own answers.

NOTE: The word *else* in *What else is Jin Won wearing?* means "additional." *What else* is a common phrase to invite more information.

Sneakers are also called "running shoes," "gym shoes," "jogging shoes" or "tennis shoes."

☐ EXERCISE 4, p. 94. Let's talk: pairwork. (Chart 4-1)

Point out that *no one* is followed by *is*.

☐ EXERCISE 5, p. 94. Let's talk: class activity. (Chart 4-1)

TEACHING SUGGESTIONS: Lead students through the example, using their names. Then continue with other actions in the list. The example shows sentences beginning with *I, we, they,* and *he/she*. It's not necessary to include all of those subjects for each item. It is also not necessary to include all 18 items if time is short or if your students have few problems with their answers. Adapt the material to your class.

Anticipate that some of the vocabulary in this exercise is new for at least some students (e.g., *ceiling, shake hands, hold up, clap*). Unfamiliar vocabulary, of course, makes following the cues in a books-closed exercise impossible for students, so take time to write new words on the board and discuss them. The definitions of the new words can come from actions you demonstrate.

If any students are visibly uncomfortable or distressed, tell them they may open their books (but not their dictionaries — they can more profitably get the meanings of the new words by paying attention to what's going on in the classroom).

☐ EXERCISE 6, p. 95. Let's talk: pairwork. (Chart 4-1)

First, go over any unfamiliar vocabulary in the list. After students complete the task, ask for volunteers to share some of their sentences with the class.

☐ EXERCISE 7, p. 96. Listening. (Chart 4-1)

TEACHING SUGGESTION: Read the story aloud first or ask a student to read it to the class. Make sure students understand the story and discuss the example before playing the audio.

ANSWERS: **1.** yes   **2.** yes   **3.** no   **4.** no   **5.** no   **6.** no   **7.** no
8. yes   **9.** no   **10.** no

☐ **EXERCISE 8, p. 96.   Pretest. (Chart 4-2)**

This pretest contains examples of all four rules found in Chart 4-2. When you introduce the chart in the next section, you may want to refer to words in the pretest (and not already in the chart) which further illustrate the rules. The *-ing* forms of many of the words in this and the following exercise are common sources of spelling errors for many learners.

SUGGESTIONS: Give students time in class to complete the exercise prior to class discussion. If you wish, students can work in pairs.

The correct spellings should be written on the board, and students should check their answers carefully. It would be helpful for students to exchange papers and check each other's answers. Some students cannot see their own spelling errors, especially beginning students whose native languages do not use the same alphabet as English.

ANSWERS: **2.** riding   **3.** running   **4.** stopping   **5.** raining   **6.** sleeping
7. pushing   **8.** counting   **9.** fixing   **10.** writing   **11.** growing
12. waiting

CHART 4-2:   SPELLING OF *-ING*

• The spelling of *-ing* forms has clear rules. Understanding these rules right from the beginning of their study of English can help students avoid lots of writing errors down the road. (If correctness of written English is not important to your students' needs, this and similar charts can be handled briefly or omitted.)

• SUGGESTION: Demonstrate the points made in the chart by writing the wrong spelling (e.g., *writting, siting, rainning*) on the board and explaining the underlying rules for correct spelling. Clearly label the wrong spellings on the board by also writing something such as WRONG or NO. Perhaps draw a circle around the misspelled word and then draw a slash through the circle.

• The unstated part of Rule 1 is that the consonant is NOT doubled. Emphasize that when we drop final *-e*, we do NOT double the consonant.

• Explain the meaning of the verb *double*.

• WORKBOOK: For additional exercises based on Chart 4-2, see *Workbook* Practices 2–4.

☐ **EXERCISE 9, p. 97.   Spelling practice. (Chart 4-2)**

EXPANSION: You could make four columns on the board with one rule written at the top of each column. Ask students to put the answers from the exercise in the correct columns.

ANSWERS: **2.** coming   **3.** dreaming   **4.** biting   **5.** hitting   **6.** joining
7. hurting   **8.** planning   **9.** dining   **10.** snowing   **11.** studying
12. warning

□ EXERCISE 10, p. 98.   Spelling practice. (Chart 4-2)

Call out the item number, pantomime the action, and ask: "What am I doing?" Students write only one word for each item. To check, their answers, they can exchange papers and mark any mistakes they see. You might sample a few items by having students spell their answers aloud as you write them on the board.

ANSWERS: **1.** smiling **2.** flying **3.** laughing **4.** sitting **5.** standing **6.** sleeping **7.** clapping **8.** writing **9.** eating **10.** running **11.** singing **12.** reading **13.** drinking **14.** sneezing **15.** crying **16.** cutting

□ EXERCISE 11, p. 98.   Let's talk: class activity. (Chart 4-1)

This exercise is meant to be fun. Books should be open because some of the vocabulary is unfamiliar.

You could also have students write the answers.

NOTE: The description must be given while the action is continuing so that the present progressive is appropriate. The short actions in items 7, 9, 16, 17, and 20 might have to be repeated until the answer is spoken.

CHART 4-3: THE PRESENT PROGRESSIVE: NEGATIVES

• Point out that *not* is added after the verb *be*.

• Some students may be accustomed to putting *no* in front of the verb and omitting *be:* *I no going.* If you have heard this error from your students, you may want to write a couple of these incorrect sentences on the board and have students supply the corrected version.

• You may want to give both contracted and non-contracted forms for (a)–(c).

• WORKBOOK: For additional exercises based on Chart 4-3, see *Workbook* Practices 5 and 6.

□ EXERCISE 12, p. 99.   Sentence practice. (Chart 4-3)

Students can complete the exercise orally with a partner in class, and then write the answers for homework.

ANSWERS: **1.** watching the news . . . talking on the phone. **2.** is listening to music . . . not playing the piano. **3.** is reading a magazine . . . not reading a book. **4.** aren't flying . . . sitting on a telephone wire.

□ EXERCISE 13, p. 101.   Let's talk: pairwork. (Chart 4-3)

Ask students to share some of their answers with the class after they have completed the task.

□ EXERCISE 14, p. 101.   Sentence practice. (Chart 4-3)

For items 2 and 3, you may want to help students by eliciting names of leaders of the students' countries, as well as names of famous actors, writers, and sports stars.

CHART 4-4: THE PRESENT PROGRESSIVE: QUESTIONS

• Short answers are quite natural, even preferred, in conversation. So are contractions, which some learners try to avoid.

• NOTE: When *be* is the main verb in an affirmative short answer (e.g., "Yes, she is. Yes, I am."), no contraction is possible, as noted in Chart 2-2, p. 25, of the student book.

• Long answers normally do not occur in conversational English. The inclusion of the long answer here is for teaching-learning reasons, so that students can understand what underlies the short answer.

• Point out again that subject-verb word order is the same in yes/no and information questions:
  BE (HELPING VERB) + SUBJECT + MAIN VERB.

• You might model the spoken contractions of *is* and *are* with *where* and *why* in examples (c) and (e): "Where's" and "Why're."

• WORKBOOK: For additional exercises based on Chart 4-4, see *Workbook* Practices 7 and 8.

□ EXERCISE 15, p. 102.   Question practice. (Chart 4-4)

This controlled exercise provides practice with the sentence structure of present progressive questions. It can be done quickly in class. Review Chart 4-4 as necessary.

ANSWERS: 2. Is John riding a bicycle?   3. Are you sleeping?   4. Are the students watching TV?   5. Is it raining outside?

□ EXERCISE 16, p. 103.   Let's talk: pairwork. (Chart 4-4)

Make sure that partners are clear about which pages they're working from before they begin the exercise. Assign two students Partner A and B roles to model the example for the class.

□ EXERCISE 17, p. 104.   Let's talk: small groups. (Chart 4-4)

You can turn this into a teacher-led class activity if students are having trouble asking questions.

□ EXERCISE 18, p. 104.   Question practice. (Chart 4-4)

This can be assigned for homework, but be sure the answers are discussed in class.
  NOTE: The name *Seung* sounds like "sung."

ANSWERS: 2. Why are you reading your grammar book?   3. What are you writing in your grammar book?   4. Where is Seung sitting?   5. Where are you living?
6. What is Roberto wearing today?   7. Why are you smiling?

□ EXERCISE 19, p. 105.   Question practice. (Chart 4-4)

Students could work in pairs to complete these exchanges; then ask for volunteers to perform them. The words in parentheses are for information only and need not be read.

ANSWERS:

3. A: Is Anna eating lunch?
   B: she is.
4. is she eating?
5. A: Is Mike drinking a cup
      of coffee?
   B: he isn't.

6. is he drinking?
7. A: Are the girls playing
      in the street?
   B: they aren't.
8. are they playing?
9. are they playing in the park?

CHART 4-5:   THE SIMPLE PRESENT vs. THE PRESENT PROGRESSIVE

- Another way to explain the difference in meaning between the simple present and the present progressive is to point out (using terms beginners can understand) that the simple present expresses more permanent or unchanging situations whereas the present progressive expresses more temporary or unique situations.

- In examples (e)–(h), point out that the subject-verb word order in the questions is the same:
  BE/DO (HELPING VERB) + SUBJECT + MAIN VERB.

- WORKBOOK: For additional exercises based on Chart 4-5, see *Workbook* Practices 9–12.

☐ EXERCISE 20, p. 107.   Sentence practice. (Chart 4-5)

TEACHING SUGGESTION: If possible, assign this exercise as homework to be discussed in class the next day. Your students need time to think this one through. It is a summary exercise that includes the affirmative, negative, and question forms of both the simple present and the present progressive. If you can't give students time to prepare out of class, go slowly as they decide which form is required.

ANSWERS: 1. . . . is talking . . . isn't talking   2. rains . . . isn't raining . . . is shining . . . Does it rain   3. sit . . . help . . . is helping   4. cooks . . . is cooking . . . Is he cooking . . . doesn't eat . . . Do you eat . . . Are you

☐ EXERCISE 21, p. 107.   Listening. (Chart 4-5)

ANSWERS: 1. every day   2. now   3. now   4. every day   5. every day   6. now   7. every day   8. now

☐ EXERCISE 22, p. 108.   Let's talk: pairwork. (Chart 4-5)

EXPANSION: After students have completed the task, you can also use the illustrations to review *what*-questions: "What is Anna doing?"

ANSWERS: Anna is . . .   1. riding her bicycle.   2. listening to music.   3. swimming.   4. watching TV.   5. talking on the phone.   6. taking a walk.   7. drinking tea.   8. playing tennis.   9. playing the guitar.   10. saying "hello" to her neighbor.

☐ EXERCISE 23, p. 108.   Sentence practice. (Chart 4-5)

This is harder than it looks. Students must know the difference between the present and the present progressive tenses, as well as question structures and forms of the verb *be*.

TEACHING SUGGESTION: This might be assigned as homework so your students have time to review past charts as they work through the exercise. The answers should be discussed in class.

ANSWERS: **1.** Are . . . is   **2.** Do   **3.** is . . . Does   **4.** do   **5.** Am
6. am . . . Do   **7.** does   **8.** is   **9.** do   **10.** Do

☐ EXERCISE 24, p. 109.   Question practice. (Chart 4-5)

ANSWERS: **2.** A: walk . . . don't take . . . Do you take   **3.** B: is she talking
A: is running   **4.** A: read   B: Do you read   A: don't read   **5.** A: are you reading
B: am reading   **6.** A: Do you want . . . Is this   B: is hanging

☐ EXERCISE 25, p. 110.   Listening. (Chart 4-5)

Exercises 25 and 26 are the first listening exercises in which students have to supply long portions of a sentence. It's important that students learn to group words or form thought groups as they listen rather than hear the discourse as individual, separate words. This is very challenging for beginning learners.

In Exercise 25, you may want to play item 1 in its entirety before having students write. Do the same for item 2. In fact, it might be necessary to play all the sentences several times. Don't be surprised if you find the verbs *be* and *do* frequently mixed up or absent. Your students will become much more proficient with this type of listening as they progress through the text.

In Exercise 25, answers that appear in parentheses are answers that are already supplied in the student book.

ANSWERS:

1. A: Does . . . have
  B: (Yes.)
  A: Does he wear
  B: (No.)
  A: Is he wearing
  B: don't know
  A: think

2. A: Do . . . dream
  B: aren't
  A: is sleeping . . . are . . . is barking
    . . . moving . . . am . . . is dreaming
    . . . dream

☐ EXERCISE 26, p. 111.   Listening. (Chart 4-5)

You may want to play the entire conversation one time, then play it a second time while students write the words they hear.

EXPANSION: If your class is advanced, two students can read this dialogue from the listening script provided in the back of the student book.

A: Are you working
B: I'm not . . . I'm writing
A: Do you write
B: don't write
A: Does she write
B: get . . . Do you get
A: like

CHART 4-6: NONACTION VERBS NOT USED IN THE PRESENT PROGRESSIVE

- "Nonaction" verbs are called "stative" verbs: they describe "states" rather than actions.

- In example (a), the verb *be* in *I'm hungry* is also an example of this rule.
  INCORRECT: **I am being hungry.*

- WORKBOOK: For additional exercises based on Chart 4-6, see *Workbook* Practices 13 and 14.

☐ EXERCISE 27, p. 112. Sentence practice. (Chart 4-6)

You could work through a few of these with your class and assign the rest as homework.

ANSWERS: **2.** is snowing . . . like   **3.** know   **4.** is talking . . . understand
5. is eating . . . likes . . . tastes   **6.** smell . . . Do you smell   **7.** is telling . . . believe
. . . think   **8.** is smoking . . . smells . . . hate   **9.** is holding . . . loves . . . is smiling

☐ EXERCISE 28, p. 113. Let's talk: interview. (Chart 4-6)

You may want to point out to students before they begin that all questions will be in the simple present.

QUESTIONS: **1.** What do you like?   **2.** What do babies around the world like?
3. What do you want?   **4.** What do children around the world want?   **5.** What do
you love?   **6.** What do teenagers around the world love?   **7.** What do you dislike or
hate?   **8.** What do people around the world dislike or hate?   **9.** What do you need?
10. What do elderly people around the world need?

CHART 4-7: *SEE, LOOK AT, WATCH, HEAR,* AND *LISTEN TO*

- As "stative" (or "nonaction") verbs, *see* and *hear* are not used in the progressive. The other verbs in this chart have more active meanings, so they can have progressive forms. This is sometimes difficult for learners to understand. The text uses these five verbs to try to convey the concept of "nonaction" vs. "action" verbs, as well as simply to give students usage information about these very common words.

- WORKBOOK: For additional exercises based on Chart 4-7, see *Workbook* Practices 15–18.

□ EXERCISE 29, p. 114.   Let's talk: class activity. (Chart 4-7)

This is a teacher-led activity. Students will need their books open for item 2; otherwise, their books should be closed for this exercise.

□ EXERCISE 30, p. 115.   Verb review. (Chart 4-7)

This exercise can be done in class or assigned as homework. As students answer, check their spelling of words that have double consonants.

> *ANSWERS:* **2.** speaks . . . is speaking   **3.** are doing . . . do   **4.** am looking . . . is writing . . . is looking . . . is biting . . . is smiling . . . is sleeping . . . is chewing
> **5.** works . . . has . . . often eats . . . usually brings . . . usually sits . . . sits . . . watches . . . watches . . . relaxes   **6.** am looking . . . isn't . . . is . . . is sitting . . . is eating . . . is running . . . is sitting . . . is eating . . . is watching . . . always watches . . . are swimming . . . are flying . . . is riding . . . rides . . . is having . . . go

---

CHART 4-8:   *THINK ABOUT* AND *THINK THAT*

• *Think about* [examples (a) and (b)] has both simple present and present progressive forms. In *think about, think* is a sort of "action" verb with thoughts actively going through one's mind. In *think that, think* is a "nonaction" verb, as introduced in Chart 4-7, p. 114, of the student book. Exercises 31–33 focus on these two different uses of the verb *think.*

• A common mistake is the use of *think that* in the present progressive: ★*I'm thinking that this is a nice city.* This chart tries to clarify when *think* can be used in the progressive and when it cannot.

• NOTE: On occasion, native speakers may use the progressive for *think:* "I'm thinking I want to leave now." But this use is infrequent and does not need to be explained at this level.

• WORKBOOK: For additional exercises based on Chart 4-8, see *Workbook* Practices 19 and 20.

□ EXERCISE 31, p. 117.   Sentence practice. (Chart 4-8)

This exercise can be done in class.

TEACHING SUGGESTION: Students should read an item and each decide his/her opinion about it. Then each student should write a statement based on examples (c)–(g) in Chart 4-8, p. 117, of the student book. You might want to expand the number of items, seeking opinions about movies, other sports, other school subjects, etc. To avoid controversy, you might wish to stay away from matters of religion or politics.

□ EXERCISE 32, p. 118.   Sentence practice. (Chart 4-8)

TEACHING SUGGESTIONS: Give students a few minutes to use their imaginations and come up with good answers, or assign the exercise as homework. The sentences can be either written or spoken, depending on your preference. During class discussion, elicit responses from several students for each item and encourage incidental conversation in which the students state (and perhaps defend) their opinions.

□ EXERCISE 33, p. 118.   Let's talk: small groups. (Chart 4-8)

Students can work in small groups, comparing their opinions. This is less threatening than having to state them in front of the whole class. Encourage students to help each other with corrections.

  The purpose of this exercise is to encourage spontaneous conversation as the students gain experience expressing their opinions in English. Grammar classes should routinely contain short periods of time devoted to spontaneous oral interaction. It's important for the teacher to give students opportunities to speak freely.

□ EXERCISE 34, p. 119.   Chapter review. (Chapter 4)

This is not a difficult or tricky multiple-choice test. Students should score 100% with little effort. Errors probably result from inattention, not lack of understanding.

ANSWERS: **2.** B **3.** C **4.** C **5.** B **6.** C **7.** B **8.** A **9.** A
10. B

□ EXERCISE 35, p. 119.   Chapter review: error analysis. (Chapter 4)

Errors in this exercise include spelling, verb forms, and words added or omitted. Finding the errors is a good way to review the grammar in this chapter, and it forces learners to pay close attention to details as they develop their self-monitoring skills.

ANSWERS: **1.** It's <u>raining</u> today. I <u>don't</u> like the rain. **2.** I like New York City. I <u>think</u> that it is a wonderful city. **3.** <u>Is</u> Abdul <u>sleeping</u> right now? **4.** Why <u>are you</u> going downtown today? **5.** I'm listening <u>to</u> you. **6.** <u>Do</u> you <u>hear</u> a noise outside the window? **7.** Kunio <u>is</u> at a restaurant right now. He usually <u>eats</u> at home, but today he <u>is eating</u> dinner at a restaurant. **8.** I <u>like</u> flowers. They <u>smell</u> good.
9. Alex is <u>sitting</u> at his desk. He <u>is</u>/He's <u>writing</u> a letter. **10.** Where <u>are they</u> sitting today?

CHAPTER 5
Talking About the Present

Overview

This chapter focuses on ways to talk about the present. It begins by showing how to use *it + be* to talk about time and weather, and *there + be* for descriptions. Two sections on prepositions of place follow. Common uses of the simple present to express needs, wants, and likes expand students' ability to talk about the present. Several pages of review for this chapter and previous ones complete the unit.

☐ **EXERCISE 1, p. 121. Preview: listening.**

> Your students may be familiar with talking about time. If so, this preview will go quickly. If not, you will know that Chart 5-1 needs to be explained in detail.
>
> *NOTE:* The abbreviation A.M. describes the period from one minute after midnight to noon. P.M. describes the period from one minute after noon to midnight. This book uses small caps, but lowercase letters (a.m./p.m.) are also correct. The letters A.M. stand for the Latin words *ante merediem,* meaning "before the half day" (before noon). P.M. stands for *post meridiem,* meaning "after the half day" (after noon).

CHART 5-1: USING *IT* TO TALK ABOUT TIME

• Speakers of the English language have developed the custom of using *it + be* to refer to time and weather. (See Chart 5-3, p. 125, in the student book.) Your students' home languages might not use this pattern. It is a very common pattern in everyday conversations, so it is helpful for learners to get used to it as soon as possible.

• These sentences use the pronoun *it* with no real meaning. Some grammar books call this "dummy *it*" or "filler *it*" because it merely fills the empty subject position in the sentence. If some students are puzzled about this required but meaningless pronoun, just assure them that languages are not always logical in their structures. Many phrases are a matter of history or custom, not pure logic.

• WORKBOOK: For additional exercises based on Chart 5-1, see *Workbook* Practices 1 and 2.

☐ **EXERCISE 2, p. 122. Question practice. (Chart 5-1)**

> Obviously, Speaker B's responses are not truthful for your students' situation. So, you might want to add a few more items about the current day, date, and time where you are.

ANSWERS: **2.** What's the date today? **3.** What time is it? **4.** What month is it? **5.** What time is it? **6.** What day is it? **7.** What's the date today? **8.** What year is it? **9.** What time is it?

CHART 5-2: PREPOSITIONS OF TIME

• Few prepositions in English have exact meanings, so they are difficult to learn. The prepositions of time in the chart are important and fairly easy to understand. Some people find it helpful to see them on a pyramid:

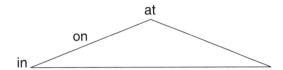

On this pyramid, *at* is at the point, a very short, specific point in time. *In* is at the broadest, most general base of the pyramid. *On* is restricted to the middle, which represents a 24-hour period of time or a 2-day weekend. (Americans say "on the weekend" whereas the British say "at the weekend.")

• The phrases "*at* night" and "*in* the evening/morning/afternoon" have no logical explanation. Students must simply memorize those phrases. Sometimes when students ask "Why?" a grammar teacher simply has to say, "That's just the way it is."

• WORKBOOK: For additional exercises based on Chart 5-2, see *Workbook* Practices 3 and 4.

☐ EXERCISE 3, p. 123. Sentence practice. (Chart 5-2)

After you lead your students through the first three items, they should be able to finish the rest of the exercise pretty quickly. Go over the answers so that difficult items can be discussed.

ANSWERS: **2.** from . . . to **3.** in . . . in **4.** in **5.** at **6.** in **7.** in **8.** on **9.** on **10.** on **11.** from . . . to **12.** at

☐ EXERCISE 4, p. 124. Listening and sentence practice. (Chart 5-2)

You may need to play the audio more than once to give everyone sufficient time to identify the persons being described in Part I. You may choose to assign Part II as pairwork so students can discuss their answers.

TEACHING SUGGESTION: Have students answer Part II without looking back at Chart 5-2. When they're done, ask them to exchange books and correct each other's work. They can use Chart 5-2 to check their answers.

PART I ANSWERS: **1.** Ann **2.** Lisa **3.** Ron **4.** Tom

PART II ANSWERS: **1.** in . . . on . . . Tom **2.** in . . . on . . . Ann **3.** in . . . at . . . Lisa **4.** Ron . . . in . . . on . . . in

☐ EXERCISE 5, p. 125.   Let's talk: pairwork. (Chart 5-3)

This is principally a vocabulary development exercise. The list of terms comes from weather reports, and learners might not need or want to know all of them.

☐ EXERCISE 6, p. 125.   Let's talk: small groups. (Chart 5-3)

In the United States, the Fahrenheit scale is used much more than Celsius (which is sometimes called "Centigrade"). This exercise allows learners to associate both scales with descriptive terms.

NOTE: In the box, 0° C is spoken "zero degrees Celsius"; −18° C is spoken "minus 18 degrees Celsius" or "18 degrees below zero Celsius."

ANSWERS: **2.** 0° C = cold, freezing   **3.** 38° C = hot   **4.** 24° C = warm
5. −18° C = very cold, below freezing

☐ EXERCISE 7, p. 126.   Let's talk: small groups. (Chart 5-3)

These formulas are handy ways of converting Fahrenheit and Celsius temperatures. If your students are not interested in these calculations, you can omit this exercise.

TEACHING SUGGESTIONS: The following can lead to interactive problem-solving that encourages creative language use.

Show students how a mathematical statement is spoken:

$$12° C \times 2 = 24 + 30 = 54° F$$

"Twelve degrees Celsius times two equals twenty-four plus thirty equals (approximately) fifty-four degrees Fahrenheit."

$$60° F − 30 = 30 \div 2 = 15° C$$

"Sixty degrees Fahrenheit minus thirty equals thirty divided by two equals (approximately) fifteen degrees Celsius."

Divide the class into groups. Give each group new temperatures, and have them figure out the answers. Encourage them to say aloud the mathematical statements as they do the calculations. Ask for volunteers to write the answers on the board (while saying them aloud).

ANSWERS: **2.** 34° F   **3.** 90° F   **4.** 50° F   **5.** 62° F   **6.** 7.5° C
7. 20° C   **8.** 14° C   **9.** 35° C   **10.** −5° C

☐ EXERCISE 8, p. 127.   Interview and paragraph practice. (Chart 5-3)

If you are teaching in an English-speaking country, your students could go outside the classroom and interview some people to practice these structures. They could take notes on a chart like the one in the book, and then write a brief report on their findings.

CHART 5-4: *THERE + BE*

- *There + be* is a way of introducing a topic or calling attention to something. The word *there* is another "dummy" subject (similar to *it* in Charts 5-1 and 5-3), also called an "expletive." *There* does not receive much stress when spoken in this phrase. This is not the same as the adverb *there*. Notice the difference:

  1. *There's a book on the shelf.* (little stress on *There's*)
  2. *There's my book! I'm glad I found it.* (heavy stress on the adverb *There*)

- Emphasize that including a place is integral to the structure in sentence 1 (above). For example, *There's a bird* is an incomplete thought. A place needs to be stated: *There's a bird in the tree.*

- WORKBOOK: For additional exercises based on Chart 5-4, see *Workbook* Practices 7 and 8.

☐ EXERCISE 9, p. 128.   Sentence practice. (Chart 5-4)

This exercise helps learners think about singular and plural subject-verb agreement. Agreement is a common problem in students' use of this structure.

> *NOTE:* Yes/no answers for items 5–12 will vary according to your classroom.

> *ANSWERS:* **3.** is (yes)   **4.** are (no)   **5.** is   **6.** are   **7.** are   **8.** is
> **9.** are   **10.** is   **11.** are   **12.** are

☐ EXERCISE 10, p. 129.   Let's talk: pairwork. (Chart 5-4)

Students need to pay special attention to singular and plural as they complete the sentences. This exercise is also a good review of classroom/community vocabulary. Go over any new words with students before they begin the exercise. They can also use words not already provided in the vocabulary list.

☐ EXERCISE 11, p. 129.   Let's talk: small groups. (Chart 5-4)

TEACHING SUGGESTION: This exercise can be done in small groups to make sure everyone can see the items. It will go more quickly too. You could then ask everyone to visualize another place (e.g., some other part of the building or a nearby street) and tell the class what things they recall seeing in that place.

EXPANSION: Tell one student to turn his/her back to the table. Put four or five items on the table. Tell the student to turn around and study the table for a certain length of time (five or ten seconds), then turn away from the table again and report what he/she remembers seeing. This is a game. It's supposed to be fun, not really a test of memory.

☐ EXERCISE 12, p. 130.   Listening. (Chart 5-4)

Point out that *there're* is very common in spoken English, but not used in writing. Students who have trouble hearing endings might not be able to tell the difference between *there're* and *there's.* You may need to play the sentences several times.

> *ANSWERS:* **1.** There're   **2.** There's   **3.** There're   **4.** There's   **5.** There's
> **6.** There're   **7.** There're   **8.** There's

□ EXERCISE 13, p. 130. Let's talk: small groups. (Chart 5-4)

You could have several students give answers to each item. Note the progression in these items from a building to the whole universe.

CHART 5-5:   *THERE* + *BE:* YES/NO QUESTIONS

• This chart explains the question form of *there* + *be,* with *there* in the subject position.

• This chart also passively introduces *any.* Students will have to use *any* in the following exercises. The determiner *any* is similar in meaning to *some* — an inexact quantity. *Any* is used with plural count nouns or noncount nouns in questions and in negative statements. (See Chart 7-8.) Exercise 14 contains only plural count nouns and noncount nouns, so students don't have to make choices at this point in their use of *any.*

• Learners have difficulty with noncount nouns, such as *milk,* because they require singular verb forms. (See Chart 7-4, p. 191, in the student book.)

• WORKBOOK: For additional exercises based on Chart 5-5, see *Workbook* Practices 9 and 10.

□ EXERCISE 14, p. 131. Let's talk: pairwork. (Chart 5-5)

You may want to tell students that all nouns that have *-s* in the list are plural and take the verb *are;* those without *-s* are singular and take the verb *is.*

EXPANSION: Students ask a new partner about his/her refrigerator (real or imagined): "Is there any cheese in your refrigerator? Is there any fruit in your refrigerator?" Etc.

□ EXERCISE 15, p. 131. Let's talk: small groups. (Chart 5-5)

Encourage free conversation in small groups.

□ EXERCISE 16, p. 132. Let's talk: class activity. (Chart 5-5)

TEACHING SUGGESTIONS: Read the information about the Johnson family. Discuss the words in the list. Choose three students (A, B, C) to model the example with you. As students complete the task, be sure that everyone gets a chance to ask a question; otherwise, a few students may dominate the conversation. Give students enough time to find each item and write the answers in the grid.

EXPANSION: Tell students to imagine the perfect hotel or vacation spot. Ask them to make a list of its attractions. Then have students describe them to a partner using *there is* and *there are.*

NOTE: If it looks like your class will figure out the answer before they have asked many questions, you can always change the answers in the key as you go along to make it more challenging.

In the Teacher's Key on the following page, the words in parentheses are answers that are already given in the student book.

TEACHER'S KEY:	a swimming pool	a beach	tennis courts	horses	ocean-view rooms
Hotel 1	(yes)	yes	yes	no	yes
Hotel 2	yes	(yes)	yes	yes	no
Hotel 3	yes	yes	(yes)	yes	yes
Hotel 4	yes	yes	no	(yes)	yes
Hotel 5	no	yes	yes	yes	(yes)

CHART 5-6: *THERE + BE:* ASKING QUESTIONS WITH *HOW MANY*

• This chart introduces the useful question phrase *how many* by putting it into one of its usual grammatical contexts: questions with *there + be*.

• Word order is difficult in these questions. Many other languages form this question with very different sequences. The following exercises give plenty of practice.

• *How many* is used only with plural count nouns. Students will be introduced to this grammar in Chapter 7. For the time being, they do not need this information since the exercises contain only plural count nouns; students can focus on word order and meaning.

• WORKBOOK: For additional exercises based on Chart 5-6, see *Workbook* Practices 11–13.

☐ EXERCISE 17, p. 133.   Let's talk: class activity. (Chart 5-6)

TEACHING SUGGESTION: Ask for a volunteer to be Speaker A. Speaker A asks another student about item 1. After answering, that student (Speaker B) then asks a different student about item 2. Continue through the exercise this way.

Students may want to omit *are there* in the question. Because word order is difficult, lead the whole class through the example. All verbs with *how many* are plural, so students can focus on the word order in this exercise.

☐ EXERCISE 18, p. 133.   Let's talk: pairwork. (Chart 5-6)

Lead the whole class in the example. As in Exercise 17, all nouns are plural.

PARTNER A'S QUESTIONS: **1.** How many chapters are there in this book?   **2.** How many doors are there in this room?   **3.** How many floors are there in this building? **4.** How many states are there in the United States? [Answer: 50]   **5.** How many countries are there in North America? [Answer: 3]

PARTNER B'S QUESTIONS: **1.** How many pages are there in this book?   **2.** How many people are there in this room?   **3.** How many letters are there in the English alphabet? [Answer: 26]   **4.** How many provinces are there in Canada? [Answer: 10] **5.** How many continents are there in the world? [Answer: 7]

CHARTS 5-7 AND 5-8:   PREPOSITIONS OF PLACE

• To help learners remember the general meanings of these prepositions, you could draw a triangle like the one below. This is the same as the one given in this *Teacher's Guide* for Chart 5-2. It illustrates that *at* is for a specific point, *in* is for large areas, and *on* is between them.

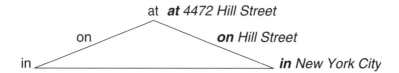

at   ***at*** *4472 Hill Street*

on   ***on*** *Hill Street*

in   ***in*** *New York City*

This relationship does not hold for other meanings of these prepositions, however.

• Lead students through a discussion of the illustrations in Chart 5-8. Compare (a) and (e); (f) and (i); (k) and (m) [note the use of *the* in (m)]; and (n) and (o). In (h), one could also say, "The cup is beneath (or below) the book." In (j), one could also say, "The cup is in the hand."

• Also in Chart 5-8, pay special attention to the difference in meaning between *in back of* vs. *in **the** back of* as well as *in front of* vs. *in **the** front of.* It's good for students to know that the inclusion or omission of *the* can change the meaning of a phrase.

• A note on the historical development of the English language: Early English used noun endings and cases to show relationships such as the location of one thing relative to another. Modern English has lost those endings and cases, so it uses prepositions to show location and other relationships. This feature of English is very different from many other languages and takes a long time to learn.

• WORKBOOK: For additional exercises based on Charts 5-7 and 5-8, see *Workbook* Practices 14–16.

☐ EXERCISE 19, p. 134.   Sentence practice. (Chart 5-7)

Items 1–7 can be done in class, and items 8–11 can be assigned as homework.

ANSWERS: **1.** in   **2.** in   **3.** on   **4.** at . . . in   **5.** First Street   **6.** Miami / Florida / Miami, Florida   **7.** 342 First Street   **8.–11.** *(free response)*

☐ EXERCISE 20, p. 136.   Sentence practice. (Charts 5-7 and 5-8)

This exercise can be done in class or assigned as homework. If done in class, lead students through the items slowly so they have time to understand. Ask for alternative answers when they are possible.

ANSWERS: **2.** under/in front of   **3.** above/behind   **4.** beside/near/next to
5. far (away) from   **6.** in/inside   **7.** between   **8.** around   **9.** outside/next to
10. front   **11.** back   **12.** the front/inside   **13.** the back/inside

☐ EXERCISE 21, p. 137.   Let's talk: pairwork. (Charts 5-7 and 5-8)

Suggest an object that's small enough for students to manipulate easily.

□ **EXERCISE 22, p. 138.   Let's talk: pairwork. (Charts 5-7 and 5-8)**

Students can also ask about things that are not in the picture. Encourage them to help each other with vocabulary as well as grammar.

If you go over the words in the list first, you may give away some answers. Let students ask questions about the vocabulary as they work through the exercise.

For a test, you might find a similar picture.

□ **EXERCISE 23, p. 138.   Listening. (Charts 5-7 and 5-8)**

Make sure that everyone is looking at the picture in Exercise 22 before you play the audio for Exercise 23.

ANSWERS: **1.** yes   **2.** no   **3.** yes   **4.** no   **5.** yes   **6.** yes   **7.** no
8. yes   **9.** yes   **10.** yes   **11.** no   **12.** yes   **13.** no   **14.** yes   **15.** yes

□ **EXERCISES 24–27, pp. 139–142.   Review. (Chapters 4 and 5)**

Exercises 24–27 build vocabulary and give students plenty of review practice.

TEACHING SUGGESTIONS: Students can work in pairs, and they don't need to do every item in every exercise. Devote whatever time your class has available. Perhaps assign an exercise for pairwork outside of class, or students could do the exercises as written homework.

Before pairwork begins, students should look at the vocabulary list and ask about words that are unfamiliar. You or their classmates can explain the meanings.

EXPANSION: After students have had time to do an exercise in pairs, hand out photocopies of the illustration for oral or written work. Students should be able to describe a picture confidently, effortlessly, clearly, and completely.

EX. 24 ANSWERS:

PART I. **1.** Mary is eating at/in a restaurant.   **2.** I see a cup of coffee, a vase of flowers, a candle, a bowl of salad, a glass of water, a plate, and a piece of meat.
3. Mary is holding a knife in her right hand. She is holding a fork in her left hand.
4. There's some salad in the bowl.   **5.** There's a steak/a piece of meat on the plate.
6. There's coffee in the cup.   **7.** A candle is burning.   **8.** No, Mary isn't eating breakfast.   **9.** No, Mary isn't at home. She's at/in a restaurant.   **10.** She's cutting a steak/a piece of meat.

PART II. **11.** at   **12.** on   **13.** in   **14.** is . . . in   **15.** at/in   **16.** isn't
17. isn't

EX. 25 ANSWERS:

PART I. **1.** John is studying.   **2.** I see a clock, a sign, some books, some bookshelves, a librarian, a desk, a plant, a table, three chairs, and two students.   **3.** No, John isn't at home. He's at the library.   **4.** No, John isn't reading a newspaper.   **5.** The librarian is standing behind the circulation desk.   **6.** John is right-handed.

PART II. **7.** at/in   **8.** at   **9.** in/on   **10.** under   **11.** on   **12.** on
13. on   **14.** isn't   **15.** is . . . behind   **16.** beside/near/next to

***EX. 26** ANSWERS:*

PART I. **1.** Mary is signing/writing a check. **2.** Mary's address is 3471 Tree Street, Chicago, Illinois 60565. **3.** Mary's full name is Mary S. Jones. **4.** Mary's middle initial is S. **5.** Mary's last name is Jones. **6.** Mary wants fifty dollars. **7.** Mary's name and address are in the upper-left corner of the check. **8.** The bank's name and address are in the lower-left corner of the check. OR Mary's bank account number is in the lower-left corner of the check. **9.** The name of the bank is First National Bank.

PART II. **10.** check **11.** her **12.** of **13.** at **14.** in **15.** in . . . of

***EX. 27** ANSWERS:*

PART I. **1.** Mary is cashing a check. **2.** No, Mary isn't at a store. She's at/in a bank. **3.** I see a bank teller, a clock, a sign, a line of people, a check, a purse/handbag/pocketbook, a briefcase, a tie/necktie, eyeglasses, a suit, a T-shirt, a beard and mustache, pants, jeans, and a dress. **4.** A woman is standing behind Mary. **5.** A man is standing at the end of the line. **6.** There are three men in the picture. **7.** There are two women in the picture. **8.** There are five people in the picture. **9.** There are four people standing in line.

PART II. **10.** at/in/inside **11.** are **12.** at/in front of **13.** behind/in back of **14.** is . . . behind/in back of **15.** isn't . . . at . . . of **16.** is . . . at . . . of **17.** is . . . between

CHART 5-9: *NEED* AND *WANT* + A NOUN OR AN INFINITIVE

- The purpose of this chart is to introduce common, simple statements formed with infinitives. Their use following these two extremely frequent verbs, *need* and *want*, is only the starting point. Students will encounter infinitives in other structures as the text progresses.
- For pedagogical purposes, this text defines an infinitive as ***to*** + *the simple form of a verb,* which is the most common form of infinitive by far. Strictly speaking, an infinitive is the uninflected form of a verb, either with or without *to* in front of it. In this text and the others in the series, the uninflected form of a verb is called the "simple form of a verb."
- A common error in infinitive usage after a main verb is the omission of *to: *I want go to a movie tonight.*
- Be sure students understand that *need* and *want* must add *-s* with a singular noun or pronoun subject, e.g., *He need**s** food; She want**s** to eat.* The text might be misleading since it gives no example of third-person singular with *need* or *want.*
- "Want to" is often reduced to "wanna" in spoken English. Because it is so common, it's likely your students have already noticed it.
- WORKBOOK: For additional exercises based on Chart 5-9, see *Workbook* Practices 17–19.

☐ EXERCISE 28, p. 143. Sentence practice. (Chart 5-9)

You could write this simplified rule on the board before students begin this exercise:

want + noun = no *to*
want + verb = *to*

ANSWERS: **3.** Linda wants <u>to</u> go to the bookstore.   **4.** *(no change)*   **5.** I need <u>to</u> make a telephone call.   **6.** *(no change)*   **7.** Do you want <u>to</u> go to the movie with us?   **8.** *(no change)*

☐ EXERCISE 29, p. 143.   Let's talk: class activity. (Chart 5-9)

TEACHING SUGGESTION: Before beginning this activity, give students time to think about their day tomorrow. What do they need to do? What do they want to do? They could jot down ideas. Then proceed to the questions.

☐ EXERCISE 30, p. 144.   Sentence practice. (Chart 5-9)

This exercise can be done in class or assigned as homework. Students don't have to limit their completions to the words in the box; they can make up their own completions.

In the verb phrase *listen to, to* is a preposition. Tell students that the word *to* has more than one grammatical use: it can be used as a preposition or as part of an infinitive.

ANSWERS: **2.** to go . . . to buy   **3.** to watch   **4.** to play   **5.** to call   **6.** to go . . . to cash   **7.** to do   **8.** to wash   **9.** to marry   **10.** to take   **11.** to go   **12.** to listen to   **13.** to take . . . to walk   **14.** to pay

☐ EXERCISE 31, p. 145.   Listening. (Chart 5-9)

As explained in Exercises 25 and 26 in Chapter 4 of this *Teacher's Guide,* supplying longer portions of sentences can be very difficult for beginners. Let them know that even though it seems hard now, it will become easier with more practice.

ALTERNATIVE PRACTICE: You can use this type of exercise for helping students predict what they might hear. Tell them beforehand that the verbs to be practiced in this exercise are *need* and *want.* Ask them to look at one or more dialogues and predict what Speakers A and B might say. Do this before they listen to the audio.

EXPANSION: After you've corrected the exercise with the class, you might ask pairs of students to read some of the dialogues aloud.

ANSWERS: **1.** do you want to go   **2.** do you want to go   **3.** doesn't want to go . . . she needs to study   **4.** I want to take   **5.** We don't need to come   **6.** wants to go back . . . he wants to change   **7.** A: do you want to go B: I want to visit   **8.** I need to look up   **9.** A: Do you want to go B: I need to get

---

CHART 5-10: *WOULD LIKE*

• Charts 5-10 and 5-11 deal with the use of *want* and *would like.* They are common words that students need to know how to use in order to express their thoughts in everyday conversation.

• *Would like* is a useful phrase that allows learners to communicate politely. It also introduces them to patterns of modal auxiliaries: i.e., both the helping and main verbs are uninflected, and the modal precedes the subject in a question. The next modal students will encounter is *will* in Chapter 10, followed closely by *may* and *might.* Chapter 12 deals with *can* and *could,* and Chapter 13 introduces *should* and *must.* The modals *be going to, be able to,* and *have to* are also included. *Would* is just the beginning.

• WORKBOOK: For additional exercises based on Chart 5-10, see *Workbook* Practice 20.

□ **EXERCISE 32, p. 147.   Sentence practice and listening activity. (Chart 5-10)**

Do this exercise in class with your students. Learners often omit final contracted sounds in their own production, both oral and written, because they don't hear them. Final contracted sounds /s/ and /d/ are unstressed and difficult for students to hear.

One of the benefits of studying grammar is that students can understand the underlying structures of what they hear; they learn what they are "supposed to hear." Say aloud to yourself, "Bob'd like some tea" and "My friend's not coming." Notice how the /d/ is practically swallowed and the /s/ is just a very tiny sound. It's easy to understand that learners are reproducing what they think they hear when they say or write ⋆*"Bob like some tea"* or ⋆*"My friend not coming."* Hearing (as opposed to seeing) the unstressed contracted sounds of basic grammatical structures helps students become more attuned to their use and frequency.

> *ANSWERS:* **3.** Ahmed and Anita would like   **4.** They would like   **5.** A: Would you like   B: I would   **6.** I would like to thank   **7.** My friends would like to thank   **8.** A: Would Robert like to ride   B: he would

□ **EXERCISE 33, p. 148.   Let's talk: class activity. (Chart 5-10)**

TEACHING SUGGESTIONS: You should ask these questions as naturally as possible, using your students' names. Keep the pace lively, and add an occasional comment (e.g., "Really? Me too!") to a student's answer so that it becomes a real exchange of information. Occasionally ask another student to follow up the first student's answer with a comment.

Depending on how much information your class gives, you may want to ask item 10 earlier.

CHART 5-11:   *WOULD LIKE* vs. *LIKE*
• Confusion between the use of *like* and *would like* is a common problem for new learners. The purpose of this chart is to clarify these uses.   • WORKBOOK: For additional exercises based on Chart 5-11, see *Workbook* Practices 21 and 22.

□ **EXERCISE 34, p. 148.   Listening. (Chart 5-11)**

Students may have trouble hearing the contracted /d/ sound. You could read the exercise more slowly to the class from the listening script in the back of the student book. Point out how subtle the /d/ sound is in spoken English contractions.

> *ANSWERS:* **1.** 'd like   **2.** like   **3.** 'd like   **4.** likes   **5.** 'd like   **6.** likes   **7.** like   **8.** like   **9.** 'd like   **10.** 'd like

□ **EXERCISE 35, p. 149.   Let's talk: class activity. (Chart 5-11)**

This exercise encourages students to express their own ideas using the target structures. See p. xv in this *Teacher's Guide* for ways of handling open-ended exercises.

NOTE: Items 9 and 10 are a little tricky. Item 9 encourages the use of parallel infinitives: e.g., *I need **to go** to the library and **(to) look** up some information.* Students have not yet been introduced to the concept of parallelism. You may need to explain it briefly, and possibly explain that *to* is usually omitted in the second parallel infinitive. Other parallel structures are possible in item 9 (e.g., *I need to talk to **Maria and Toshi**.)*

Item 10 is looking for a question word: *Where would you like to go this evening? What would you like to do this evening? What time would you like to leave this evening?*

☐ EXERCISE 36, p. 149.   Let's talk: pairwork. (Chart 5-11)

This exercise should clarify the difference in meaning between *would like* and *like*.

☐ EXERCISES 37–40, pp. 150–153.   Review. (Chapters 4 and 5)

Exercises 37–40 build vocabulary and give students plenty of practice.

TEACHING SUGGESTIONS: Students can work in pairs. They don't need to do every item in every exercise. Devote whatever time your class has available. Perhaps assign an exercise for pairwork outside of class or have students do one as written homework.

Before the pairwork begins, students should look at the vocabulary list and ask about words that are unfamiliar. You or their classmates can explain the meanings.

EXPANSION: After students have had time to do an exercise in pairs, hand out photocopies of the illustration for oral or written work. Students should be able to describe a picture confidently, effortlessly, clearly, and completely.

EX. 37 ANSWERS:

PART I.   **1.** John/He is cooking/making dinner.   **2.** I see a kitchen, a stove, a pot, a salt shaker, a pepper shaker, a clock, a refrigerator, a spoon, and a shopping/grocery list. **3.** John is in the kitchen. / John is at the stove.   **4.** Yes, John/he is tasting his dinner. **5.** No, John isn't a good cook. [because he doesn't like the taste of the food]   **6.** The refrigerator is beside/near/next to the stove. [behind John]   **7.** There's a shopping/grocery list on the refrigerator.   **8.** The food on the stove is hot.   **9.** The food in the refrigerator is cold.

PART II.   **10.** in   **11.** on   **12.** beside/near/next to   **13.** on   **14.** to go **15.** on   **16.** on . . . of   **17.** in

EX. 38 ANSWERS:

PART I.   **1.** John and Mary are sitting on a sofa. They're watching TV.   **2.** I see a TV set, a table, a fishbowl, a fish, a rug, a dog, a cat, a lamp, a clock, and a sofa.   **3.** No, John and Mary aren't in the kitchen. They're in the living room.   **4.** The lamp is on the floor. The lamp is beside/near/next to the sofa.   **5.** The rug is on the floor in front of the sofa.   **6.** The dog is on the rug.   **7.** The cat is on the sofa. OR The cat is beside/next to Mary.   **8.** No, the cat isn't walking. The cat's sleeping.   **9.** The dog is sleeping (too).   **10.** A fishbowl is on top of the TV set. OR There's a fishbowl on top of the TV set.   **11.** No, the fish isn't watching TV.   **12.** There's a singer on the TV screen. John and Mary are watching a singer on TV.

PART II.   **13.** are . . . to   **14.** are . . . on   **15.** aren't   **16.** on   **17.** is . . . on **18.** is . . . on

EX. **39** ANSWERS:

PART I. **1.** John and Mary are talking to each other on the phone. **2.** I see a clock, a refrigerator, a calendar, two phones, a table, a pen, a chair, a piece of paper, a telephone book, and a picture on the wall. **3.** Yes, John/he is happy. Yes, Mary/she is happy. Yes, John and Mary/they are smiling. **4.** No, they aren't sad./No, they're not sad. **5.** John is standing. Mary is sitting. **6.** No, John isn't in his bedroom. He's in his kitchen. **7.** Mary is drawing a heart. **8.** There's a telephone book on Mary's table. OR There's a piece of paper. OR There's/are a telephone book and a piece of paper on Mary's table. **9.** There's a clock on the wall next to the refrigerator. OR There's a calendar on the wall next to the refrigerator. OR A clock and a calendar are on the wall next to the refrigerator. **10.** The clock is on the wall next to the refrigerator. **11.** It's eight-thirty/half past eight. **12.** There's a picture of a mountain on the wall above the table.

PART II. **13.** are . . . on **14.** is . . . to . . . is . . . to . . . are . . . each **15.** in . . . in front of/near/next to/beside **16.** on **17.** is . . . at . . . drawing **18.** talk **19.** on **20.** of . . . above

EX. **40** ANSWERS:

PART I. **1.** Mary is sleeping. She's dreaming about John. **2.** John is sleeping. He's dreaming about Mary. **3.** Mary and John are sleeping and dreaming about each other. **4.** I see an alarm clock, two pillows, two heads, and two beds. **5.** Yes, she is. Mary is in her bedroom. **6.** No, John isn't in class. He's in his bedroom. **7.** John is/He's lying down. **8.** Yes, Mary is/she's dreaming. **9.** Yes, Mary and John/they are dreaming about each other. **10.** Yes, Mary and John/they are in love.

PART II. **11.** are . . . in **12.** is . . . about/of . . . is . . . about/of . . . are . . . about/of **13.** on **14.** aren't **15.** are . . . aren't **16.** in **17.** to

☐ **EXERCISE 41, p. 154.   Let's talk: pairwork. (Chapters 4 and 5)**

ALTERNATIVE PRACTICE: You could supply the picture(s). Students could work in small groups and check one another's work.

☐ **EXERCISE 42, p. 154.   Paragraph practice. (Chapters 4 and 5)**

Students could correct one another's papers.

ALTERNATIVE PRACTICE: You could use this exercise as homework or a test. Check for verb tenses, spelling, and prepositions.

☐ **EXERCISE 43, p. 154.   Chapter review. (Chapter 4)**

This is not a difficult or tricky multiple-choice test. Students should score 100% with little effort. Errors probably result from inattention, not lack of understanding.

ANSWERS: **2.** B **3.** A **4.** C **5.** B **6.** C **7.** C **8.** C

□ EXERCISE 44, p. 154.   Chapter review: error analysis. (Chapter 4)

Errors in this exercise include spelling, verb forms, singular-plural agreement, prepositions, and words omitted or added. Finding the errors is a good way to review the grammar in this chapter, and it forces learners to pay close attention to details as they develop their self-monitoring skills.

ANSWERS: **1.** Do you want <u>to</u> go downtown with me?   **2.** There <u>are</u> many problems in big cities today.   **3.** I'd like <u>to</u> see a movie tonight.   **4.** We <u>need</u> to find a new apartment soon.   **5.** Mr. Rice <u>would like</u> to have a cup of tea.   **6.** How many students <u>are there</u> in your class?   **7.** Yoko and Ivan are <u>studying</u> grammar right now. They want <u>to</u> learn English.   **8.** I <u>would</u> like to leave now. How about you? **9.** Please put the chair in <u>the</u> middle <u>of</u> the room.   **10.** The teacher needs to <u>check</u> our homework now.

□ EXERCISE 45, p. 154.   Review. (Chapters 4 and 5)

Students can complete this exercise orally with a partner, or you may collect their written work.

□ EXERCISE 46, p. 156.   Review. (Chapters 1 → 5)

Students must think about the verb tenses that match the adverbs of time, some irregular forms, and using *is/are/do/does/did* with negatives.

Assign this and other review exercises as homework whenever possible. If that is not practical, be sure to give students time to think before they respond. There is no benefit to the students going through a fill-in-the-blanks review exercise by writing in the correct answers they hear other students give. It's important for students to come up with their own completions before the correct answers are discussed.

You may want to assign this exercise in parts.

ANSWERS:

1. is sitting	**16.** is rising	**31.** needs
2. is reading	**17.** doesn't like	**32.** to go
3. is sitting	**18.** knows	**33.** is eating
4. is studying	**19.** is making/makes	**34.** thinks
5. is listening to	**20.** is thinking about	**35.** tastes
6. hears	**21.** gets	**36.** doesn't see
7. isn't listening to	**22.** loves	**37.** doesn't smell
8. is reading	**23.** wants	**38.** is sleeping
9. is studying	**24.** take	**39.** is dreaming about
10. likes	**25.** is standing	**40.** is playing
11. thinks	**26.** is taking off	**41.** doesn't see
12. is thinking about	**27.** is wearing	**42.** is looking at
13. understands	**28.** is thinking about	**43.** is singing
14. is cooking	**29.** wants	**44.** isn't listening to
15. is making	**30.** to watch	

CHAPTER 6
Nouns and Pronouns

Overview

This chapter begins with the basic parts of a simple sentence, leading students to identify the parts with the traditional grammatical terms "subject," "verb," "object," "preposition," and "object of a preposition." These terms are used in the charts and exercises in the rest of the student book. The basic notions of countability and plurality are introduced, as well as some commonly used irregular forms.

☐ EXERCISE 1, p. 158. Let's talk: small groups.

If you don't have much time, shorten the exercise or limit the number of nouns to three per item.

EXPANSION: You could make this a game by dividing students into teams and giving them just one minute per item to come up with a list of nouns. The team with the highest number of correct nouns wins.

CHART 6-1: NOUNS: SUBJECTS AND OBJECTS

• The purpose of this section is to introduce basic terms that will be used throughout the rest of the book. Most grammar books use these same terms. There are two types of terms: "categories" and "functions." "Noun" is a grammatical category; "subject" is one of the functions (or uses) of a noun in a sentence. "Verb" is both a category and a function; verbs are further divided into types such as "transitive" and "intransitive," which are usually identified in dictionaries. "Prepositions" and "prepositional phrases" are categories which have a variety of functions, but those functions are not important in this lesson.

• The important point for learners is that these grammatical units work together to communicate meanings from one person to another. They follow a certain predictable order in English that students benefit from learning and understanding.

• WORKBOOK: For additional exercises based on Chart 6-1, see *Workbook* Practices 1–7.

☐ EXERCISE 2, p. 159. Noun practice. (Chart 6-1)

This is a quick review of nouns, verbs, and adjectives. Students should not have trouble with this. If there are questions, take a few minutes to review Charts 1-1 and 1-6 with your class.

NOUNS: dog, eyes, English, mathematics, flowers, juice, Paris

☐ EXERCISE 3, p. 159. Sentence practice. (Chart 6-1)

Initially, some learners may be confused by this exercise because it can present them with a completely different way of looking at a sentence. They might like to work it out in small groups and talk over their solutions. This is an excellent way to deepen everyone's understanding. A thorough understanding of the grammar in this exercise will greatly benefit students as they work their way through the rest of the text — and the mysteries of English. You may want to work through items 1–7 in class and assign the rest as homework.

This exercise sneaks in the concept of parallel structure (in items 8, 9, 10, and 12). Point out that two nouns connected by *and* can function as a subject or object.

EXPANSION: For further practice, make up your own simple sentences, using only simple present and present progressive verbs.

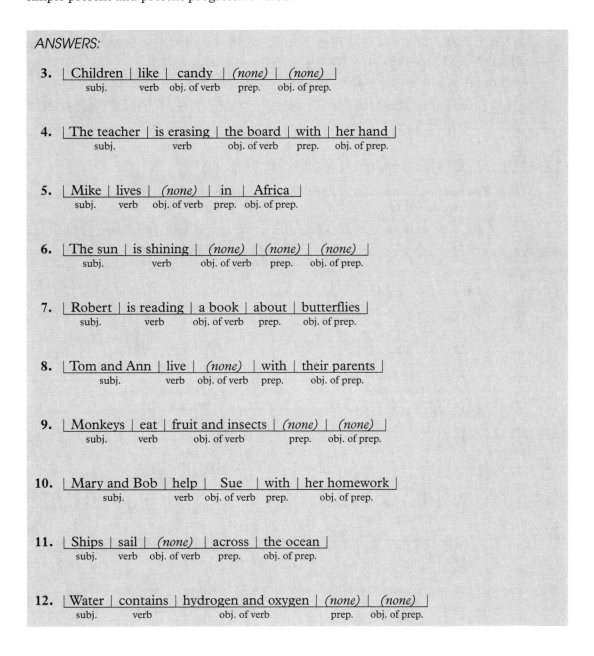

ANSWERS:

3. | Children | like | candy | *(none)* | *(none)* |
    subj.   verb   obj. of verb   prep.   obj. of prep.

4. | The teacher | is erasing | the board | with | her hand |
    subj.   verb   obj. of verb   prep.   obj. of prep.

5. | Mike | lives | *(none)* | in | Africa |
    subj.   verb   obj. of verb   prep. obj. of prep.

6. | The sun | is shining | *(none)* | *(none)* | *(none)* |
    subj.   verb   obj. of verb   prep.   obj. of prep.

7. | Robert | is reading | a book | about | butterflies |
    subj.   verb   obj. of verb   prep.   obj. of prep.

8. | Tom and Ann | live | *(none)* | with | their parents |
    subj.   verb   obj. of verb   prep.   obj. of prep.

9. | Monkeys | eat | fruit and insects | *(none)* | *(none)* |
    subj.   verb   obj. of verb   prep.   obj. of prep.

10. | Mary and Bob | help | Sue | with | her homework |
     subj.   verb obj. of verb   prep.   obj. of prep.

11. | Ships | sail | *(none)* | across | the ocean |
    subj.   verb   obj. of verb   prep.   obj. of prep.

12. | Water | contains | hydrogen and oxygen | *(none)* | *(none)* |
    subj.   verb   obj. of verb   prep.   obj. of prep.

Nouns and Pronouns **61**

CHART 6-2: ADJECTIVE + NOUN

• "Adjective" is another grammatical category; its function is the modification of nouns. Most adjectives in English come before a noun, which may be different from the word order in your students' languages. The other normal location for an adjective is after the main verb *be;* in this case, *be* is a "linking verb" which links the subject noun with its adjective modifier; *be* is like the equals sign (=) in an equation: *The weather = cold.*

• Students were introduced to the term "adjective" in Chapter 1. This chart expands upon that information a bit. It includes many of the adjectives used in Chapter 1 and also introduces some new vocabulary. Students will encounter adjectives again in Chapter 14.

• Note that the first two columns of "common adjectives" in Chart 6-2 are pairs with opposite meanings. Take time to discuss any unfamiliar words in this list. Demonstrate them or use them in sentences for the students. Ask them leading questions using adjectives, such as "What is your favorite food?" or "What color is a ripe banana?"

• See if the class can come up with a few other adjectives to add to the list.

• WORKBOOK: For additional exercises based on Chart 6-2, see *Workbook* Practices 8–13.

□ EXERCISE 4, p. 161.   Sentence practice. (Chart 6-2)

You may want to work through a few of these with your class and assign the rest as homework.

Some students may recall that *my* (item 2) and *her* (item 4) are possessive adjectives (see Chart 2-5, p. 33, in the student book). This category is not included in this exercise, but you might want to remind students of it.

ANSWERS:

2. sister = *noun*
   beautiful = *adjective*
   house = *noun*

3. Italian = *adjective*
   restaurant = *noun*

4. Maria = *noun*
   favorite = *adjective*
   songs = *noun*
   shower = *noun*

5. Olga = *noun*
   American = *adjective*
   hamburgers = *noun*

6. sour = *adjective*
   apples = *noun*
   sweet = *adjective*
   fruit = *noun*

7. Political = *adjective*
   leaders = *noun*
   important = *adjective*
   decisions = *noun*

8. Heavy = *adjective*
   traffic = *noun*
   noisy = *adjective*
   streets = *noun*

9. Poverty = *noun*
   serious = *adjective*
   problems = *noun*
   world = *noun*

10. Young = *adjective*
    people = *noun*
    interesting = *adjective*
    ideas = *noun*
    modern = *adjective*
    music = *noun*

□ **EXERCISE 5, p. 162. Let's talk: small groups. (Chart 6-2)**

Give students a few minutes to think of some opinions before you ask for their responses. If giving an opinion seems embarrassing to them, give them permission to say what "some people" think, or allow them to not tell the truth.

In items 5, 6, and 8 there is a choice between *a* and *an*. This was explained in Chart 1-1, but students may need to be reminded of the difference.

SAMPLE COMPLETIONS: **2.** hot, spicy, cold, frozen, fried, broiled, Italian, Thai, etc. **3.** honest, strong, generous, intelligent, courageous, trustworthy, truthful, etc. **4.** Rude, impolite, unkind, cruel, dishonest, selfish, etc. **5.** large/big, serious, common, widespread, significant, undeniable, etc. **6.** good, bad, terrible, funny, wonderful, odd, strange, terrific, unforgettable, interesting, etc. **7.** large/big, noisy, polluted, dirty, crowded, impoverished, ugly, etc. **8.** early, late, delicious, quick, frozen, Greek, horrible, marvelous, great, etc.

□ **EXERCISE 6, p. 162. Sentence practice. (Chart 6-2)**

You can work through a few of the items in class and assign the rest as homework.

The "use" of a noun is its grammatical function in a sentence.

ANSWERS: **2.** Jack = *a noun used as the subject;* radio = *a noun used as the object of the verb "have";* car = *a noun used as the object of the preposition "in"* **3.** Monkeys, apes = *nouns used as the subject;* thumbs = *a noun used as the object of the verb "have"* **4.** Janet = *a noun used as the subject;* office = *a noun used as the object of the preposition "in"* **5.** Scientists = *a noun used as the subject;* origin = *a noun used as the object of the preposition "on";* earth = *a noun used as the object of the preposition "of"* **6.** Egypt = *a noun used as the subject;* summers, winters = *nouns used as objects of the verb "has"* **7.** farmers = *a noun used as the subject;* villages = *a noun used as the object of the preposition "in";* fields = *a noun used as the object of the preposition "near"* **8.** cities = *a noun used as the subject;* problems = *a noun used as the object of the verb "face"* **9.** problems = *a noun used as the subject;* poverty, pollution, crime = *nouns used as objects of the verb "include"* **10.** hour = *a noun used as the subject;* minutes = *a noun used as the object of the preposition "of";* day = *a noun used as the subject;* minutes = *a noun used as the object of the preposition "of"* [Yes, there are 1440 minutes in a day. 60 × 24 = 1440.]

□ **EXERCISE 7, p. 163. Let's talk: small groups. (Chart 6-2)**

This exercise can be as short or as long as you want. At the end, students will have a list of countries and the adjective for each country. Students enjoy talking about foods, and this is a natural context for use of the adjective.

EXPANSION: You could also have students make a list of languages for the countries they name. In some cases, the language is the same as the adjective; in other cases it's different (e.g., *Egypt = Arabic; Mexico = Spanish*).

SAMPLE ANSWERS: **2.** (Mexico)/Mexican
3.–8. France/French Japan/Japanese
Egypt/Egyptian Korea/Korean
Indonesia/Indonesian Malaysia/Malaysian
Italy/Italian America/American

CHART 6-3: SUBJECT PRONOUNS AND OBJECT PRONOUNS

• The pronouns are listed in the traditional order: (a) and (b) first-person singular; (c) and (d) second-person singular; (e)–(j) third-person singular; (k) and (l) first-person plural; (m) and (n) second-person plural; (o) and (p) third-person plural. The term "first person" indicates the speaker/writer; the "second person" is someone who is spoken/written to; the "third person" is someone spoken/written about.

• Speakers of some languages may find it odd that English uses *he* for male and *she* for female but only *they* for the plural form with no distinction between the genders.

• WORKBOOK: For additional exercises based on Chart 6-3, see *Workbook* Practices 14–21.

☐ EXERCISE 8, p. 164.   Sentence practice. (Chart 6-3)

This exercise can be done in class or assigned as homework. Ask students to identify the antecedents. You could introduce the term "antecedent" if you wish, or simply use the verb *refer* to ask leading questions (e.g., "In item 1, what nouns do *he* and *her* refer to?").

ANSWERS: **2.** She . . . him   **3.** They . . . her   **4.** They . . . him   **5.** He . . . her
6. She . . . them   **7.** He . . . them   **8.** They . . . them

☐ EXERCISE 9, p. 165.   Sentence practice. (Chart 6-3)

This exercise can be done in class or assigned as homework. In this exercise, you may need to tell students if a name is for a male or a female. The text uses a core of common English names that students will encounter over and over, but at this point they may be unfamiliar with some of the names.

ANSWERS: **2.** them   **3.** it   **4.** He   **5.** him   **6.** her . . . She . . . I
7. them. They   **8.** us   **9.** It   **10.** We . . . it

☐ EXERCISE 10, p. 165.   Let's talk: find someone who . . . . (Chart 6-3)

Point out that *it* and *them* are not optional and cannot be omitted here.

QUESTIONS: When do you . . .   **1.** do it?   **2.** visit them?   **3.** read them?
4. talk to her?   **5.** watch it?   **6.** buy them?   **7.** wear them?   **8.** use it?

☐ EXERCISE 11, p. 166.   Sentence practice. (Chart 6-3)

This exercise can be done in class or assigned as homework.

ANSWERS: **2.** it . . . It   **3.** we . . . I . . . you   **4.** they . . . They . . . them
5. it. It   **6.** he . . . him

☐ EXERCISE 12, p. 166.   Listening practice. (Chart 6-3)

It's more important that students hear these reduced forms than pronounce them. In fact, in the early stages of language learning, it can sound strange for students to use reduced speech because they haven't yet grasped the basics of stress and rhythm of English (which is integral to reduced speech).

NOTE: In item 4 *(There's Bill and Julie)*, notice that "There's" + a plural subject is frequently heard in spoken English. Although very common, it is generally not considered to be grammatically correct. It has been included to give students more exposure to authentic spoken discourse.

☐ EXERCISE 13, p. 167.   Listening. (Chart 6-3)

Words like *her* and *him* may at first glance appear easy to understand, but when spoken with reduced speech, they are actually quite difficult to hear clearly (even for more proficient students). Encourage your students not to give up. Hearing these words accurately will take lots of exposure to and practice with English.

> *ANSWERS:*
> 1. A: I are going . . . with us
>   B: I are going . . . We need to
>
> 2. B: It's . . . know her? She's from
>   A: know her . . . with her
>   B: we enjoy . . . visit us . . . you
>   A: I'd like
>
> 3. they do . . . them . . . He's . . . him

CHART 6-4:   NOUNS: SINGULAR AND PLURAL

• In Chapter 3, students learned the spelling and pronunciation of verbs that end in *-s/-es*. This chart presents the spelling of nouns that end in *-s/-es*. Examples (d) and (f) present new information. The other examples represent spelling rules students were introduced to in Chapter 3.

• The pronunciation of final *-s/-es* follows the same rules presented in Chapter 3 in Charts 3-5, 3-6, and 3-8. In (a), point out the two pronunciations of final *-s*: /z/ and /s/ (pen/z/, apple/z/, cup/s/, elephant/s/). Example (e) gives the third possible pronunciation of final *-s/-es*: /əz/.

• WORKBOOK: For additional exercises based on Chart 6-4, see *Workbook* Practices 22–25.

☐ EXERCISE 14, p. 168.   Sentence practice. (Chart 6-4)

This exercise can be done in class or assigned as homework. Discuss the meaning, spelling, and pronunciation of each answer when you correct the exercise.

> *LIST A ANSWERS:*   2. countries   3. babies   4. keys   5. cities   6. parties
> 7. trays   8. dictionaries   9. ladies   10. Cowboys

> *LIST B ANSWERS:*   11. leaves   12. wives   13. lives   14. thieves   15. knives

> *LIST C ANSWERS:*   16. glasses   17. sexes   18. dishes   19. taxes
> 20. bushes   21. matches   22. tomatoes   23. potatoes   24. sandwiches
> 25. classes   26. zoos

☐ **EXERCISE 15, p. 170.   Pronunciation practice. (Chart 6-4)**

TEACHING SUGGESTIONS: Review the meaning of "voiced" and "voiceless" sounds. You could model one or two examples in each list and then play the audio (or simply have the class repeat the words after you). Unless you have an advanced beginning class, it's more important that your students be able to produce an ending that approximates /s/ and /z/ rather than pronounce it like a native speaker.

☐ **EXERCISES 16 and 17, pp. 171–172.   Listening. (Chart 6-4)**

Both exercises test students' ability to hear plural noun endings. Exercise 16 requires them to listen to single words for plural noun endings, whereas in Exercise 17 they are asked to identify the plural nouns within a sentence. Your students may want to practice the pronunciation, but accuracy in pronunciation should not be the emphasis; it's more important at this stage that they hear the endings correctly.

> *EX. 16 ANSWERS:*   **2.** table   **3.** face   **4.** hats   **5.** offices   **6.** boxes
> **7.** package   **8.** chairs   **9.** edge   **10.** tops

> *EX. 17 ANSWERS:*   **2.** places   **3.** sandwich   **4.** sentences   **5.** apple
> **6.** exercise   **7.** pieces   **8.** roses   **9.** bush   **10.** college

☐ **EXERCISE 18, p. 172.   Pronunciation practice. (Chart 6-4)**

This exercise has two parts: (1) identifying plural nouns, and (2) pronouncing them correctly. In item 7, *people* and *feet* are also plural nouns, but have not been included here because they're irregular. Irregular plural nouns will be explained in Chart 6-5.

TEACHING SUGGESTIONS: In class, students can work in pairs, but you should review the plural nouns with the whole group so that everyone can check the pronunciations.

If you have a language lab, you could record these sentences so that students could practice their pronunciation.

> *PLURAL NOUNS:*   **1.** students /s/ . . . books /s/ . . . backpacks /z/   **2.** stores /z/ . . .
> sizes /əz/ . . . clothes /z/   **3.** cats /s/ . . . dogs /z/   **4.** teachers /z/ . . . offices /əz/
> **5.** Engineers /z/ . . . bridges /əz/   **6.** tigers /z/, monkeys /z/, birds /z/, elephants /s/,
> bears /z/ . . . snakes /s/   **7.** ears /z/ . . . eyes /z/ . . . arms /z/ . . . hands /z/ . . . legs /z/
> **8.** tables /z/ . . . tables /z/ . . . edges /əz/   **9.** pages /əz/   **10.** apples /z/, bananas /z/,
> strawberries /z/ . . . peaches /əz/   **11.** cockroaches /əz/

CHART 6-5: NOUNS: IRREGULAR PLURAL FORMS

• The most frequent irregular forms are given in this chart.

• Another common plural that fits into the category with (g) *sheep* and (h) *fish* (no change for the plural) is *deer*.

• The word *people* seems difficult for many learners to use correctly. In English, this is a plural word like *women, children,* or *men*. It has no singular form. In the singular, one would use *a man, a woman, a child, a person*.

NOTE: The subject-verb agreement in the footnote under Chart 6-5, p. 173, in the student book might be confusing. *People is always plural* means the <u>word</u> *people*. The word *people* is one item; therefore, the verb in the footnote is singular. However, when we are talking about *people* (many persons), then the verb must be plural.

• The spelling of *woman* and *women* changes in the second syllable. However, the pronunciation changes in the first syllable: *woman* /wʊmən/; *women* /wɪmən/. This strange phenomenon is the result of changes during the historical development of the English language.

• WORKBOOK: For additional exercises based on Chart 6-5, see *Workbook* Practice 26.

☐ EXERCISE 19, p. 173. Game. (Chart 6-5)

This game can challenge your more advanced and competitive students while still being fun for the less advanced.

Students can work in small groups or alone. They can use their dictionaries or not, as you wish.

TEACHING SUGGESTIONS: During discussion, you could have students simply call out answers. Or you could have groups write their lists on the board. Another possibility would be to have students first work alone, then form groups where they pool their answers and try to come up with a noun for as many letters of the alphabet as possible. The group that has the most answers "wins."

Be sure to stress that all the answers students come up with are called "nouns." At this point, students should be quite familiar and comfortable with that term.

☐ EXERCISE 20, p. 175. Let's talk: class activity. (Chart 6-5)

TEACHING SUGGESTIONS: For variation, you could divide the class into two halves and have them alternate in responding to your cues: one half answering items 1, 3, 5, etc., and the other half answering items 2, 4, 6, etc.

Another possibility would be pairwork or small groups, with one student in each group acting as leader with his/her book open.

ANSWERS:		
2. two women	10. two bananas	17. two knives
3. two teeth	11. two children	18. two sexes
4. two feet	12. two desks	19. two girls
5. two men	13. two sentences	20. two exercises
6. two mice	14. two men	21. two teeth
7. two fish	15. two oranges	22. two women
8. two pages	16. two feet	23. two boys and two women
9. two places		

☐ **EXERCISE 21, p. 175.** Review. (Chapter 6)

TEACHING SUGGESTION: You could call out the grammatical term, and a student could say the word(s) that has/have that particular function in the sentence.

ANSWERS:

2. | Anita | carries | her books | in | her backpack |
      subj.   verb   obj.   prep.   obj. of prep.

3. | Snow | falls | *(none)* | *(none)* | *(none)* |
      subj.   verb   obj.   prep.   obj. of prep.

4. | Monkeys | sleep | *(none)* | in | trees |
      subj.   verb   obj.   prep. obj. of prep.

5. | The teacher | is writing | words | on | the chalkboard |
      subj.   verb   obj.   prep.   obj. of prep.

6. | I | like | apples | *(none)* | *(none)* |
      subj. verb   obj.   prep.   obj. of prep.

☐ **EXERCISE 22, p. 176.** Review. (Chapter 6)

All along, your students have been learning what a "complete sentence" is in English. Now they have a term for it. Define the word *complete* for them.

ANSWERS: **4.** This class ends at two o'clock.   **5.** *Inc.*   **6.** My mother works.
7. *Inc.*   **8.** My mother works in an office.   **9.** Does your brother have a job?
10. *Inc.*   **11.** Rain falls.   **12.** My sister lives in an apartment.   **13.** *Inc.*
14. The apartment has two bedrooms.   **15.** *Inc.*   **16.** *Inc.*

☐ **EXERCISE 23, p. 177.** Review. (Chart 6-3)

This is a review of subject and object pronouns.

ANSWERS: **2.** B   **3.** C   **4.** C   **5.** C   **6.** A   **7.** D   **8.** B   **9.** B
10. A

☐ **EXERCISE 24, p. 178.** Chapter review: error analysis. (Chapter 6)

Most students enjoy the challenge of using their knowledge of English grammar to correct errors in this kind of exercise.

ANSWERS: **2.** Our teacher gives <u>difficult tests</u>.   **3.** Alex helps Mike and <u>me</u>.
4. <u>Babies</u> cry.   **5.** Mike and Tom <u>live</u> in an apartment.   **6.** There are seven <u>women</u> in this class.   **7.** There are nineteen <u>people</u> in my class.   **8.** Olga and Ivan <u>have</u> three <u>children</u>.   **9.** There <u>are</u> twenty <u>classrooms</u> in this building.   **10.** Mr. Jones is our teacher. I like <u>him</u> very much.

CHAPTER 7
Count and Noncount Nouns

Overview

The basic notions of countability and plurality are introduced in this chapter as well as several elements of noun phrases, including adjectives, articles, and phrases of measurement. Questions and negatives with *some* and *any* complete the chapter.

☐ **EXERCISE 1, p. 179. Preview: noun practice.**

You can use this exercise as a preview or for practice immediately after you've taught Chart 7-1. In either case, review the first four items with the class before asking them to complete the exercise. Because this is a pretest, you can correct the answers without giving explanations. As you go through Chart 7-1, refer to items in the pretest for more clarification.

ANSWERS: **5.** s **6.** x **7.** x **8.** x **9.** s **10.** s **11.** x **12.** s
13. x **14.** x **15.** s

CHART 7-1: NOUNS: COUNT AND NONCOUNT

• Countability (singular/plural/mass/collective nouns) is a peculiar feature of English, and it causes problems for many learners whose languages do not have such categories. Do not expect students to master this point now; they will come across it repeatedly in this course and others that use the Azar grammar series.

• "Noncount" (also called "mass") nouns cannot be counted (*one money, *two moneys, etc.), so they cannot use *a* or *one* or a plural form. A list of common noncount nouns is given to help students get an initial understanding and usage ability. The use of count vs. noncount nouns is difficult for all learners and is the underlying cause of many article usage errors and singular-plural errors at all levels of proficiency, from beginner to advanced.

• Dictionaries for nonnative speakers identify the category of each noun as "count" or "noncount." However, most dictionaries written for native speakers of English usually do not note this point.

• For more information about count vs. noncount, see Chapter 11 in *Fundamentals of English Grammar, Third Edition,* and Chapter 7 in *Understanding and Using English Grammar, Third Edition,* as well as the *Teacher's Guides* for those texts.

• WORKBOOK: For additional exercises based on Chart 7-1, see *Workbook* Practices 1–8.

□ EXERCISE 2, p. 181. Noun practice. (Chart 7-1)

This exercise contrasts count and noncount nouns in sentence contexts so that learners can begin to understand the differences between them. There is a lot of information in Chart 7-1; it will take time for it to make sense. You may want to work through some of these with your class and assign the rest as homework.

ANSWERS: **3.** coin (count)   **4.** money (noncount)   **5.** traffic (noncount)   **6.** cars (count)   **7.** fact (count)   **8.** information (noncount)   **9.** homework (noncount)   **10.** assignment (count)   **11.** music (noncount)   **12.** coffee (noncount)   **13.** library (count)   **14.** vocabulary (noncount)   **15.** advice (noncount)   **16.** job (count)   **17.** work (noncount)   **18.** bracelets (count)

□ EXERCISE 3, p. 182. Let's talk: small groups. (Chart 7-1)

Walk around the room to help students with unfamiliar vocabulary.

ANSWERS: (NC = noncount; C = count)   **2.** advice (NC); a suggestion (C)   **3.** furniture (NC); a desk (C)   **4.** homework (NC); an assignment (C)   **5.** information (NC); a fact (C)   **6.** jewelry (NC); a bracelet (C)   **7.** money (NC); a coin (C)   **8.** music (NC); a song (C)   **9.** weather (NC); a cloud (C)   **10.** work (NC); a job (C)

□ EXERCISE 4, p. 183. Let's talk: class activity. (Chart 7-1)

This exercise stresses the idea of countability and points out that the great majority of nouns are count nouns. Check a dictionary if disagreements arise about a noun's category, but also be aware that many nouns have both count and noncount uses. For example, one can say *breads, cheeses, coffees, foods, fruits, meats,* etc., in certain contexts. If these forms come up in class, tell students this is more advanced grammar, and they will study it later.

CHART 7-2: USING *AN* vs. *A*

• The use of *an* before vowel sounds makes the words seem easier or smoother to pronounce, in the opinion of native speakers of English. For example, saying "an apple" is easier than saying "a apple."

• Some students want to use an article before possessive adjectives: *a my father, a his book.* If this is the case, point out that this is never correct.

• WORKBOOK: For additional exercises based on Chart 7-2, see *Workbook* Practices 9–11.

□ EXERCISE 5, p. 183. Sentence practice. (Chart 7-2)

This exercise can be done in pairs, with students checking each other's accuracy. You could lead a discussion of difficult items.

ANSWERS: **1.** an apple   **2.** a banana   **3.** an office   **4.** an idea   **5.** a good idea   **6.** a class   **7.** an easy class   **8.** an island   **9.** An hour   **10.** A healthy person   **11.** A horse   **12.** an honest worker   **13.** a math tutor   **14.** A university . . . an educational institution   **15.** an unusual job

☐ EXERCISE 6, p. 184. Listening. (Chart 7-2)

You may find that some students can't even hear *a* or *an*, much less make a distinction between them. To them it's a blur of words. You might read the sentences yourself at a slower speed before you play the audio CD.

> ANSWERS: **2.** a small apartment   **3.** an hour   **4.** an interesting class   **5.** a new teacher   **6.** an office   **7.** an insurance office   **8.** a nurse   **9.** a hospital **10.** a difficult job

---

CHART 7-3:   USING *A/AN* vs. *SOME*

• If you want to understand what an amazingly complicated word *some* is, look it up in several dictionaries. It does not lend itself to easy definition or grammatical explanation. You might tell your students that the basic meaning of *some* is "an inexact amount." You could tell them that people use *some* when the exact amount is unknown or unimportant.

• Be sure students understand that *some* can be used with both plural count nouns and noncount nouns, but NOT with singular count nouns.

• WORKBOOK: For additional exercises based on Chart 7-3, see *Workbook* Practices 12 and 13.

☐ EXERCISE 7, p. 185. Noun practice. (Chart 7-3)

This exercise is designed to show students in a very visual way that *a* and *an* are used for singular count nouns only. It also shows them that *some* can be used with both plural and noncount nouns, but never with singular count nouns. As students progress through the exercise, they should begin to see this pattern for themselves.

> ANSWERS: **4.** a (sing. count)   **5.** some (pl. count)   **6.** some (noncount) **7.** a (sing. count)   **8.** some (pl. count)   **9.** some (pl. count)   **10.** some (noncount)   **11.** some (noncount)   **12.** an (sing. count)

☐ EXERCISE 8, p. 185. Sentence practice. (Chart 7-3)

This exercise can be done in class or assigned as homework.

> *NOTE:* This exercise contains only count nouns; there are no noncount nouns in it.

> ANSWERS: **3.** a desk   **4.** some desks   **5.** an apple   **6.** some apples   **7.** an exercise   **8.** some exercises

---

☐ EXERCISE 9, p. 186. Sentence practice. (Chart 7-3)

This exercise contrasts singular count nouns and noncount nouns. It can be done in class or assigned as homework.

> *NOTE:* For the students' sake, it's regrettable that English has this very confusing and difficult feature known as countability. Tell students not to get frustrated; countability will eventually become less of a problem as they gain experience with English. Make sure they know that this feature of English is difficult for <u>all</u> learners.

☐ EXERCISE 10, p. 186.   Let's talk: small groups. (Chart 7-3)

This is a good vocabulary builder. Walk around the room to assist groups with new words, but encourage students to help one other before asking you for help. Write some of the most useful vocabulary on the board.

☐ EXERCISE 11, p. 187.   Sentence practice. (Chart 7-3)

This exercise can be assigned for homework or used as a quiz to test students' understanding of *a, an,* and *some.*

☐ EXERCISE 12, p. 188.   Let's talk: pairwork. (Chart 7-3)

This exercise should move quickly between partners. If either one challenges an answer, that person should produce the correct form. It may not be necessary to include all 30 items.

☐ EXERCISE 13, p. 189.   Sentence practice. (Chart 7-3)

This exercise can be done in class or assigned as homework. It focuses on nouns again: which ones are count and which are noncount. It also includes irregular noun plurals. All the sentences use the word *some,* so the task is to decide whether the nouns following *some* are plural count nouns or noncount nouns.

   The other point to stress is that noncount nouns do NOT have a final *-s.*

☐ EXERCISE 14, p. 190.   Sentence practice. (Chart 6-4)

This exercise can be done in class or assigned as homework. Students will see how a change from singular to plural requires grammatical changes in a sentence. They are also reminded that noncount nouns cannot be plural.

CHART 7-4:   MEASUREMENTS WITH NONCOUNT NOUNS

• This is a lesson in vocabulary as well as in the grammar of counting quantities. Take time to connect the pictures in the chart with the list of common expressions of measure.

• When speakers say these expressions at normal speed, the word *of* becomes just a vowel sound /ə/. The sound of *a* and *of* are then the same: *a bag of rice* = /ə bæg ə rais/.

• NOTE: a *loaf* of bread refers to the whole bread, but one piece of bread cut from the loaf with a knife is often called a *slice* of bread. Similarly, one piece of cut cheese or meat is called a *slice*. Since the text neglects to introduce the term *slice*, you might want to do so.

• The expressions of quantity in this chart are called "partitives."

• WORKBOOK: For additional exercises based on Chart 7-4, see *Workbook* Practices 14–17.

☐ EXERCISE 15, p. 191.   Noun practice. (Chart 7-4)

Students could complete this exercise in pairs. Ask for volunteers to share a few of their answers with the class. This exercise and the next are designed to reinforce new vocabulary.

The partitives students choose may reflect cultural differences. For example, some cultures typically use glasses, not cups, for tea.

☐ EXERCISE 16, p. 192.   Let's talk: pairwork. (Chart 7-4)

This exercise affords students the chance to talk about a familiar daily routine while reinforcing their understanding of count and noncount nouns.

☐ EXERCISE 17, p. 192.   Sentence practice. (Chart 7-4)

This exercise can be done in class or assigned as homework. Its purpose is to explore common noncount nouns used with the given expressions of quantity. See how many completions students can come up with.

EXPANSION: With quick learners, you might turn this into a memory game. The first student answers the second item by repeating the first item, then adding the answer to the second. The next student must repeat items 1 and 2 before adding the response to item 3. As the game continues, the responses get longer and harder to remember. No writing is allowed. The last student has the most difficult answer.

☐ **EXERCISE 18, p. 193. Review. (Chart 7-4)**

> *TEACHING SUGGESTION:* You could ask some students to read from their lists while the rest of the class listens carefully for correct uses of nouns and their markers.

☐ **EXERCISE 19, p. 193. Review: pairwork. (Chart 7-4)**

> *TEACHING SUGGESTION:* Collect students' lists. The next day, write some of the more common errors on the board, and ask students (in pairs or groups) to correct them.

☐ **EXERCISE 20, p. 194. Let's talk: pairwork. (Chart 7-4)**

> This is a cumulative review exercise. If your students can do this exercise easily, be sure to congratulate them. This seemingly simple exercise contains some difficult and complicated grammar.
>
> > *NOTE:* If your students have only Volume A, you will need to photocopy the following answers for each partner.

PARTNER B'S ANSWERS:	PARTNER A'S ANSWERS:
1. a. some food.	6. a. a snack.
b. an apple.	b. some fruit.
c. a sandwich.	c. an orange.
d. a bowl of soup.	d. a piece of chicken.
2. a. a glass of milk.	7. a. some juice.
b. some water.	b. a bottle of water.
c. a cup of tea.	c. a glass of ice tea.
3. a. some medicine.	8. a. a doctor.
b. an ambulance.	b. some help.
4. a. a coat.	9. a. some boots.
b. a hat.	b. a blanket.
c. some warm clothes.	c. a hot bath.
d. some heat.	d. some gloves.
5. a. some sleep.	10. a. some strong coffee.
b. a break.	b. a break.
c. a relaxing vacation.	c. a vacation.
	d. a nap.

CHART 7-5: USING *MANY, MUCH, A FEW, A LITTLE*

• Point out the difference in usage between *many* (used only with plural count nouns) and *much* (used only with noncount nouns).

• *Much* is more common in questions and negatives than affirmative statements. *A lot* is generally used for affirmative statements.

• Point out the differences in usage between *a few* and *a little*.

• *Few* and *little* (meaning *not many/not much*) are taught in *Understanding and Using English Grammar*. *Few* and *little* give a negative idea and mean *not many* or *not much*, as opposed to *a few* and *a little*, which give a positive idea and mean *some*. If students ask about this, tell them it's advanced grammar that they will study later.

• WORKBOOK: For additional exercises based on Chart 7-5, see *Workbook* Practices 18–21.

☐ EXERCISE 21, p. 195.   Sentence practice. (Chart 7-5)

You may want to work through some of these with your class and assign the rest as homework. Each item in this exercise contains *a lot of* as the quantifier. Point out that *a lot of* is used with both plural count nouns and noncount nouns, but *many* is used only with plural count nouns and *much* only with noncount nouns.

> *ANSWERS:*   **3.** many cities   **4.** much sugar   **5.** many questions   **6.** much furniture   **7.** many people   **8.** much mail ... many letters   **9.** many skyscrapers ... many tall buildings   **10.** much work   **11.** much coffee   **12.** many friends   **13.** much fruit   **14.** much coffee   **15.** many letters

☐ EXERCISE 22, p. 195.   Sentence practice. (Chart 7-5)

You may want to do this exercise in class. After one student has formed the complete question, that student could ask another student to give a truthful answer, including "I don't know."

> *ANSWERS:*   **3.** many languages   **4.** much homework   **5.** much tea   **6.** much sugar   **7.** many sentences   **8.** much water

☐ EXERCISE 23, p. 196.   Let's talk: pairwork. (Chart 7-5)

The purpose of this exercise is to give students practice forming a typical question pattern with *how many* and *how much*. These questions require students to be aware of the countability of the noun and to make subjects and verbs agree in number (singular or plural), as well as to put *is there/are there* in the correct place in the sentence. Not easy!

> *QUESTIONS:*   **1.** How many restaurants are there in *(name of this city)*?   **2.** How many desks are there in this room?   **3.** How much furniture is there in this room?   **4.** How many letters are there in your mailbox today?   **5.** How much mail is there in your mailbox today?   **6.** How much chicken is there in your refrigerator?   **7.** How many bridges are there in *(name of this city)*?   **8.** How much traffic is there on the street right now?   **9.** How many cars are there in the street outside the window?   **10.** How many people are there in this room?

☐ EXERCISE 24, p. 197.   Sentence practice. (Chart 7-5)

This exercise can be done in class. Some learners cannot understand why the article *a* is used with *few* and plural nouns. This is just a strange development in the English language. This exercise gives practice in the expression of small quantities with common count and noncount nouns.

> *ANSWERS:*   **2.** a little salt   **3.** a few questions   **4.** a little help ... a few problems ... a little advice   **5.** a few clothes   **6.** a little homework   **7.** a little mail   **8.** a few letters   **9.** a little cheese   **10.** a few oral exercises

☐ EXERCISE 25, p. 197.   Let's talk: pairwork. (Chart 7-5)

Pairs that complete the task quickly can change roles, or they can do the exercise again with new partners.

PARTNER A'S QUESTIONS:	PARTNER B'S ANSWERS:
1. many pens	1. a few
2. much tea	2. a little
3. much rice	3. a little
4. many apples	4. a few
5. much money	5. a little
6. much help	6. a little
7. many toys	7. a few

PARTNER B'S QUESTIONS:	PARTNER A'S ANSWERS:
1. much salt	1. a little
2. many bananas	2. a few
3. much soup	3. a little
4. much coffee	4. a little
5. many assignments	5. a few
6. much cheese	6. a little
7. many books	7. a few

☐ EXERCISE 26, p. 198.   Sentence review. (Charts 7-1 → 7-5)

This exercise can be done in class; it puts the grammar and vocabulary students have been learning into sentence-level contexts. (A context does not have to be long to be a context. "Contextualized grammar" comes in many forms.) Be sure to include spelling and pronunciation in the discussion of the correct answers.

ANSWERS: 2. Leaves   3. sexes   4. knives   5. information   6. paper
7. dishes   8. women   9. bushes   10. homework   11. pages   12. pieces
13. edges   14. valleys   15. weather   16. Thieves   17. Strawberries
18. trays   19. sizes   20. glasses   21. fish   22. centimeters   23. inches
24. feet

CHART 7-6:   USING *THE*

• For learners, *the* is perhaps the most difficult word in the English language. It is also possibly the most difficult word for teachers to teach. This chart simply scratches the surface. It provides a beginning point.

• Emphasize the idea that when the speaker uses *the*, he/she knows that the listener has the same thing or person in mind. (Students may well ask if they have to be mind readers in order to use *the* correctly.)

• WORKBOOK: For additional exercises based on Chart 7-6, see *Workbook* Practices 22 and 23.

☐ EXERCISE 27, p. 200.   Sentence practice. (Chart 7-6)

You may choose to do this exercise in class. Learners need time to understand the use of articles. This exercise, which is confined to the use of *the* for second mention, allows you to clarify some of the information in Chart 7-6. Go slowly. Make up additional examples from the classroom context or things you draw on the board. For example, for item 1 use an actual notebook and a grammar book in the classroom to demonstrate the use of *a* vs. *the*.

ANSWERS:
1. (a notebook) . . . a grammar book . . . The notebook . . . The grammar book
2. a woman . . . a man . . . The woman . . . The man
3. a ring . . . a necklace . . . The ring
4. a magazine . . . a newspaper . . . the newspaper . . . the magazine
5. a circle . . . a triangle . . . a square . . . a rectangle . . . The circle . . . the triangle . . . The square . . . the triangle . . . the rectangle
6. an apartment . . . an old building . . . the apartment . . . The building
7. a card . . . a flower . . . The card . . . the card . . . the flower
8. a hotel . . . The hotel

☐ EXERCISE 28, p. 201.   Let's talk: pairwork. (Chart 7-6)

This exercise, which gives the context of a picture to help students practice the use of articles, is confined to the use of *the* for second mention, contrasting it with the use of *a/an*.

ANSWERS: 1. a chair   2. a desk   3. a window   4. a plant   5. the chair
6. The chair   7. the window   8. the plant   9. The plant   10. the chair
11. a man   12. a woman   13. The man   14. The woman   15. a dog
16. a cat   17. a bird   18. a cage   19. the dog   20. the cat   21. The cat
22. the bird

☐ EXERCISE 29, p. 202.   Review. (Charts 7-2 → 7-6)

In addition to the use of *the* for second mention, this exercise includes the use of *the* for something that is "one of a kind," e.g., *the sun, the weather, the moon.*

TEACHING SUGGESTION: Students can work in pairs to perform these conversations. They can discuss any difficult answers or ask you for help. In item 2, you might want to explain the use of exclamation points (!); they indicate expressions of greeting, surprise, or strong feeling. They are NOT used in formal writing and are found mostly in conversational writing such as letters to friends or family.

ANSWERS:
1. A: a coat
   B: an umbrella
2. B: The weather
   A: the coat . . . the umbrella
      . . . the kitchen
3. a good job . . . an office . . .
   a computer
4. the computer
5. a stamp
6. A: an egg
   B: a glass
7. the floor
8. the moon . . . The moon
9. a telephone
10. the telephone

CHART 7-7: USING Ø (NO ARTICLE) TO MAKE GENERALIZATIONS

• This grammar is not easy for learners. A beginning (or even advanced) textbook cannot cover all the contingencies of article usage. Be aware that you are just giving your students a small introduction to articles.

• Don't expect proficiency in article usage from your students in their creative language use. Learning how to use articles in English takes a long time. Tell your students not to get frustrated. Articles are just one small part of English.

• A typical error students from diverse language groups make is to use *the* in generalizations:
  ★*The life is hard.* ★*We need the food to live.*

• Explain as best you can the meaning of the word *generalization*. Basically, a generalization says that something is usually or always true, e.g., *Sugar is sweet.*

• Be sure that students understand that the symbol "Ø" is never written in English. This textbook uses it to call attention to the absence of an article before a noun.

• WORKBOOK: For additional exercises based on Chart 7-7, see *Workbook* Practices 24–26.

☐ EXERCISE 30, p. 203. Sentence practice. (Chart 7-7)

You may want to work through some of these with your class and assign the rest as homework. You might mention in item 1 that the "s" in *sugar* should be capitalized because it is the first word in the sentence.

   NOTE: In item 2, *the sugar* means that there is a bowl of sugar on the table where the speaker and listener are eating.

> ANSWERS: 3. Ø 4. the bananas 5. Ø 6. The food 7. Ø . . . Ø
> 8. the salt . . . the pepper 9. Ø 10. The coffee . . . the tea 11. The pages
> 12. Ø . . . Ø 13. the fruit . . . the vegetables 14. Ø . . . Ø

☐ EXERCISE 31, p. 204. Listening. (Chart 7-7)

> ANSWERS: 2. general 3. specific 4. general 5. general 6. specific
> 7. specific 8. specific

☐ EXERCISE 32, p. 205. Listening: article review. (Charts 7-2 → 7-7)

EXPANSION: If you feel your students are fairly competent at hearing articles in connected speech, you can use this as a review quiz. Have students write their answers on a separate sheet of paper and hand them in. Or students can exchange papers and correct one another's mistakes. Be sure to discuss the correct answers in class.

> ANSWERS:
> 1. A: a pen   4. A: a university
>   B: the counter . . . the kitchen   B: an English professor
> 2. A: the keys . . . the car   A: the department
>   B: a set   5. B: an hour
> 3. A: a noise   A: the clock
>   B: a bird . . . a woodpecker   B: a new battery

CHART 7-8: USING *SOME* AND *ANY*

• Note that *any* is not used with singular count nouns. One would say, "I don't have a pencil."

• The text purposefully does not make a distinction between *any* and *some* in examples (c) and (d). The distinction is subtle and difficult for beginning students to understand as well as for teachers and textbooks to explain.

• WORKBOOK: For additional exercises based on Chart 7-8, see *Workbook* Practices 27 and 28.

☐ EXERCISE 33, p. 206.   Sentence practice. (Chart 7-8)

This exercise can be done in class or assigned as homework. It requires learners to recognize noncount and plural count nouns and then decide whether a statement is negative or affirmative. In a question, either *some* or *any* can be used.

ANSWERS: **4.** some/any help   **5.** any help   **6.** some help   **7.** any mail
8. any fruit . . . any apples . . . any bananas . . . any oranges   **9.** any people
10. some paper . . . some/any paper   **11.** any paper   **12.** any problems
13. some food . . . some/any groceries   **14.** any homework   **15.** any money
16. some beautiful flowers

☐ EXERCISE 34, p. 206.   Let's talk: class activity. (Chart 7-8)

Students can have fun with this exercise because some of the items are completely unexpected. Discuss any confusion about expressing quantities in the answers.

In item 20, *light bulbs* are the glass globes in electric fixtures that produce light.

☐ EXERCISE 35, p. 207.   Sentence practice. (Chart 7-8)

This exercise can be done in class or assigned as homework. It provides practice with negative statements. Students must recognize noncount and plural count nouns, then add *any* or *a* correctly.

ANSWERS: **4.** any new furniture   **5.** any children   **6.** any coffee . . . any coffee
7. a cup   **8.** any windows   **9.** any friends   **10.** any help   **11.** a comfortable
chair   **12.** any problems   **13.** a car   **14.** any homework   **15.** any new
clothes   **16.** a new suit

☐ EXERCISE 36, p. 208.   Chapter review: error analysis. (Chapter 7)

Most students enjoy the challenge of using their knowledge of English grammar to correct mistakes in this kind of exercise.

ANSWERS: **2.** I don't like hot <u>weather</u>.   **3.** I usually have <u>an</u> egg for breakfast.
4. <u>The sun</u> rises every morning.   **5.** The students in this class do a lot of <u>homework</u>
every day.   **6.** How many <u>languages</u> do you know?   **7.** I don't have <u>much</u> money.
8. John and Susan don't have <u>any</u> children.   **9.** <u>The</u> pictures are beautiful. You're a
good photographer.   **10.** There isn't <u>any</u> traffic early in the morning.   **11.** I can't
find <u>a</u> bowl for my soup.

☐ **EXERCISE 37, p. 208.   Review: pairwork.   (Chapter 7)**

The purpose of this exercise is for students to use the target structures in this chapter in semi-structured conversation. Students usually have fun with this.

☐ **EXERCISE 38, p. 210.   Sentence practice.   (Chapter 7)**

Incorrect singular-plural usage of nouns is common among learners at all proficiency levels. This exercise reviews the grammar your students now know about noun usage and asks them to apply it. Attention to grammatical number is an important part of the self-monitoring skills all learners need to develop.

   EXPANSION: To make this a game, you could announce in advance the total number of errors and have students compete to find them all as fast as possible.

> *ANSWERS:* **3.** Horses **4.** *(no change)* **5.** children **6.** stories **7.** minutes **8.** toys **9.** shelves **10.** women . . . men **11.** islands **12.** glasses **13.** Tomatoes **14.** dishes, spoons, forks, knives . . . napkins **15.** friends . . . enemies

☐ **EXERCISE 39, p. 210.   Let's talk: review.   (Chapter 7)**

This is a very challenging exercise. It reviews *a/an/the* in first mention/second mention contexts, *there is*, and prepositions of place. Divide students into pairs and discuss the meanings of the vocabulary words before they begin the exercise.

   TEACHING SUGGESTION: You might assign Part I for homework so that students have time to experiment with the blueprint. Point out the "front" and "back" so that they understand the building's orientation to the street. Ask students to think about the kinds of businesses that do better in the front vs. the back of a building. In other words, would they rather have a restaurant in the back of this building or in the front where customers will see it when they first drive in?

CHAPTER 8

Expressing Past Time, Part 1

Overview

As with the other chapters, this one contains far more information than the title suggests. The focus is first on the past tense forms of the verb *be* in statements, negatives, and questions. Then *-ed* verbs are introduced in statements, negatives, and questions along with common past time words. The first four groups of frequently used irregular verbs come next, followed by chapter review exercises.

CHART 8-1: USING *BE*: PAST TIME

• The chart uses the adverbs *today* and *yesterday* to show the meanings of the verb forms. The text consistently uses adverbs of time with verb tenses; together they establish the time period more clearly for learners than the verbs do alone.

• The bottom half of the chart organizes the forms of *be* in the past tense in two ways: on the left is the traditional list of first-, second-, and third-person pronouns in singular and plural; on the right is a list of pronouns associated with the two past forms of *be*. Your learners may have a preference for one list or the other to help them remember the forms.

• Point out that noun subjects require *was* if singular or *were* if plural. The chart includes some noun subjects in examples (c)–(f).

• WORKBOOK: For additional exercises based on Chart 8-1, see *Workbook* Practices 1 and 2.

☐ **EXERCISE 1, p. 213. Sentence practice. (Chart 8-1)**

This exercise can easily be done in class. It's simply a quick check of how well students understand the forms presented in Chart 8-1. Although it is natural to use contractions (*I'm, we're, she's,* etc.) in the present tense, they are not used with past tense forms of *be*. However, in normal, rapid, contracted speech, the form *was* has the unstressed pronunciation /wz/.

ANSWERS: **3.** Mary was at the library yesterday too.   **4.** We were in class yesterday too.   **5.** You were busy yesterday too.   **6.** I was happy yesterday too.   **7.** The classroom was hot yesterday too.   **8.** Ann was in her office yesterday too.   **9.** Tom was in his office yesterday too.   **10.** Ann and Tom were in their offices yesterday too.

□ **EXERCISE 2, p. 214.** Let's talk: class activity. (Chart 8-1)

> Substitute the names of your students for the words in parentheses. Remind students to close their books.
>
> > *TEACHING SUGGESTION:* Adapt or add more examples to fit the classroom situation.

CHART 8-2: PAST OF *BE:* NEGATIVE

- The text introduces *was* and *were* gradually. Each of the three basic patterns (statement, negative, and question) has its own chart (see Charts 8-2 → 8-4). This is to ensure that information doesn't get lost or buried. In all likelihood, you can cover these three charts quickly.

- Students should try to use negative contractions in their speaking.
  - Pronunciations: *wasn't* = /wəznt/
  -                  *weren't* = /wɚnt/

- Remind students that a noun subject requires *wasn't* if it is singular and *weren't* if it is plural.

- WORKBOOK: For additional exercises based on Chart 8-2, see *Workbook* Practices 3–6.

□ **EXERCISE 3, p. 214.** Sentence practice. (Chart 8-2)

> This exercise can be done in class or assigned as homework. The main point of this exercise is to ensure that students understand the negative contractions *wasn't* and *weren't* presented in Chart 8-2.
>
> Another purpose is to introduce a few adverbs of time (prior to a fuller presentation in Chart 8-5). In the boxed list of adverbial time phrases, students should understand that each item on the left (in the present) is equivalent to the item on the right (in the past). The oddity is that English speakers use *yesterday* with *morning, afternoon,* and *evening,* but use *last* with *night.*
>
> A third possible point of discussion in this exercise is the use of *but.* You could point out that the conjunction *but* requires a contrast between the fact in the first clause and the fact in the second clause. You might show that the sentences in the previous exercise (Exercise 2) could be joined by *and* because there is no contrast (e.g., *I am in class today,* **and** *I was in class yesterday too.*).
>
> Students must use pronouns to complete each sentence, so they need to pay attention to the antecedents (e.g., in item 1, *he* is the pronoun and *Ken* is the antecedent that *he* refers to).
>
> This is an easy exercise — but fertile ground for the aware teacher. Students are focusing on the past tense of *be* in negative contractions. But they're also learning (or reviewing) adverbial time phrases; being passively introduced to the meaning and use of *but;* and having to demonstrate control of personal pronoun references.

> *ANSWERS:* **3.** she wasn't busy yesterday.   **4.** he wasn't at the library last night.
> **5.** they weren't at work yesterday afternoon.   **6.** you weren't here yesterday.
> **7.** she wasn't in her office yesterday morning.   **8.** it wasn't cold last week.

☐ **EXERCISE 4, p. 215.   Let's talk: class activity. (Chart 8-2)**

> *TEACHING SUGGESTIONS:* Discuss the vocabulary in all six items before students begin the exercise. If necessary, model or pantomime each adjective for the class.

☐ **EXERCISE 5, p. 215.   Listening. (Chart 8-2)**

> The /t/ in *wasn't* can be hard for students to hear. Many native speakers use a glottal stop instead of /t/. (A glottal stop is the sound you hear in the negative utterance "uh-uh.")

> *ANSWERS:* **2.** was   **3.** was   **4.** wasn't   **5.** were   **6.** weren't   **7.** was   **8.** was   **9.** weren't   **10.** were

☐ **EXERCISE 6, p. 215.   Let's talk: find someone who . . . . (Chart 8-2)**

> *TEACHING SUGGESTIONS:* Review the vocabulary with the class before you begin. For additional practice, students can write the answers for homework.

CHART 8-3:   PAST OF *BE:* QUESTIONS

- You might review Charts 2-1 → 2-3 with your students. They can see the similarities between questions with *be* in the present and in the past. The word order is the same.

- In short answers, the verb *was* is stressed and must be fully pronounced: /waz/ or /wəz/.

- In questions, the verb *was* is unstressed and its pronunciation is shortened: /wz/.

- Speakers of some languages (e.g., Japanese) may have difficulty answering with *yes* and *no* as speakers of English expect. They often say "Yes" and mean "What you just asked is true" — something like the old song "Yes, We Have No Bananas." In English, *yes* or *no* must express the truth of the situation: *No, we don't have any bananas.* Also, in Japanese a way of saying "No, thank you" is to say something that roughly translates as "Yes, that's perfect."

- WORKBOOK: For additional exercises based on Chart 8-3, see *Workbook* Practices 7–9.

☐ **EXERCISE 7, p. 217.   Question practice. (Chart 8-3)**

> *TEACHING SUGGESTIONS:* Students could work in pairs to complete the dialogues (orally or in writing); then you could ask pairs to perform the dialogues. Students can look in their books before speaking, but must look at their partners while talking. (If they don't write the answers in class, they should write them for homework.)
>
> Occasionally, students have difficulty following *yes* or *no* with an appropriate short answer. Be prepared to deal with this, as explained in Chart 8-3, p. 216, in the student book. *Yes* must be followed by an affirmative verb and *no* by a negative verb.

　2. A: Was Mr. Yamamoto absent from class yesterday?
　　 B: he was.
　3. A: Were Oscar and Anya at home last night?
　　 B: they were.
　4. A: Were you nervous the first day of class?
　　 B: I wasn't.
　5. A: Was Ahmed at the library last night?
　　 B: he was.
　6. A: Was Mr. Shin in class yesterday?
　　 B: he wasn't.
　　 A: was he?
　7. A: Were you and your family in Canada last year?
　　 B: we weren't.
　　 A: were you?
　8. A: Are you at the library right now?
　　 B: I'm not.
　　 A: are you?

☐ EXERCISE 8, p. 218.　Let's talk: pairwork.　(Chart 8-3)

　　TEACHING SUGGESTION: Set up this exercise carefully. First, decide who will be Partner A (book open) and who will be Partner B (book closed). Make sure that students understand that with a *no* response, they need to ask a follow-up question. Note that students change roles after item 8 so that each person has practice in asking and answering questions.

　　The note at the bottom of p. 219 in the student book brings up grammar that is introduced in Chart 10-5. At this point, you probably don't need to explain that present and past tenses can be used with the same adverbial time phrases depending on the relation of the adverb to the moment of speaking. The footnote should be sufficient to allow the students to use the appropriate tense with the adverbial phrase *this morning.*

☐ EXERCISE 9, p. 219.　Question practice.　(Chart 8-3)

　　In this exercise, both present and past answers are required. Students have to pay attention to the adverbs of time. This exercise can be done in class or as homework.

ANSWERS:
　3. A: Were you tired last night?
　　 B: I was
　4. A: Are you hungry right now?
　　 B: I'm not
　5. A: Was the weather hot in New York City last summer?
　　 B: it was
　6. A: Is the weather cold in Alaska in the winter?
　　 B: it is
　7. A: Were Yoko and Mohammed here yesterday afternoon?
　　 B: they were.
　8. A: Are the students in this class intelligent?
　　 B: they are
　9. A: Is Mr. Tok absent today?
　　 B: he is.
　　 A: is he?
　　 B: He is . . . . *(free response)*

10. A: Were Tony and Benito at the party last night?
 B: they weren't.
 A: were they?
 B: They were . . . . (*free response*)
11. A: Was Amy out of town last week?
 B: she was.
 A: was she?
 B: She was . . . . (*free response*)
12. A: Are Mr. and Mrs. Rice in town this week?
 B: they aren't
 A: are they?
 B: They're . . . . (*free response*)

CHART 8-4: THE SIMPLE PAST TENSE: USING *-ED*

- After practicing forms of *be*, students now learn about other verbs in the past tense. This chart presents the regular form, the *-ed* ending.

- WORKBOOK: For additional exercises based on Chart 8-4, see *Workbook* Practices 10–15.

☐ EXERCISE 10, p. 221. Sentence practice. (Chart 8-4)

 TEACHING SUGGESTION: Model the *-ed* endings clearly for the class so that students can hear them. *-Ed* pronunciation is not introduced until Exercise 13, so you don't need to be concerned with your students' pronunciation at this point.

 ANSWERS: **1.** walked **2.** worked **3.** shaved **4.** watched **5.** cooked
 6. smiled **7.** rained **8.** asked **9.** talked **10.** listened

☐ EXERCISE 11, p. 222. Sentence practice. (Chart 8-4)

 This exercise can be done in class or assigned as homework. Its purpose is to convey the idea that *-ed* signifies past time.

 ANSWERS: **2.** walk . . . walked **3.** asks . . . asked **4.** watched . . . watch
 5. cooked . . . cooks **6.** stay . . . stayed **7.** work . . . worked **8.** dream . . .
 dreamed/dreamt **9.** waits . . . waited **10.** erased **11.** smiles **12.** shaved
 . . . shaves

☐ EXERCISE 12, p. 223. Let's talk: pairwork. (Chart 8-4)

 TEACHING SUGGESTION: Pairs that finish early can begin writing their partner's answers.

☐ EXERCISE 13, p. 223. Pronunciation practice. (Chart 8-4)

 This exercise expands the discussion of pronunciation of *-ed* endings. Clearly model the pronunciation of the words in each group. Have students repeat the words after you. Stress the /t/, /d/, and /əd/ pronunciations. For many students, their goal will be simply to <u>have</u> an ending. It's not realistic to expect that they will produce these endings correctly at this stage of their learning.

☐ **EXERCISE 14, p. 224.   Listening. (Chart 8-4)**

TEACHING SUGGESTION: If your students have trouble hearing the different endings on the audio, you may want to read the sentences yourself from the listening script in the back of the student book.

> *ANSWERS:* **2.** plays   **3.** watched   **4.** enjoyed   **5.** watch   **6.** asked
> **7.** answered   **8.** listened   **9.** like   **10.** works

☐ **EXERCISE 15, p. 224.   Let's talk: class activity. (Chart 8-4)**

TEACHING SUGGESTION: You may first need to review vocabulary from the exercise (e.g., *sneeze, point, yawn,* etc.). Write each word on the board and ask students to pantomime the action.

CHART 8-5:   PAST TIME WORDS: *YESTERDAY, LAST,* **AND** *AGO*

• These adverbs of time are very useful for students learning the past tense system. Help them understand that the lists are separate; elements from one list cannot be mixed with the other. For example, it is not possible to say *yesterday night* or *last afternoon.* (There is one exception the text chooses not to mention: *last evening* is also correct.)

• As a pedagogical note, the text continually connects adverbs of time with verb tenses (present, past, or future) so that students are learning both at once; learning one helps students learn the other.

• WORKBOOK: For additional exercises based on Chart 8-5, see *Workbook* Practices 16 and 17.

☐ **EXERCISE 16, p. 225.   Sentence practice. (Chart 8-5)**

This exercise can be done in class or assigned as homework. Exercises 16 and 17 will help students learn the separate uses of the adverbs in Chart 8-5.

Make sure students do not use the article *the* with *last* in their answers. *Last* has various uses and meanings. When used with *the, last* usually means "final": *Tom arrived the last week in April.* The meaning of *last* in the adverbial phrases in Chart 8-5 is more or less "the most recent one" or "the previous one." In *I saw her last week,* the phrase *last week* means "the week previous to this one" or "the week most recent to this week."

> *ANSWERS:* **2.** yesterday   **3.** last   **4.** last   **5.** yesterday   **6.** last   **7.** last
> **8.** yesterday   **9.** last   **10.** last   **11.** yesterday   **12.** last   **13.** last
> **14.** last   **15.** yesterday

☐ **EXERCISE 17, p. 226.   Sentence practice. (Chart 8-5)**

This exercise can be done in class or assigned as homework.

Items 3 and 4 might not be suitable for your students' situation. You could substitute other items that mention events that occurred at a specific time in the past, such as *visited a museum, graduated from high school,* or *had a part-time job.*

> *SAMPLE COMPLETIONS:* **2.** two days ago   **3.** two years ago   **4.** Caracas a week ago   **5.** 15 years ago   **6.** one month ago   **7.** two weeks ago   **8.** a day ago
> **9.** four hours ago   **10.** a week ago

☐ EXERCISE 18, p. 226. Listening. (Chart 8-5)

Give students plenty of time to answer each question. You'll probably want to pause the audio after each item.

ANSWERS: *(These will vary depending on the current date and time.)*

CHART 8-6: THE SIMPLE PAST: IRREGULAR VERBS (GROUP 1)

• This chart is the students' introduction to the phenomenon of irregular verbs in English. This chart presents a selection of frequently used irregular verbs as a starting point. Others are introduced later in this chapter and in Chapter 9, ten to twelve words at a time. There is a list of irregular verbs in the student book *Appendix,* p. 487.

• Many of the most commonly used verbs in English are irregular verbs. Students cannot avoid them.

• How best to learn them? Some teachers believe students should not try to memorize these lists; they believe that it's better to do exercises and learn the forms in the context of sentences. Other teachers assign lists of irregular verbs for memorization; they believe it helps students to know the principal parts of all irregular verbs.

• Each irregular verb chart in this text is followed by an oral (books-closed) exercise (e.g., Exercise 19 following this chart). These exercises only suggest a way for you to help your students learn the given irregular verbs. You don't have to follow the "script" verbatim. The idea is for you to put the verbs in meaningful contexts, demonstrating their use and eliciting correct usage from your students. The script is written out because teachers sometimes find a little priming useful to get a drill like this one moving.
   Remind yourself that these are odd, unfamiliar words for your students. Try to put students into situations where they have to use these words, and then make sure they know they have communicated the correct meaning by assuring them you understood what they said.

• Go through the list with the class, pronouncing each word clearly and following the example.

• WORKBOOK: For additional exercises based on Chart 8-6, see *Workbook* Practices 18–20.

☐ EXERCISE 19, p. 227. Let's talk: class activity. (Chart 8-6)

Read the notes in Chart 8-6 (above) for information on how to use this type of exercise. You might want to photocopy the exercise so you don't have to hold the heavy student book as you interact with your class.

TEACHING SUGGESTIONS: First, pronounce the verb forms and have students repeat them after you. Then use them in the given contexts. You may want to write the verb forms on the board as you read out the sentences. When you ask the questions, you could allow the whole class to call out short answers, or you could ask individuals to respond. Then ask a follow-up question of just one student, who should answer truthfully, trying to use the same verb you used in your question. Keep the pace lively and interesting.

☐ EXERCISE 20, p. 228. Let's talk: pairwork. (Chart 8-6)

TEACHING SUGGESTION: Pairs that finish early can write the past tense form of the verb in each sentence on a piece of paper.

PARTNER A SENTENCES: **1.** Rita got some mail yesterday. **2.** They went downtown yesterday. **3.** The students stood in line at the cafeteria yesterday. **4.** I saw my friends yesterday. **5.** Hamid sat in the front row yesterday. **6.** I slept for eight hours last night.

PARTNER B SENTENCES: **1.** We had lunch yesterday. **2.** I wrote e-mails to my parents last week. **3.** Wai-Leng came to class late yesterday. **4.** I did my homework yesterday. **5.** I ate breakfast yesterday morning. **6.** Roberto put his books in his briefcase yesterday.

☐ **EXERCISE 21, p. 229.** Verb review. (Chapters 2, 3, and 8)

This exercise mixes the three tenses students have studied thus far. The time expressions are the keys to the tenses. Remind students that spelling is important when they write the answers.

ANSWERS: **2.** talked **3.** is talking **4.** talks **5.** ate **6.** eat **7.** went **8.** studied **9.** wrote **10.** writes **11.** is sitting **12.** did **13.** saw **14.** had . . . dreamed/dreamt . . . slept **15.** happened **16.** comes **17.** came **18.** is standing **19.** stood **20.** put **21.** puts **22.** sits . . . sat . . . is . . . was

☐ **EXERCISE 22, p. 230.** Listening. (Chart 8-6)

This exercise may lead to questions as to why the wrong answers don't work. For example, students may want to know why in item 3, *They came* and *car* don't go together. Be prepared to explain that more is needed: *by car, in a car,* etc. You may want to prepare explanations for the wrong answers beforehand.

ANSWERS: **1.** some rice **2.** on the floor; together **3.** late; yesterday **4.** an answer; a book **5.** a good grade; a new truck **6.** next to my parents; at the bus stop

☐ **EXERCISE 23, p. 230.** Let's talk: small groups. (Chart 8-6)

Divide the class into small groups of four or five.

TEACHING SUGGESTIONS: One student can be the secretary for the group. All students contribute to the story, but the secretary does all the writing. You can then collect and correct this copy and make photocopies for all the students in that group. Each student can then rewrite the story independently and turn it back to you for final correction and/or a grade.

Students don't need to write a long story; they may just add two or three additional sentences. The point is that they have a chance to practice the verbs in Chart 8-6, both orally and in writing.

NOTE: Items 8 and 9 are interchangeable.

ANSWERS: **1.** One night, John went camping. **2.** He looked up at the stars. **3.** They were beautiful. **4.** He wrote a postcard to his girlfriend. **5.** He put the postcard down and went to sleep. **6.** The next morning, John sat up and rubbed his eyes. **7.** He saw a bear. **8.** The bear stood next to his tent. OR The bear had his postcard. **9.** The bear had his postcard. OR The bear stood next to his tent. **10.** *(Group story endings will vary.)*

CHART 8-7:   THE SIMPLE PAST: NEGATIVE

• This chart introduces *did* as a helping verb. Relate these sentences to simple present sentences to show the relationship between the use of *do* and the use of *did*.
> Simple present: *I **do** not walk to school every day.*
> Simple past: *I **did** not walk to school yesterday.*

• Some grammarians call these sentences examples of "*do*-support." English adds the "helping (auxiliary) verb *do*" in order to support the verb tense which is not attached to the main verb. In other words, we could say that the *-ed* has moved from the main verb and attached itself to *do*, forming the word *did*.

• Learners often make the mistake of adding the past tense to both *do* and the main verb (e.g., *★They didn't came yesterday.*).

• Encourage students to use contractions when they speak.

• WORKBOOK: For additional exercises based on Chart 8-7, see *Workbook* Practices 21–23.

☐ EXERCISE 24, p. 231.   Sentence practice. (Chart 8-7)

Students can give their answers orally in class and write them for homework.

> *ANSWERS:*   **2.** didn't have   **3.** didn't sit   **4.** didn't talk

☐ EXERCISE 25, p. 231.   Let's talk: pairwork. (Charts 3-9 and 8-7)

Remind yourself that at least some of your students have never used *didn't* before, and it may seem like an odd word to them. They need a little time to get used to it, and this exercise gives students the chance to produce *didn't* creatively. They will need to pay attention to time adverbs, tenses, and contractions, so give them enough time to finish the exercise. Pairs that finish early can write the past tense negative for each sentence.

> *PARTNER A SENTENCES:*   **1.** I don't eat breakfast every day. I didn't eat breakfast yesterday.   **2.** I don't watch TV every day. I didn't watch TV yesterday.   **3.** I don't go shopping every day. I didn't go shopping yesterday.   **4.** I don't read a newspaper every day. I didn't read a newspaper yesterday.   **5.** I don't study every day. I didn't study yesterday.

> *PARTNER B SENTENCES:*   **1.** I don't go to the library every day. I didn't go to the library yesterday.   **2.** I don't visit my friends every day. I didn't visit my friends yesterday.   **3.** I don't see (. . .) every day. I didn't see (. . .) yesterday.   **4.** I don't do my homework every day. I didn't do my homework yesterday.   **5.** I don't get on the Internet every day. I didn't get on the Internet yesterday.

☐ EXERCISE 26, p. 232.   Let's talk: class activity. (Charts 3-9 and 8-7)

This exercise can be fun and challenging. The students need to speak loudly enough for their classmates to hear, and everyone needs to listen carefully.

> *TEACHING SUGGESTION:* You could stand behind one student and ask another about the first student's response; then, move to another student and continue. This allows everyone to focus on the student seated in front of him/her rather than looking at you in another part of the classroom.

1. A: I don't eat breakfast every morning. I didn't eat breakfast yesterday morning.
   B: She/He doesn't eat breakfast every morning. She/He didn't eat breakfast yesterday morning.

2. A: I don't watch TV every night. I didn't watch TV last night.
   B: She/He doesn't watch TV every night. She/He didn't watch TV last night.

3. A: I don't talk to Georgio every day. I didn't talk to Georgio yesterday.
   B: She/He doesn't talk to Georgio every day. She/He didn't talk to Georgio yesterday.

4. A: I don't play soccer every afternoon. I didn't play soccer yesterday afternoon.
   B: She/He doesn't play soccer every afternoon. She/He didn't play soccer yesterday afternoon.

5. A: I don't study grammar every evening. I didn't study grammar last evening.
   B: She/He doesn't study grammar every evening. She/He didn't study grammar last evening.

6. A: I don't dream in English every night. I didn't dream in English last night.
   B: She/He doesn't dream in English every night. She/He didn't dream in English last night.

7. A: I don't visit my aunt and uncle every year. I didn't visit my aunt and uncle last year.
   B: She/He doesn't visit her/his aunt and uncle every year. She/He didn't visit her/his aunt and uncle last year.

8. A: I don't write to my parents every week. I didn't write to my parents last week.
   B: She/He doesn't write to her/his parents every week. She/He didn't write to her/his parents last week.

9. A: I don't read the newspaper every morning. I didn't read the newspaper yesterday morning.
   B: She/He doesn't read the newspaper every morning. She/He didn't read the newspaper yesterday morning.

10. A: I don't pay all of my bills every month. I didn't pay all of my bills last month.
    B: She/He doesn't pay all of her/his bills every month. She/He didn't pay all of her/his bills last month.

☐ EXERCISE 27, p. 232.   Sentence practice. (Charts 3-9 and 8-7)

This exercise can be done in class or as homework. Students must think about the verb tenses that match the adverbs of time, irregular forms, and using *is/are* and *do/does/did* with negatives.

ANSWERS: **1.** (didn't come) . . . stayed   **2.** went . . . didn't enjoy . . . wasn't
3. is reading . . . isn't watching . . . doesn't like   **4.** doesn't eat . . . doesn't have . . . didn't have . . . got

☐ EXERCISE 28, p. 233.   Let's talk: small groups. (Chart 8-7)

TEACHING SUGGESTION: Ask students to answer truthfully about what they "didn't" do yesterday. Go over a few of the suggested phrases before beginning the exercise.

CHART 8-8: THE SIMPLE PAST: YES/NO QUESTIONS

• Students are now aware of the use of *did* as a helping verb in the simple past negative. You might tell them that in forming a question in the simple past, the helping verb *did* moves to the beginning of the sentence. The subject and main verb do not change positions.

• Perhaps write the following on the board and ask students what's wrong:
    *Did Mary walked to school?
    *Did Mary walks to school?
    *Did Mary to walk to school?
    *Did Mary walking to school?

• WORKBOOK: For additional exercises based on Chart 8-8, see *Workbook* Practices 24–28.

☐ EXERCISE 29, p. 234.   Question practice. (Chart 8-8)

TEACHING SUGGESTION: Give students time to work out their responses. You can have students work through the exercise with a partner, and then select some items for pairs to present to the whole class. When they perform the dialogues, remind them that they can look at their books before speaking, but they must look at their partners while speaking.

NOTE: You may wish to point out that Olga, Yoko, and Gina /jinə/ are feminine names, whereas Benito and Ali are masculine names.

ANSWERS:
3. A: Did you eat lunch at the cafeteria?   B: Yes, I did.
4. A: Did Mr. Kwan go out of town last week?   B: No, he didn't.
5. A: Did you have a cup of tea this morning?   B: Yes, I did.
6. A: Did you and Benito go to a party last night?   B: Yes, we did.
7. A: Did Olga study English in high school?   B: Yes, she did.
8. A: Did Yoko and Ali do their homework last night? B: No, they didn't.
9. A: Did you see Gina at dinner last night?   B: Yes, I did.
10. A: Did you dream in English last night?   B: No, I didn't.

☐ EXERCISE 30, p. 235.   Listening. (Chart 8-8)

Although some of your students may ask about reductions with *did,* this exercise does not include reduced speech (e.g., *dih-juh* for *did you,* etc.). That will be introduced in Exercise 33.

ANSWERS: 1. Did we   2. Did you   3. Did it   4. Did I   5. Did they
6. Did he   7. Did I   8. Did they   9. Did you   10. Did she

☐ EXERCISE 31, p. 235.   Let's talk: pairwork. (Chart 8-8)

TEACHING SUGGESTION: Tell students that they must answer truthfully. To make a kind of game, tell them not to answer any question that is not grammatically correct. The phrase *this morning* is intended to refer to a time before now, even if it is still before noon at this moment. *This morning* should be interpreted to mean "before you came to class today."

☐ **EXERCISE 32, p. 236. Let's talk: find someone who . . . . (Chart 8-8)**

> *TEACHING SUGGESTIONS:* Lead the class through the example. Make sure students understand that they're to give both a short and a long answer when they answer "yes." You may want to take notes during the exercise and go over the most common mistakes with the class afterward.

☐ **EXERCISE 33, p. 237. Listening. (Chart 8-8)**

> These reduced forms are very common in spoken English, but they can be hard for students to understand. You might pronounce these yourself for the class after each sentence on the audio. Tell students that it's important they hear these forms, but they don't need to practice the pronunciation at this stage of their learning. In fact, it may sound odd if they try.

> *PART II ANSWERS:* **1.** Did you   **2.** Did it   **3.** Did you   **4.** Did they
> **5.** Did I   **6.** Did he   **7.** Did she   **8.** Did you   **9.** Did I   **10.** Did he

---

CHART 8-9: IRREGULAR VERBS (GROUP 2)

• The concept of irregular verbs was introduced in Chart 8-6. Additional irregular verbs are introduced in Charts 8-9 → 8-11 in this chapter and again in Chapter 9, Charts 9-4 → 9-6. The text asks students to learn only a few irregular verbs at a time, rather than expecting them to learn all 76 irregular verbs at once. The list is found in the student book *Appendix*, p. 487.

• The words *brought, bought, thought, caught,* and *taught* have the same pronunciation after the first sound: /_ɔt/. Unfortunately for learners, the historical development of English has produced some odd spellings.

• Again, go through the list with the class, pronouncing each word clearly and following the example.

• WORKBOOK: For additional exercises based on Chart 8-9, see *Workbook* Practices 29 and 30.

☐ **EXERCISE 34, p. 238. Let's talk: class activity. (Chart 8-9)**

> *TEACHING SUGGESTION:* See the notes for Chart 8-6 and subsequent Exercise 19 for ideas on how to present irregular verbs to your students.

> Items 5 and 11 require students to remember what has just been discussed in the classroom. The items are intended as another way of eliciting irregular verb usage in a meaningful classroom context.

> In item 3, the idiom *catch the bus* means "get on the bus."

☐ **EXERCISE 35, p. 239. Sentence practice. (Chart 8-9)**

> This exercise can be done in class or assigned as homework. It contextualizes the irregular verbs. The dialogues are models of how these verbs are used.

> *TEACHING SUGGESTIONS:* Make the models more memorable for your students by asking them to say the dialogues without looking at their texts. Assign pairs to memorize particular dialogues and say them for the class. Don't make this too stressful. Students can check the text if they need to, but they should look at their partners while speaking. Make it a fun activity.

Alternatively, students can work with partners, discussing any difficult items, including spelling and pronunciation. Or, if class time is limited or your students are advanced, assign the exercise for homework and review the answers in your next class session.

> *ANSWERS:* **1.** ran **2.** A: rode B: drove **3.** thought **4.** A: Did you go B: bought **5.** A: Did you study B: read . . . went **6.** drank . . . was
> **7.** brought **8.** taught . . . taught **9.** caught

☐ **EXERCISE 36, p. 240. Let's talk: pairwork. (Chart 8-9)**

This is a review of simple past verb forms. Students can use any adverbs about the past, not just *this morning.*

☐ **EXERCISE 37, p. 241. Listening. (Chart 8-9)**

See the notes for Exercise 22 in this chapter.

> *ANSWERS:* **1.** a fish **2.** very fast; to the store **3.** books; the newspaper
> **4.** yesterday; a horse **5.** some food **6.** into town; home

☐ **EXERCISE 38, p. 241. Writing practice. (Chart 8-9)**

TEACHING SUGGESTION: Before you collect your students' papers, have them exchange their lists with partners and make their own corrections.

EXPANSION: Collect your students' work. Write the most common errors (15–20 sentences) on a piece of paper. Make photocopies for all your students. At the next class session, divide students into groups for a game. First, have them correct the sentences you handed out; then call out a sentence number at random. The first group to raise their hands with the correct answer gets one point.

CHART 8-10: IRREGULAR VERBS (GROUP 3)

- See the notes for Chart 8-6 for information on how to present irregular verbs.

- Pronunciation note: *flew* is either /flu/ or /fliu/; *paid* is /peid/.

- Vocabulary note: *wake up* = "open your eyes after sleeping."

- WORKBOOK: For additional exercises based on Chart 8-10, see *Workbook* Practices 31 and 32.

☐ **EXERCISE 39, p. 242. Let's talk: class activity. (Chart 8-10)**

See the notes for Chart 8-6 and subsequent Exercise 19 for ideas on how to present irregular verbs to your students.

☐ **EXERCISE 40, p. 243. Sentence practice. (Chart 8-10)**

TEACHING SUGGESTION: Students enjoy doing this exercise with partners. Ask for volunteers to perform the dialogues. Remind them that they can look at their books before they speak, but they must look at their partners while they speak. Then follow up with questions about the dialogue, such as "What happened to *(Speaker B)*'s finger?"

ANSWERS: **1.** broke **2.** spoke **3.** left **4.** sent **5.** met **6.** heard
7. took **8.** rang **9.** sang **10.** woke **11.** flew **12.** paid

☐ **EXERCISE 41, p. 244. Listening. (Chart 8-10)**

TEACHING SUGGESTION: Play the audio twice before asking students to answer the questions. Then play it as many times as needed for students to understand the correct answers. You may need to write key parts of sentences on the board. Students are not accustomed to listening to discourse of this length, so this exercise may be challenging for them. For homework, they can read the audioscript for this exercise at the back of the student book and recheck their answers.

ANSWERS: **1.** no **2.** yes **3.** no **4.** no **5.** no

CHART 8-11: IRREGULAR VERBS (GROUP 4)

• The text asks students to learn only a few irregular verbs at a time, not the entire list at once (see the *Appendix,* p. 487, of the student book for the entire list). See the comments in Chart 8-6 for ways of teaching this chart and the exercises that follow.

• Using Exercise 42, lead the class through the list of verbs, having them pronounce both forms. Discuss any meanings that are not clear.

• There are two verbs *hang* in English. The one in this chart means "to suspend, or to fasten something above with no support below." The other verb *hang* means "to kill a person by suspending with a rope around the neck"; the past tense of this second verb is *hanged.*

• WORKBOOK: For additional exercises based on Chart 8-11, see *Workbook* Practices 33 and 34.

☐ **EXERCISE 42, p. 244. Let's talk: class activity. (Chart 8-11)**

See the notes for Chart 8-6 and subsequent Exercise 19 for ideas on how to present irregular verbs to your students.

PRONUNCIATIONS:

In item 1, *lose* is pronounced /luz/. This should not be confused with the adjective *loose,* which is pronounced /lus/.

In item 7, *wear* /wɛr/; *wore* /wɔr/ (the same as *war).*

In item 8, *steal* /stil/.

In item 9, *said* /sɛd/.

☐ **EXERCISE 43, p. 245. Sentence practice. (Chart 8-11)**

TEACHING SUGGESTION: Students could work in pairs. Some of the items contain phrases and situations that might lead to discussions about cultural traditions.

ANSWERS: **1.** began **2.** told **3.** lost **4.** hung **5.** found **6.** sold
7. said **8.** stole **9.** wore **10.** tore

☐ **EXERCISE 44, p. 247.** Listening. (Chart 8-11)

See teaching notes for Exercise 41 in this chapter.

> *ANSWERS:* **1.** no   **2.** no   **3.** yes   **4.** yes   **5.** yes

☐ **EXERCISE 45, p. 247.** Chapter review. (Chapter 8)

TEACHING SUGGESTION: Review the following with students: *Did* + subject + verb; *was/were* + subject + adjective or noun.   For example: *Did you go?* vs. *Were you happy? / Was Tom a student? / Was Tom at work?*

> *ANSWERS:* **1.** Did   **2.** Were   **3.** Was   **4.** Were   **5.** Did   **6.** Did
> **7.** Did   **8.** Was   **9.** Were   **10.** Did

☐ **EXERCISE 46, p. 247.** Chapter review. (Chapter 8)

EXPANSION: You might ask for volunteers to perform the dialogues in items 3–5.   Remind students that they can look at their books before speaking, but they must look at their partners while speaking.

> *ANSWERS:* **2.** was . . . did   **3.** A: Was . . . Did   B: was   **4.** A: Were . . . Did
> B: was . . . Were   **5.** A: were   B: was   A: Did   B: was . . . were . . . was . . . did

☐ **EXERCISE 47, p. 248.** Chapter review. (Chapter 8)

This exercise reviews simple present or simple past, the correct form of *be* or *do,* and correct word order.   It can be done in class or as homework.

> *ANSWERS:*   **3.** A: Do you want a roommate?   B: No, I don't.   **4.** A: Did you have a roommate last year?   B: Yes, I did.   **5.** A: Was he difficult to live with?   B: Yes, he was.   **6.** A: Did you ask him to keep the apartment clean?   B: Yes, I did.
> **7.** A: Were you glad when he left?   B: Yes, I was.

☐ **EXERCISE 48, p. 249.** Class activity. (Chapter 8)

TEACHING SUGGESTIONS: To keep other students alert, you could occasionally ask Speaker A, "What did *(Speaker B)* answer?" or "Do you think that's the truth?"

Explore interesting responses and engage your students in short, meaningful conversations.   This exercise is not intended to be a rote drill.

Items 14 and 15 passively introduce the structure *go + -ing (go shopping, go swimming, go dancing, go fishing, go camping,* etc.).   This structure is not presented in a chart in this text. You may want to mention it briefly.

☐ **EXERCISE 49, p. 250.** Let's talk: game. (Chapter 8)

ALTERNATIVE: For a different version of the game, try this: Divide students into groups of three to five.   Have them choose a team leader.   Say the verb to the entire class.   Students should consult with team members; when they agree on the answer, the team leader can raise his/her hand and give the answer.   If incorrect, ask the next team.   The team with the most points at the end of the game wins.   Students may want to answer without consulting others.   Discourage this so that everyone participates.

1. flew	11. paid	21. left
2. brought	12. heard	22. had
3. read	13. caught	23. paid
4. told	14. found	24. met
5. stood	15. slept	25. sat
6. taught	16. thought	26. took
7. drank	17. rode	27. rang
8. wore	18. broke	28. wrote
9. bought	19. said	29. sang
10. spoke	20. got	30. woke up

☐ EXERCISE 50, p. 250. Chapter review: error analysis. (Chapter 8)

ANSWERS: **1.** Someone <u>stole</u> my bicycle two <u>days</u> ago. **2.** Did you <u>go</u> to the party <u>last</u> weekend? **3.** I <u>heard</u> a really interesting story yesterday. **4.** The teacher <u>was not/wasn't</u> ready for class yesterday. **5.** Did <u>Joe come</u> to work last week? **6.** <u>Last</u> night I <u>stayed</u> home and <u>worked</u> on my science project. **7.** Several students <u>weren't</u> on time for the final exam yesterday. **8.** Your fax came ten minutes <u>ago</u>. Did you <u>get</u> it? **9.** Did you <u>invite</u> all your friends to your graduation party? **10.** I <u>slept</u> too late this morning and ~~was~~ missed the bus. **11.** The market <u>didn't have</u> any bananas yesterday. I <u>got</u> there too late. **12.** <u>Were</u> you nervous about your test ~~the~~ last week? **13.** I didn't <u>see</u> you at the party. <u>Were</u> you there?

☐ EXERCISE 51, p. 251. Review. (Chapter 8)

TEACHING SUGGESTION: Ask for volunteers to write sentences on the board for the rest of the class to check.

CHAPTER 9
Expressing Past Time, Part 2

Overview

This chapter begins with how to use information questions in the past tense, then moves on to include three more groups of irregular verbs. Time clauses are explained in two successive charts followed by a comparison of the present progressive and past progressive tenses. This leads to the importance of *wh*-clauses *(while and when)*. The chapter ends with the differences between the simple past and the past progressive.

CHART 9-1:   THE SIMPLE PAST: USING *WHERE, WHEN, WHAT TIME,* AND *WHY*

• You might point out the similarity with present tense questions in Charts 3-11 and 3-12 in the student book, pp. 78 and 80, respectively.

• It's useful to point out that learners need to listen to the first word of a question. If they can't hear that word *(When, Where, Why,* etc.), they can't answer the question meaningfully.

• WORKBOOK: For additional exercises based on Chart 9-1, see *Workbook* Practices 1–4.

☐ EXERCISE 1, p. 252.   Question practice. (Chart 9-1)

TEACHING SUGGESTION: Students can work in pairs; if so, they should exchange A and B roles after seven items. Give them time to think about these items because they have to work with word order and the correct question word.

ANSWERS: 2. When did Mr. Chu arrive in Canada?   3. When/What time did your plane arrive?   4. Why did you stay home last night?   5. Why were you tired?
6. Where did Sara go for her vacation?   7. When/What time did you finish your homework?   8. When did you come to this city?   9. Why did you laugh?
10. Where is Kate?   11. When/What time does the movie start?   12. Why was Tina behind the door?   13. Why does Jim lift weights?

☐ EXERCISE 2, p. 254.   Let's talk: class activity. (Chart 9-1)

You supply the answer, and the student asks the question that produced your answer. This is a kind of "backward conversation," just for practice. It's an enjoyable language game and a useful tool in the language classroom.

For many of the items in this exercise, there is more than one correct question. Accept any correct question a student gives you.

□ **EXERCISE 3, p. 254.   Let's talk: pairwork. (Chart 9-1)**

> *TEACHING SUGGESTION:* Students may need some help getting started because the questions are so open-ended. Review the example carefully before dividing the class into pairs. Then walk around the room to check on your students' progress as they work.

□ **EXERCISE 4, p. 255.   Listening. (Chart 9-1)**

> *TEACHING SUGGESTIONS:* Have students look at the four datebook pages. Say the names of the four people. Ask students to tell you what information the pages give (appointment, time, place). Then play the audio example. When you are sure students understand the task, continue with item 1. Be sure to give students enough time to look for the answer and write it.
>
> > *NOTE:* The prepositions in the answers are optional, as shown by the example (and the answers below). If your students have trouble with the prepositions, skip them.

> *ANSWERS:* **1.** (To the) City Café   **2.** (For a) business meeting   **3.** (To the) gym   **4.** (At) 1:00 P.M.   **5.** (For a) workout   **6.** (To) school   **7.** (For a meeting with the) teacher   **8.** (At) 12:00 noon   **9.** (To) Dr. Clark / (To the) dentist   **10.** (At) 10:00 A.M.   **11.** (For) a dental checkup   **12.** (At) 7:00 A.M.

□ **EXERCISE 5, p. 256.   Question practice. (Chart 9-1)**

The use of negative verbs after *why* is relatively straightforward and common. In *why didn't* questions, the speaker knows that something didn't happen and wants to know the reason. Typical errors with this pattern:
* ⋆ *Why you didn't come to class?*
* ⋆ *Why you not come to class?*

This is an open-ended exercise, so students need to use their imaginations for the questions. See p. xv in this *Teacher's Guide* for ways this type of exercise can be used.

> *ANSWERS:* **2.** you finish your homework   **3.** you eat breakfast   **4.** you clean your apartment   **5.** you answer the phone

□ **EXERCISE 6, p. 256.   Question practice: pairwork. (Chart 9-1)**

> *TEACHING SUGGESTION:* Students can use their imaginations and perhaps add some humor to their questions. Ask each pair to repeat their best question and answer for the class.

CHART 9-2:   QUESTIONS WITH *WHAT*

• In examples (c) and (d), a form of *be* is a helping (auxiliary) verb, not the main verb. The helping verb is part of the present progressive tense. (See Chart 4-1, p. 92, in the student book.)

• Compare Chart 2-8, p. 42, in the student book for questions with *what,* when *be* is the main verb.

• In (a) and (b), a form of *do* is a helping verb because the main verb is not *be* and is not in a progressive tense.

• Learners frequently make this mistake: ⋆*What Carol bought?*

• WORKBOOK: For additional exercises based on Chart 9-2, see *Workbook* Practice 5.

EXERCISE 7, p. 257. Question practice. (Chart 9-2)

There is a lot to think about in this exercise: the kind of question, the verb tense, helping verbs, irregular forms, and word order. If done in class, give students time to work out their answers.

> *ANSWERS:* **3.** Is Mary carrying a suitcase? **4.** What is Mary carrying?
> **5.** Do you see an airplane? **6.** What do you see? **7.** What did Bob eat for lunch?
> **8.** Did Bob eat some soup for lunch? **9.** What does Bob usually eat for lunch?
> **10.** Does Bob like salads? **11.** Are you afraid of snakes? **12.** What is the teacher pointing to?

EXERCISE 8, p. 258. Question practice: pairwork. (Chart 9-2)

This may be very difficult for some learners because it is so open-ended. Walk around the room, helping students as needed.

EXERCISE 9, p. 259. Question practice. (Chart 9-2)

Students enjoy this vocabulary-building exercise. Encourage them to give their own definitions of the words (in any form they choose, including gestures or pictures), but allow them to consult their dictionaries if they are stuck.

NOTE: In item 3, *quite* is an error that will be corrected in subsequent printings of the student book. The correct word is *quiet*.

> *ANSWERS:* **1.** humid, damp **2.** disagreeable; dreadful **3.** make little or no
> sound **4.** 100 years **5.** kill a person **6.** a big store; a large self-serve retail
> store that sells food and other household goods **7.** containing nothing **8.** sick
> **9.** the part of a house directly under the roof; garret **10.** easy to understand
> **11.** the spoken or written form used to ask a person to join another in an activity
> **12.** take pleasure in; like a lot **13.** a large area covered with trees **14.** *pretty* = an
> informal intensifier indicating an intensity less than *very; difficult* = hard, not easy
> **15.** something from a former time that is no longer in style

EXERCISE 10, p. 259. Listening. (Chart 9-2)

This exercise focuses on *wh*-questions with *do, does,* and *did.* Your students may have trouble distinguishing past from present, as well as the various *wh*-words from one another. You may need to play the sentences two or more times.

> *ANSWERS:* **1.** When did you **2.** Why did you **3.** Where do they **4.** What
> did she **5.** What does this **6.** Why didn't you **7.** Where did he **8.** When
> does class

CHART 9-3: QUESTIONS WITH *WHO*

• This is not an easy chart for students. Those who understand the basic S-V-O (Subject-Verb-Object) structure of a simple sentence will have a much easier time than those who don't. Give ample additional examples when you present this chart. Draw arrows and circles around words on the board to show relationships and ordering.

• Some teachers and grammar books insist that only (d) is correct and that (b) and (c) are incorrect. Most people today, however, rarely use *whom* at the beginning of a question. For this reason, (e) shows the letter *m* as optional: *who(m)*.

• Many learners have difficulty grasping the difference between (b) and (h). They need a lot of practice with *who* as subject and *who* as object before they begin to understand the patterns.

• WORKBOOK: For additional exercises based on Chart 9-3, see *Workbook* Practices 6–9.

☐ EXERCISE 11, p. 260.   Question practice. (Chart 9-3)

This exercise shows students the two different patterns in a very systematic way. It's important that students write out all the answers even though it may seem repetitive. Note that in item 3, the questions alternate between subject and object. At this point, students may really begin to see the difference in patterns.

ANSWERS:
1. Who called Yuko?
   Who visited Yuko?
   Who studied with Yuko?
   Who did John call?
   Who did John visit?
   Who did John study with?

2. Who did Mary carry?
   Who did Mary help?
   Who did Mary sing to?
   Who carried the baby?
   Who helped the baby?
   Who sang to the baby?

3. Who talked to the children?
   Who did Ron watch?
   Who played with the children?
   Who did Ron talk to?
   Who watched the children?
   Who did Ron play with?

☐ EXERCISE 12, p. 261.   Question practice. (Chart 9-3)

This exercise can be done in class (in pairs) or assigned as homework. If done in pairs, students should alternate A and B roles.

ANSWERS: 1. Who did you see at the party?   2. Who came to the party?
3. Who lives in that house?   4. Who did Janet call?   5. Who did you visit?
6. Who visited you?   7. Who did you talk to?   8. Who helped Ann?
9. Who did Bob help?   10. Did Bob help Ann?   11. Who are you thinking about?
12. Are you confused?

☐ EXERCISE 13, p. 262.   Let's talk: pairwork. (Chart 9-3)

If students have worked in pairs to finish Exercise 12, have them change partners for this exercise. Ask for volunteers to write some of their questions on the board.

EXPANSION: Have students write their questions on another piece of paper to turn in. Compile 15–20 questions that have common errors, put them on one page, and make photocopies for students. At the next class session, divide the class into small groups. Call out a sentence number; the first group to give the proper correction wins a point.

☐ EXERCISE 14, p. 263. Listening. (Chart 9-3)

Only one answer in each group is correct. Give students enough time to process each question and choose their response.

EXPANSION: For extra practice, create questions for other responses in the items. Read them to your students and have them circle the answers in their books. Examples: 1. *When did John wake up? (Ten minutes ago.)* 2. *Why didn't you finish your homework? (Because it was late.).* Etc.

> *ANSWERS:* **1.** In a small town. **2.** At midnight. **3.** Some help. **4.** I am.
> **5.** Mary did. **6.** An apartment downtown. **7.** Two hours ago. **8.** Because I didn't have time.

CHART 9-4: IRREGULAR VERBS (GROUP 5)

• Note that *cost, cut, hit,* and *hurt* have no change in their past tense forms.

• Use Exercise 15 to lead students through this list of verb forms.

• WORKBOOK: For additional exercises based on Chart 9-4, see *Workbook* Practices 10 and 11.

☐ EXERCISE 15, p. 264. Let's talk: class activity. (Chart 9-4)

TEACHING SUGGESTION: See the notes for Chart 8-6 and subsequent Exercise 19 in this *Teacher's Guide* for ideas on how to present irregular verbs to your students.

You might point out that *give* is the opposite of *receive; lend* is the opposite of *borrow; forget* is the opposite of *remember; spend* is the opposite of *save;* and *shut* is the same as *close* and the opposite of *open.*

☐ EXERCISE 16, p. 265. Sentence practice. (Chart 9-4)

This exercise can be done in class or assigned as homework.

> *ANSWERS:* **1.** A: does a new car cost B: costs **2.** cost **3.** gave **4.** hit
> **5.** B: forgot A: forgot **6.** made **7.** puts **8.** put **9.** spent **10.** lent
> **11.** cuts **12.** cut

☐ EXERCISE 17, p. 266. Listening. (Chart 9-4)

TEACHING SUGGESTION: Prepare explanations for the wrong answers beforehand since your students may ask why the answer they chose didn't work.

> *ANSWERS:* **1.** the answer; the conversation; the teacher **2.** money **3.** your hair; some paper **4.** a tree; an animal **5.** his appointment; the question

CHART 9-5: IRREGULAR VERBS (GROUP 6)

- Lead students through the list, pointing out spelling patterns.
- Some learners mix up the past forms of *fall* and *feel*. Give extra attention to those words.
- WORKBOOK: For additional exercises based on Chart 9-5, see *Workbook* Practices 12 and 13.

☐ EXERCISE 18, p. 266.   Let's talk: class activity. (Chart 9-5)

TEACHING SUGGESTION: See the notes for Chart 8-6 and subsequent Exercise 19 in this *Teacher's Guide* for ideas on how to present irregular verbs to your students.

☐ EXERCISE 19, p. 267.   Sentence practice. (Chart 9-5)

TEACHING SUGGESTION: Students enjoy doing this exercise with partners. Ask for volunteers to perform the dialogues. Remind them that they can look at their books before they speak, but they must look at their partners while they speak.

ANSWERS: **1.** won   **2.** fell   **3.** kept   **4.** drew   **5.** grew   **6.** blew
7. knew   **8.** swam   **9.** felt   **10.** threw

☐ EXERCISE 20, p. 268.   Listening. (Chart 9-5)

TEACHING SUGGESTION: Prepare explanations for the wrong answers beforehand, as your students may ask why an answer they chose didn't work.

ANSWERS: **1.** on a car; in the park   **2.** the game; a prize   **3.** on the paper; a picture; with some chalk   **4.** happy; excited   **5.** a ball; a pillow

CHART 9-6: IRREGULAR VERBS (GROUP 7)

- Pronounce each word and have the class repeat it. Then ask one student to spell the word aloud.
- Clarify the meanings of the words.
- WORKBOOK: For additional exercises based on Chart 9-6, see *Workbook* Practices 14 and 15.

☐ EXERCISE 21, p. 269.   Let's talk: class activity. (Chart 9-6)

TEACHING SUGGESTION: See the notes for Chart 8-6 and subsequent Exercise 19 in this *Teacher's Guide* for ideas on how to present irregular verbs to your students.

☐ EXERCISE 22, p. 270.   Sentence practice. (Chart 9-6)

This exercise can be done in class or assigned as homework.

ANSWERS: **2.** hid   **3.** built   **4.** fed   **5.** became   **6.** held   **7.** fought
8. bit   **9.** bent

☐ **EXERCISE 23, p. 271.   Listening. (Chart 9-6)**

> *TEACHING SUGGESTION:* Prepare explanations for the wrong answers beforehand, as your students may ask why an answer they chose didn't work.
>
> > *ANSWERS:* **1.** the dog; her baby   **2.** a new house   **3.** a stick; my hand   **4.** in the bedroom; behind a tree; their money   **5.** some chalk; some papers

☐ **EXERCISE 24, p. 271.   Class activity. (Chart 9-6)**

> Every answer must begin with "Yes." Keep the pace fairly fast. If a student can't answer, he/she can say "Pass" so you can continue to the next student quickly. Later, come back to the student who passed and ask a different question.
>
> > *EXPANSION:* You may want to use this exercise as pairwork, or you may want to make it a team contest.
>
> For a contest, divide the class into two or three equal teams. Ask the first person on one team one question. That person must answer immediately and correctly to get two points for the team. If the answer is not correct, the second person on the same team has a chance to answer correctly for one point. Ask a different team the next question. At the end of the game, the team with the most points is the winner.

CHART 9-7:   *BEFORE* AND *AFTER* IN TIME CLAUSES

- Time clauses give learners a way to combine information into complex sentences. This chart is the students' introduction to complex (compared to simple) sentence structure in English.

- A time clause is a type of dependent clause usually called an "adverb(ial) clause" or a "subordinate clause." *After* and *before* are called "subordinating conjunctions." The text prefers to minimize terminology.

- Call attention to the punctuation: In (d) and (f), a comma is necessary when the time clause comes at the beginning of the sentence. In speaking, there is a short pause where the comma appears. (See the footnote below Chart 9-7, p. 273, of the student book.)

- Point out the prepositional phrases in (g) and (h). They do NOT contain a subject and verb as required in a clause.

- WORKBOOK: For additional exercises based on Chart 9-7, see *Workbook* Practices 16–18.

☐ **EXERCISE 25, p. 273.   Sentence practice. (Chart 9-7)**

> In item 1, some students may ask about the pronoun *it*. They might want to say, "Before I ate it, I peeled the banana." It is more common, however, to place the noun in the first part of the sentence and the pronoun later.
>
> > *TEACHING SUGGESTION:* Ask one student to analyze a sentence for the class. Ask him/her about the placement of commas.
>
> > *ANSWERS:* **2.** *main clause* = We arrived at the airport; *time clause* = before the plane landed   **3.** *main clause* = I went to the movie; *time clause* = after I finished my homework   **4.** *main clause* = they watched TV; *time clause* = After the children got home from school   **5.** *main clause* = I lived at home with my parents; *time clause* = Before I moved to this city

□ EXERCISE 26, p. 274. Sentence practice. (Chart 9-7)

A common error is for students to write adverb clauses as though they were complete sentences. Learners need to understand that time clauses must be connected to the main (or independent) clause.

> *ANSWERS:* **4.** *Inc.*   **5.** We went to the zoo.   **6.** We went to the zoo before we ate our picnic lunch.   **7.** The children played games after they did their work.   **8.** The children played games.   **9.** *Inc.*   **10.** The lions killed a zebra.   **11.** *Inc.*
> **12.** They ate it.   **13.** After the lions killed a zebra, they ate it.

□ EXERCISE 27, p. 274. Let's talk: small groups. (Chart 9-7)

> *ANSWERS:* **1.** She ate breakfast before she went to work. Before she went to work, she ate breakfast. She went to work after she ate breakfast. After she ate breakfast, she went to work.   **2.** He did his homework before he went to bed. Before he went to bed, he did his homework. He went to bed after he did his homework. After he did his homework, he went to bed.   **3.** We bought tickets before we entered the movie theater. Before we entered the movie theater, we bought tickets. We entered the movie theater after we bought tickets. After we bought tickets, we entered the movie theater.

□ EXERCISE 28, p. 276. Sentence practice. (Chart 9-7)

You may want students to write their answers on a separate piece of paper so you can collect their work and correct it yourself. When you check it, watch for comma placement as well as logical combinations of ideas.

CHART 9-8: *WHEN* IN TIME CLAUSES

• *When* basically means "at that time." It has variations of meaning that students at this level probably aren't ready for. For example, in (a) *when* means "as soon as" or "immediately after," compared with (b) where it means "for the same period of time."

• WORKBOOK: For additional exercises based on Chart 9-8, see *Workbook* Practices 19–21.

□ EXERCISE 29, p. 276. Sentence practice. (Chart 9-8)

Students can do this exercise in class (alone or with partners) or for homework.

> *ANSWERS:* **2.** When I was in Japan, I stayed in a hotel in Tokyo. I stayed in a hotel in Tokyo when I was in Japan.   **3.** Maria bought some new shoes when she went shopping yesterday. When she went shopping yesterday, Maria bought some new shoes.
> **4.** I took a lot of photographs when I was in Hawaii. When I was in Hawaii, I took a lot of photographs.   **5.** Jim was a soccer player when he was in high school. When he was in high school, Jim was a soccer player.   **6.** When the rain stopped, I closed my umbrella. I closed my umbrella when the rain stopped.   **7.** The antique vase broke when I dropped it. When I dropped it, the antique vase broke.

☐ EXERCISE 30, p. 277. Sentence practice. (Chart 9-8)

After students complete this exercise, they can compare their answers with partners and discuss any differences.

EXPANSION: Have students work in small groups to write completions for the incomplete sentences.

ANSWERS: **3.** *Inc.*   **4.** When were you in Iran?   **5.** When did the movie end?
6. *Inc.*   **7.** *Inc.*   **8.** *Inc.*   **9.** *Inc.*   **10.** When does the museum open?

☐ EXERCISE 31, p. 277. Sentence practice. (Chart 9-8)

Praise your students for their ability to complete these sentences. The underlying grammar is quite complicated. You could tell them that they have shown that they can distinguish between the use of *when* as a subordinating conjunction and its use as an interrogative pronoun — just to impress them with their knowledge of English grammar. They know and can correctly use the grammar whether they know the terminology or not — just like native speakers.

You could include items such as these on a test.

CHART 9-9: THE PRESENT PROGRESSIVE AND THE PAST PROGRESSIVE

• You might have the class cover the right side of this chart and talk about the differences they see between examples (a) and (b). Then look at the illustrations (below the chart) and ask the class about the clocks and how they relate to the meanings of the sentences.

• The progressive has other meanings and functions, but "activity in progress" is the most basic one.

• Grammarians call the progressive an "aspect" instead of a verb tense. However, learners do not need this specialized vocabulary. Here we just call it "the progressive" or "the progressive form." Calling the present progressive or the past progressive a tense works well in the classroom. "Tense" is a term students are familiar and comfortable with.

• Some grammars use the term "continuous" instead of "progressive."

• WORKBOOK: For additional exercises based on Chart 9-9, see *Workbook* Practices 22 and 23.

☐ EXERCISE 32, p. 279. Sentence practice. (Chart 9-9)

The progressive tense is useful in referring to two activities at the same time. The continuing (or background) activity uses the progressive, and the interrupting activity uses the simple tense. Discuss this with the class after they look at the drawings and complete the answers. Write some of their answers on the board.

ANSWERS: **1.** was eating . . . came   **2.** called . . . was watching   **3.** was playing

□ EXERCISE 33, p. 280. Let's talk: class activity. (Chart 9-9)

The activities in the illustration were in progress at midnight. They began before midnight and were happening at the time the thief stole Mrs. Gold's jewelry. Hence, the past progressive is used for all the responses.

The purpose of this exercise is for students to understand the meaning of the past progressive, i.e., that it expresses an activity in progress at a particular time in the past when another event occurred.

EXPECTED RESPONSES (from bottom to top of illustration):

Mr. Brown and Miss Gray were playing pool in the basement. Mr. White was playing the piano for Mrs. Blue, who was singing. Mr. Black and Mr. Green were playing cards and smoking cigars. Ms. Orange was reading in bed at midnight. Mr. Blue was watching TV in his bedroom. Mr. and Mrs. Gold were sleeping in their bedroom. A bat was hanging in the attic. A mouse was running toward a piece of cheese.

CHART 9-10:   USING *WHILE* WITH THE PAST PROGRESSIVE

• The word *while* is a subordinating conjunction. It subordinates (makes less important, puts in the background) the ongoing, progressive activity.

• *While* introduces a time clause. (See also Chart 9-7, p. 273, in the student book.)

• Ask students to explain the comma in example (b). (See the footnote below Chart 9-10, p. 281, of the student book.)

• WORKBOOK: For additional exercises based on Chart 9-10, see *Workbook* Practices 24–26.

□ EXERCISE 34, p. 281. Let's talk: class activity. (Chart 9-10)

Ask two students to answer each item differently, as in the example. The drawing illustrates item 6; note the different times on the clocks.

ANSWERS: **2.** Someone knocked on my apartment door while I was eating breakfast yesterday morning. While I was eating breakfast yesterday morning, someone knocked on my apartment door.   **3.** While I was cooking dinner yesterday evening, I burned my hand. I burned my hand while I was cooking dinner yesterday evening.   **4.** Yoko raised her hand while the teacher was talking. While the teacher was talking, Yoko raised her hand.   **5.** A tree fell on my car while I was driving home yesterday. While I was driving home yesterday, a tree fell on my car.   **6.** While I was studying last night, a mouse suddenly appeared on my desk. A mouse suddenly appeared on my desk while I was studying last night.

CHART 9-11: *WHILE* vs. *WHEN* IN PAST TIME CLAUSES

• Tell the class to look closely at examples (a) and (c). Ask them to tell you the differences. Then do the same with (b) and (d). Ask the class to explain in their own words how the word *when* is different from *while*.

• Note that the explanation says that these forms are "often" used, not always (not 100% of the time). Your students should learn these patterns well, but they might see other verb forms with *when* and *while*. For example:

Jack and I got home at 5:00 P.M. Then, while I took a bath, he cooked dinner. We ate at 6:00.

The bath and dinner were in the same time period but unrelated. Neither was a background for the other. Therefore, neither was in progress before the other. (Don't teach this now.)
Another example: Sometimes the verbs in the main clause and the *while*-clause are both past progressive: *While I was washing the dishes, Jane was sweeping the floor.* Students can learn these patterns later in their study of English grammar.

• In the next exercises, it is easy for students to become confused. Ask your class to think about which activity was in progress; *while* means "in progress."

• WORKBOOK: For additional exercises based on Chart 9-11, see *Workbook* Practice 27.

□ **EXERCISE 35, p. 282. Sentence practice. (Chart 9-11)**

This exercise can be done in class or assigned as homework.

> *ANSWERS:* **2.** called . . . was washing   **3.** came . . . was eating   **4.** was eating . . . came   **5.** came . . . was watching . . . invited   **6.** was watching . . . came   **7.** was wearing . . . saw   **8.** was watching . . . relaxing . . . took

□ **EXERCISE 36, p. 283. Let's talk: class activity. (Chart 9-11)**

TEACHING SUGGESTION: Explain and demonstrate the instructions and the example so that the class understands what to do. Then for item 1, tell Student A what to do. After Student A begins, tell Student B what to do. After they stop, ask Student C to describe the two actions. This is a fun exercise that gives the grammar an immediate and real context.

CHART 9-12: SIMPLE PAST vs. PAST PROGRESSIVE

• This chart seeks to clarify the differences between the simple past and the past progressive.

• Example (g) can be difficult for students to understand. Point out that there was a sequence of actions; one followed the other. Nothing was in progress.

• Compare examples (h) and (i). The students should see that nothing was in progress in (h).

• WORKBOOK: Only review *Workbook* practices include information from Chart 9-12.

☐ **EXERCISE 37, p. 284.   Sentence practice. (Chart 9-12)**

This exercise can be done in class or assigned as homework. Students have to think about the relationship of events in time. Some are sequences. Others are in progress, then interrupted. The verb forms must show these relationships.

> *ANSWERS:* **1.** were having . . . saw . . . introduced   **2.** heard . . . walked . . . opened . . . opened . . . saw . . . greeted . . . asked   **3.** were watching . . . came . . . watched
> **4.** was walking . . . saw . . . said . . . walked

☐ **EXERCISE 38, p. 285.   Sentence practice. (Chart 9-12)**

This is similar to Exercise 37 — but with longer contexts.

> *ANSWERS:* **1.** turned . . . was driving . . . was listening . . . heard . . . looked . . . saw . . . pulled . . . waited   **2.** A: was . . . were eating . . . jumped . . . didn't seem   B: did you say . . . didn't you ask   A: didn't want

☐ **EXERCISE 39, p. 286.   Sentence practice. (Charts 9-10 → 9-12)**

Your students may know who Bill Gates is, but they are more likely familiar with a computer software program called "Word." If they don't know who Gates is, explain that he started Microsoft Corporation, which created Word. Explain that they are going to learn more about Bill Gates' life.

Go over the example sentences on the board. Students can work in pairs or small groups to make two or three more sentences using the dates in Exercise 39. Select a few of their sentences to write on the board (or have students write them). You can assign the rest as homework.

> *SAMPLE SENTENCES:*
> In 1955, Bill Gates was born.
> In 1967, he entered Lakeside School.
> While Bill Gates was studying at Lakeside School, he wrote his first computer program.
> While Bill Gates was studying at Lakeside School, he started his first software company.
> In 1973, he graduated from Lakeside.
> While he was studying at Harvard University, he began to design programs for personal computers.
> In 1977, he left Harvard.
> While he was working as Chief Executive Officer for Microsoft, he got married.
> In 1996, his first child was born.

☐ **EXERCISE 40, p. 287.   Listening. (Chapter 9)**

Play the audio once through without stopping. Then play it again, pausing after each sentence so students can complete the sentences. If a sentence is long, you may want to pause after the first completion.

Discuss the answers in class. Write the verbs in two columns on the board: one headed *simple past* and the other *past progressive*. Call attention to the two negative verbs.

I <u>had</u> a strange experience yesterday. I <u>was reading</u> my book on the bus when a man <u>sat</u> down next to me and <u>asked</u> me if I wanted some money. I <u>didn't want</u> his money. I <u>was</u> very confused. I <u>stood</u> up and <u>walked</u> toward the door.

While I <u>was waiting</u> for the door to open, the man <u>tried</u> to give me the money. When the door <u>opened</u>, I <u>got</u> off the bus quickly. I still <u>don't know</u> why he <u>was trying</u> to give me money.

☐ **EXERCISE 41, p. 287.   Verb review. (Charts 9-9 → 9-12)**

This exercise can be used as a quiz.

ANSWERS: **2.** C   **3.** C   **4.** A   **5.** C   **6.** B   **7.** C   **8.** A   **9.** C
10. D

☐ **EXERCISE 42, p. 288.   Let's talk: interview. (Chapter 9)**

Conduct the interviews in class, but assign the paragraph as homework. If it's to be graded, be sure the students understand what you'll be grading. At this stage, it's best to concentrate on the time expressions and the verb tenses.

☐ **EXERCISE 43, p. 288.   Chapter review: error analysis. (Chapter 9)**

ANSWERS: **1.** Did you <u>go</u> downtown yesterday?   **2.** Yesterday I <u>spoke</u> to Ken before he <u>left</u> his office and <u>went</u> home.   **3.** I <u>heard</u> a good joke last night.   **4.** ~~When~~ Pablo finished his work. OR When Pablo finished his work, (he went home).   **5.** I <u>visited</u> my relatives in New York City last month.   **6.** Where <u>did you</u> go yesterday afternoon?   **7.** Ms. Wah ~~was~~ flew from Singapore to Tokyo last week.   **8.** When I <u>saw</u> my friend yesterday, he didn't <u>speak</u> to me.   **9.** Why <u>didn't Mustafa come</u> to class last week?   **10.** Where <u>did</u> you <u>buy</u> those shoes? I like them.   **11.** Mr. Adams <u>taught</u> our class last week.   **12.** I <u>wrote</u> a letter last night.   **13.** Who <u>did</u> you <u>write</u> a letter to?   **14.** Who <u>opened</u> the door? Jack <u>opened</u> it.

☐ **EXERCISE 44, p. 289.   Verb review. (Chapters 8 and 9)**

Don't make this exercise a test or work. It's supposed to be fun and interesting. It's meant to be a reward. Expand upon this exercise as time allows. You may want to do it in three parts, covering one part each day.

EXPANSION: Students can do role-plays, write summaries, discuss the meaning of the story in small groups, do artwork as a basis for retelling the story, continue the story (Will Bear eventually eat Fish?), etc.

PART I ANSWERS:

1. was	**6.** sit	**11.** is
2. saw	**7.** need	**12.** don't trust
3. are you	**8.** don't need/do not need	**13.** do you want
4. am doing	**9.** are you doing	**14.** want
5. Would you like	**10.** am getting	**15.** had

PART II ANSWERS:

16. saw
17. love
18. stopped
19. reached
20. came
21. was

22. don't believe/do not believe
23. don't believe/do not believe
24. are
25. aren't/are not
26. is it
27. did the bee sting

28. are you doing
29. are you holding
30. am holding
31. tricked
32. happened

PART III ANSWERS:

33. got
34. wanted
35. to catch
36. caught
37. looks
38. don't believe/do not believe

39. is
40. is coming
41. don't see/do not see
42. dropped
43. fooled
44. tricked

45. taught
46. learned
47. am
48. have
49. Would you like

CHAPTER 10
Expressing Future Time, Part 1

Overview

This chapter introduces the phrases that express future time in English. The first of these is *be going to,* which is especially common in conversation. The present progressive to express future time is next. Time words for future and past time are also introduced and practiced. The last section introduces *will*, followed by a review of all verb tenses studied thus far, including forms of the verb *be*.

☐ **EXERCISE 1, p. 294. Preview: let's talk.**

This exercise will show you how familiar your students are with *be going to.* You can use this as a diagnostic to see how much explanation and practice your students will require.

TEACHING SUGGESTION: Ask several students each question so that all students have a chance to speak.

SAMPLE ANSWERS: **1.** Yes, I am. I'm going to come to class tomorrow. OR No, I'm not. I'm not going to come to class tomorrow. **2.** Yes, he/she is. (. . .) is going to be here tomorrow. OR No, he/she isn't. (. . .) isn't going to be here tomorrow. **3.** Yes, they are. (. . .) and (. . .) are going to be here tomorrow. OR No, they aren't. (. . .) and (. . .) aren't going to be here tomorrow. **4.** At ten/ten o'clock. I'm going to bed tonight at 10:00/ten o'clock. **5.** At eight/eight o'clock. I'm going to get up at 8:00/ eight o'clock tomorrow morning. **6.** To the drugstore. She/He is going to go to the drugstore tomorrow after class.

CHART 10-1: FUTURE TIME: USING *BE GOING TO*

• Contractions with both *be* and *going to* are the most common use of these forms in spoken English. Thus, *I am going to go downtown* is spoken, "I'm gonna go downtown." *Gonna* = /gənə/. It is unusual for a speaker to say this phrase without contractions, but *gonna* is not a standard written form.

• Model "gonna" for the class, but don't teach it as the only way of saying "be going to." Students learn to use *gonna* naturally as they gain experience with English.

• When students learn to say "gonna" for *going to,* they sometimes make the mistake of adding *to* again: ★*"I'm gonna to* go downtown." This is like saying ★*"I am going to to* go downtown."

• The general meaning of *be going to* is "expressing a plan or intention."

• Chart 10-1 includes negative statements and questions that use *be going to.* Lead students through these forms, pointing out parallels with the word order in present progressive sentences (compare with Charts 4-4 and 4-5).

• WORKBOOK: For additional exercises based on Chart 10-1, see *Workbook* Practices 1–7.

□ **EXERCISE 2, p. 295. Let's talk: pairwork. (Chart 10-1)**

Divide the students into pairs.

TEACHING SUGGESTIONS: Write *go downtown* (from the example) on the board, and have one pair perform the rest of the example in the book. Tell students to change Partner A and Partner B roles after item 10. Only the partner asking the question should have his/her book open. As the students work, walk around the classroom listening to their efforts. Interrupt as little as possible, but take note of which items need discussion after everyone is finished.

□ **EXERCISE 3, p. 295. Let's talk: class interview. (Chart 10-1)**

TEACHING SUGGESTIONS: Remind students to ask a different person each question. You can also be one of the "students." Make sure there is time for students to share their answers.

□ **EXERCISE 4, p. 296. Sentence practice. (Chart 10-1)**

This exercise can be done in class or as homework.

TEACHING SUGGESTIONS: Lead students through the list of phrases to be sure they know the meanings and pronunciations. Note that the instructions suggest adding the students' own words — to make their answers more real and truthful.

ANSWERS: **2.** am going to go to bed. **3.** is going to get something to eat.
4. am going to take them to the laundromat. **5.** am going to see a dentist.
6. am going to look it up in my dictionary. **7.** is going to take it to the post office.
8. are going to take a long walk in the park. **9.** are going to go to the beach.
10. am going to lie down and rest for a while. **11.** am going to call the police.
12. am going to major in psychology. **13.** am going to stay in bed today.
14. are going to go to an Italian restaurant. **15.** is going to call the manager.

□ **EXERCISE 5, p. 297. Let's talk: class activity. (Chart 10-1)**

TEACHING SUGGESTION: You might ask students to close their eyes and picture the situation that your words describe. Model the example with one student. Substitute names of your students and perhaps other teachers for the parentheses (. . .).

EXPANSION: Divide students into small groups. Ask each group to come up with a couple of scenarios similar to the items they just completed. Have one group present its scenarios to another group or to the entire class.

VOCABULARY NOTES:

In item 6, a *laundromat* /lɔndrəmæt/ is a kind of shop with many washing machines where people can wash their clothes for a few coins.

In item 9, an *engagement ring* is given by a man to the woman he is planning to marry. In the United States, this ring is worn on what is called the "ring finger" of the left hand (the finger next to the little finger), and the wedding ring will also be worn on that finger.

In item 10, *swimming suits* (or *swimsuits)* are worn for swimming in the water or sunbathing on the beach; *sandals* are shoes that are open at the toes and heels.

□ **EXERCISE 6, p. 298. Let's talk: interview. (Chart 10-1)**

TEACHING SUGGESTIONS: Lead the class in the example. Remind students to give short answers. After they have finished, ask them to share their answers for each item. If your class has trouble with this exercise, write the complete question for each item on the board at the end of the exercise.

□ **EXERCISE 7, p. 299.   Let's talk: class activity. (Chart 10-1)**

> *TEACHING SUGGESTION:* This is a teacher-led activity; students' books are closed. Keep the pace lively with a little humor. In item 14, you should substitute a local food if *pizza* is not appropriate.

CHART 10-2:   USING THE PRESENT PROGRESSIVE TO EXPRESS FUTURE TIME

- Write sentences (a) and (b) on the board. Ask students if they think they have the same or different meanings. Do the same for (c) and (d).

- Explain that this use of the present progressive is for plans that have already been made; there is no difference in meaning.

- Ask students to name verbs they might use when talking about plans. You may need to give students a context, for example, taking a trip. See how many verbs students list; then have them look at the list in the chart. Tell students they don't need to memorize these verbs; they just need to be familiar with their use.

- WORKBOOK: For additional exercises based on Chart 10-2, see *Workbook* Practices 8 and 9.

□ **EXERCISE 8, p. 300.   Sentence practice. (Chart 10-2)**

This exercise can be done in class or as homework.

> *EXPANSION:* For paragraph practice, you might ask students to write their sentences (without numbering them) on a separate sheet of paper. They should begin with the example sentence, then add each new sentence immediately after the others. When they're done, they'll have a complete paragraph. Explain that a paragraph is about one unifying idea. Here, it is a trip that the narrator ("I") plans to take with his/her mother and brother.

> *ANSWERS:*   **2.** We are flying to Athens.   **3.** We are spending a week there.   **4.** My brother is meeting us there.   **5.** He is taking the train.   **6.** We are going sightseeing together.   **7.** I am coming back by boat, and they are returning by train.

□ **EXERCISE 9, p. 300.   Listening. (Chart 10-2)**

All the present sentences in this exercise begin with a context that indicates immediacy: "Look," "Oh no," "Hurry," or "Shhh." Students will find it helpful to learn to recognize these cues.

> *ANSWERS:*   **2.** future   **3.** present   **4.** future   **5.** present   **6.** present
> **7.** future   **8.** future

□ **EXERCISE 10, p. 300.   Let's talk: interview. (Chart 10-2)**

> *VOCABULARY NOTE:* A DVD (digital video disk) is a computer disk that contains a movie you can watch in your own home. The disk is inserted into a DVD player. DVDs have nearly replaced the older VHS movie tapes.

This exercise includes both *going to* and *gonna*. The spelling of the word *gonna* should not be taught. Simply mention that it is the usual American pronunciation for *going to*. Students will hear "gonna" more often, so they should be aware of it. The focus here is on listening, not pronunciation.

> *ANSWERS:* **2.** am leaving   **3.** starts   **4.** is coming   **5.** is going to call
> **6.** Are you going to study   **7.** are having   **8.** aren't going   **9.** rides
> **10.** is going to help

CHART 10-3: WORDS USED FOR PAST TIME AND FUTURE TIME

• You might begin with the sentences on the right side of the chart, asking students what differences they see in each pair.

• You might divide the class in half and have one group say a word from the "Past" list followed by the other group saying the contrasting word from the "Future" list.

• NOTE: We do not use the article *the* before *last* or *next* in these time phrases. Also note that we can say *last night* but not *next night;* we must say *tomorrow night*.

• WORKBOOK: For additional exercises based on Chart 10-3, see *Workbook* Practice 10.

□ EXERCISE 12, p. 302. Sentence practice. (Chart 10-3)

This exercise can be done in class or as homework. Students must identify the verb tense before completing each sentence correctly. Make sure students don't use *the* before *last* or *next*.

> *ANSWERS:* **3.** next   **4.** last   **5.** yesterday   **6.** Tomorrow   **7.** next
> **8.** last   **9.** next   **10.** Last   **11.** next   **12.** last   **13.** tomorrow
> **14.** Last   **15.** Tomorrow   **16.** yesterday

□ EXERCISE 13, p. 303. Sentence practice. (Chart 10-3)

This exercise can be done in class or as homework. Again, students must identify the verb tense before they can complete each sentence correctly.

> *ANSWERS:* **3.** an hour ago.   **4.** in an hour.   **5.** in two more months.   **6.** two
> months ago.   **7.** a minute ago.   **8.** in half an hour.   **9.** in one more week.
> **10.** a year ago.

□ EXERCISE 14, p. 303. Sentence practice. (Chart 10-3)

This exercise gives students practice with *ago* and *in* in a realistic context.

TEACHING SUGGESTIONS: Tell your class that for the purposes of this exercise, "today" is September 9. Point out that it's circled in red on the calendar for easy reference. Lead the class through the example. You can do the first two or three items as a class, and then students can complete the exercise in pairs. Correct the answers as a class. It is helpful to put the calendar on the board or project it onto a screen.

For item 8, write the months *September, October, November,* and *December* on the board to make the time (in months) easier for the students to calculate.

> ANSWERS: **2.** They are going to leave for their honeymoon in six days. **3.** Beth and Tom got engaged three months ago. **4.** They are going to return from their honeymoon in two weeks / in fourteen days. **5.** Beth and Tom met (three years ago, four years ago, etc.). *(Answers will vary.)* **6.** They began dating (two years ago, three years ago, etc.). *(Answers will vary.)* **7.** Tom is going to quit his job in three weeks / in twenty-one days. **8.** Beth and Tom are going to open a restaurant together in three months.

☐ EXERCISE 15, p. 304.   Listening. (Chart 10-3)

If you choose to read from the listening script instead of playing the audio, be sure to let your voice rise at the end of each phrase. This signals to the students that you have not reached the end of the sentence. This is important because they are completing the sentence.

> ANSWERS: **2.** in one hour **3.** two weeks ago **4.** one year ago **5.** in ten minutes **6.** a few minutes ago **7.** next spring **8.** last summer **9.** next weekend **10.** yesterday evening

☐ EXERCISE 16, p. 304.   Let's talk: interview. (Chart 10-3)

Students need to pay special attention to the verb forms. You may find many mistakes with their question forms. Take note of these and discuss them afterward.

☐ EXERCISE 17, p. 304.   Sentence practice. (Chart 10-3)

This exercise can be done in class or as homework.

> ANSWERS:
> **2.** ago
> **3.** next
> **4.** in
> **5.** yesterday
> **6.** tomorrow
> **7.** last
> **8.** tomorrow
> **9.** ago
> **10.** in
> **11.** Tomorrow
> **12.** Last
> **13.** Yesterday
> **14.** last
> **15.** in
> **16.** Next

CHART 10-4:   USING *A COUPLE OF* OR *A FEW* WITH *AGO* (PAST) AND *IN* (FUTURE)

- This is a usage expansion lesson.
- WORKBOOK: For additional exercises based on Chart 10-4, see *Workbook* Practices 11–13.

☐ EXERCISE 18, p. 306.   Let's talk: small groups. (Chart 10-4)

TEACHING SUGGESTION: Students should give truthful answers to make the exercise more realistic.

SAMPLE ANSWERS: **3.** a few hours ago   **4.** in a couple of hours   **5.** a few minutes ago   **6.** in thirty (more) minutes   **7.** twenty years ago   **8.** thirty years ago   **9.** ten weeks ago . . . in a few months

☐ EXERCISE 19, p. 306.   Sentence practice. (Chart 10-4)

This exercise can be done in class or as homework.

TEACHING SUGGESTION: Have students read their answers aloud to the whole class or to a small group. They can correct one another as necessary.

NOTE: Your students may choose to use the present progressive for future meaning.

☐ EXERCISE 20, p. 307.   Listening. (Chart 10-4)

This exercise may prove challenging for your students. Give enough time for them to think about the meaning of the time words. You may need to play the audio two or more times for each sentence.

ANSWERS: **2.** same   **3.** different   **4.** same   **5.** different   **6.** different   **7.** same   **8.** different

---

CHART 10-5:   USING *TODAY, TONIGHT,* AND *THIS* + *MORNING, AFTERNOON, EVENING, WEEK, MONTH, YEAR*

• It is difficult for some learners to understand that the time expressions in this list can be used with present, past, or future verb forms. The tense depends on the relationship between the time of the event (or activity) and the moment of speaking.

• Make up additional examples from the class context. For instance, if you are teaching an afternoon class, show how *this morning* refers to a past time and *this evening* to a future time. Show how past, present, and future tenses can truthfully be used with *this afternoon.* For example:

> *I ate breakfast this morning. I'm going to eat dinner this evening.*
> *I saw Pedro before class this afternoon. We're in class this afternoon.*
> *I'm going to go to the bookstore after class this afternoon.*

• WORKBOOK: For additional exercises based on Chart 10-5, see *Workbook* Practices 14–16.

☐ **EXERCISE 21, p. 307.   Sentence practice. (Chart 10-5)**

Students can work with partners, in small groups, or as a class.

   TEACHING SUGGESTION: Students should answer truthfully. You may want them to give the answers orally in class and write them later for homework.

> *SAMPLE ANSWERS:* **4.** I ate breakfast earlier today.   **5.** I am sitting in English class today (right now).   **6.** I am going to meet my friends later today.   **7.** I brushed my teeth earlier this morning.   **8.** I am going to read the newspaper later this evening.

☐ **EXERCISE 22, p. 308.   Sentence practice. (Chart 10-5)**

   TEACHING SUGGESTIONS: Pairs of students can work together to discuss appropriate sentences for each item, or you could lead a general discussion in which students call out various completions. Alternatively, students can write their answers at home and then share them with the class.

☐ **EXERCISE 23, p. 308.   Let's talk: small groups. (Chart 10-5)**

   TEACHING SUGGESTION: Divide the class into small groups and lead them through the example. All sentences will include *be going to.* The groups should change roles after each item so that everyone gets a chance to be Speakers A, B, and C. (In other words, the role of Speaker A rotates.)

☐ **EXERCISE 24, p. 309.   Let's talk: pairwork. (Chart 10-5)**

This exercise gives more practice with past and future verb phrases and with time words.

   TEACHING SUGGESTIONS: Partners should change roles after item 9. Have them share a few of their answers after most of the pairs have finished.

☐ **EXERCISE 25, p. 310.   Listening. (Chart 10-5)**

   TEACHING SUGGESTION: Briefly review what students need to listen for in order to recognize past, present, and future verb tenses (e.g., helping verbs, *-ed*, etc.). The *-ed* ending (as well as some helping verbs) may be hard to hear, but this will help students see the importance of time words, which can be used with any of the tenses.

> *ANSWERS:* **2.** future   **3.** past   **4.** future   **5.** past   **6.** future
> **7.** present   **8.** past   **9.** future   **10.** past

CHART 10-6: FUTURE TIME: USING *WILL*

• In most cases, there is little difference in meaning between *will* and *be going to;* both are used to make predictions about the future.

• This text does not present the differences between *will* and *be going to,* but some questions may arise. *Be going to* (but not *will*) is used to express a preconceived plan (e.g., *I bought some wood because I'm going to build a bookcase*). *Will* (but not *be going to*) is used to volunteer or express willingness (e.g., *This chair is too heavy for you to carry alone. I'll help you.*). In this case, the use of *will* is related to its historical meaning of willingness or promise.

An easy way for the teacher to connect the idea of "plan" with *be going to* is to think of the sentence *I was going to call you.* This has the same meaning as *I was planning to call you.* Similarly, *I am going to call you* means *I am planning to call you.* Native speakers more often associate the idea of "plan" with the past progressive, and it is easier to remember it that way. This is not something students will understand (or need to know) at this level.

• This text does not present *shall,* but you may be asked questions about it. *Shall* is used instead of *will* (with "*I*" and *we* as subjects) far more frequently in British English than American English. The use of *shall* to express future time is infrequent in American English.

Shall has another meaning besides future. In expressions such as *Shall I call you tomorrow?* or *Shall we leave at eight?*, *shall* is not synonymous with *will;* rather, it expresses a polite offer of help or an invitation.

• *Won't* is pronounced /wount/.

• WORKBOOK: For additional exercises based on Chart 10-6, see *Workbook* Practices 17–20.

☐ EXERCISE 26, p. 311.   Let's talk: class activity. (Chart 10-6)

Be sure students understand that they have not changed the meaning of the sentence by using *will* instead of *be going to.* (There are some very subtle distinctions between *will* and *be going to* that students will come to understand much later in their experience with English. They cannot understand these distinctions at this point.)

Model spoken contractions of *will* with nouns (e.g., "Fred'll") as well as with pronouns.

☐ EXERCISE 27, p. 312.   Listening. (Chart 10-6)

For many learners the *'ll* contraction cannot be heard, so students do not think a form of *will* is there. This is good practice for them because the contracted form of *will* is very common in spoken English. It's important that your students become more attuned to its use.

ANSWERS: 2. teacher will   3. We'll   4. We will   5. I'll   6. students'll
7. John will   8. doctor'll   9. nurse will   10. You'll

☐ EXERCISE 28, p. 312.   Listening. (Chart 10-6)

TEACHING SUGGESTION: Be sure all the students have a dream vacation spot in mind before you play the audio. Give them enough time to think about and write their answers.

CHART 10-7: ASKING QUESTIONS WITH *WILL*

- You might ask students to compare these questions with those in Chart 10-1, looking for similarities in word order.
- WORKBOOK: For additional exercises based on Chart 10-7, see *Workbook* Practices 21–23.

☐ EXERCISE 29, p. 313. Question practice. (Chart 10-7)

This exercise can be done in class or as homework.

TEACHING SUGGESTIONS: The words in parentheses should not be spoken. They simply give the information necessary for completing the questions and answers. For additional practice, you might have students repeat part of this exercise, using *be going to.*

> *ANSWERS:* 4. A: Will the plane be on time?   B: it will.   5. A: Will dinner be ready in a few minutes?   B: it will.   6. When will dinner be ready?   7. When will you graduate?   8. Where will Mary go to school next year?   9. A: Will Jane and Mark be at the party?   B: they won't.   10. A: Will Mike arrive in Chicago next week?   B: he will.   11. Where will Mike be next week?   12. A: Will you be home early tonight?   B: I won't.   13. When will Dr. Smith be back?   14. A: Will you be ready to leave at 8:15?   B: I will.

☐ EXERCISE 30, p. 314. Let's talk: pairwork. (Chart 10-7)

Part I should be done individually before the class is divided into pairs. After students have completed Part II, ask them to share a few of their answers with the class.

TEACHING SUGGESTION: Bring in several different pictures of Paris landmarks to spark student interest. Include some of the places listed in the exercise. Find out if any of your students have been to Paris; if so, ask them about their favorite places.

EXPANSION: Your students may also enjoy bringing in pictures or postcards of other famous landmarks from their own countries. Ask your class what they would like to do if they visited one (or more) of these places.

☐ EXERCISE 31, p. 315. Listening. (Chart 10-7)

TEACHING SUGGESTIONS: You can read the story to the class, or have one or two of your best students read it (divided into sections). Discuss any new vocabulary before you play the audio. Review the answers with your class.

If your class is advanced, have students read the story silently before you play the audio. After they listen, have them exchange papers. Then play the audio again, so they can correct one another's work. Do a spot-check to see which items were incorrect and to discuss the most common mistakes.

> *ANSWERS:* 2. No, she won't.   3. No, she won't.   4. No, she won't.   5. No, she won't.   6. Yes, she will.   7. No, she won't.   8. Yes, she will.

☐ EXERCISE 32, p. 316. Listening. (Chart 10-7)

TEACHING SUGGESTION: For some students, these words will sound identical. Review the meanings of the verbs *want* (to desire something) and *won't* (the contraction of *will not*).

> *ANSWERS:* **2.** won't **3.** won't **4.** want **5.** won't **6.** won't **7.** want
> **8.** want

CHART 10-8: VERB SUMMARY: PRESENT, PAST, AND FUTURE

• This is a good review of the verb forms studied so far. You might divide the class into three groups. Have one group say the statement, one the negative, and one the question. Another possibility is to hand out a grid of the chart with the vertical and horizontal labels but no examples. Ask students to make up their own examples or place those you dictate into the proper place in the grid.

• Discuss any questions students have about these forms.

• WORKBOOK: For additional exercises based on Chart 10-8, see *Workbook* Practices 24 and 25.

☐ EXERCISE 33, p. 317. Sentence practice. (Chart 10-8)

This exercise can be done in class or as homework.

> *ANSWERS:* **2.** is not doing / isn't doing . . . is writing **3.** writes **4.** doesn't write
> **5.** don't expect **6.** wrote . . . started **7.** rang . . . was **8.** didn't finish . . .
> talked . . . went **9.** is going to write / will write **10.** isn't going to write / won't
> write **11.** Do you write **12.** Did you write **13.** Are you going to write / Will
> you write

☐ EXERCISE 34, p. 318. Listening. (Chart 10-8)

TEACHING SUGGESTIONS: Make sure students know the word *vegetarian* (a person who doesn't eat meat) before you play the audio. This exercise is challenging because the students have to listen for several things: affirmative and negative verbs, contractions, helping verbs, and reductions. You may need to play the sentences two or more times. Discuss problem grammar spots.

> *ANSWERS:* **1.** doesn't like **2.** is . . . doesn't eat . . . didn't eat **3.** doesn't eat . . .
> isn't **4.** doesn't enjoy **5.** are going to try **6.** will . . . have **7.** won't have
> . . . 'll . . . ask **8.** Are they going to enjoy **9.** Will they go

CHART 10-9:   VERB SUMMARY: FORMS OF *BE*

• *Be* is the main verb in these sentences. It is also the helping (auxiliary) verb in the present progressive and in *be going to*. It is useful for learners to compare all the forms.

• It is difficult to explain the meaning of *be* as a main verb. It may mean "exist" or "occupy a specific place" or "occur." Sometimes it is like the equals sign (=) in an equation: *Ann was late. (Ann = late.)*

• You might divide the class into three groups. Have one group say the statement, one the negative, and one the question. Or you could make a grid, as suggested in the notes for Chart 10-8, and have your students fill it in.

• WORKBOOK: For additional exercises based on Chart 10-9, see *Workbook* Practices 26–30.

☐ EXERCISE 35, p. 319.   Sentence practice: review of BE. (Chart 10-9)

TEACHING SUGGESTION: This exercise can be done in class or as homework. Tell students to read each complete item before answering. They have to relate the verb form to the time words as well as to the singular or plural subject.

ANSWERS: **1.** am . . . wasn't / was not . . . was . . . Were you . . . Was Carmen
2. were . . . were not / weren't   **3.** will be / are going to be . . . will be / am going to be
. . . Will you be / Are you going to be . . . Will Yuko be / Is Yuko going to be   **4.** isn't / is
not . . . is . . . aren't / are not . . . are

☐ EXERCISE 36, p. 319.   Listening: review of BE. (Chart 10-9)

Forms of the *be* verb can be very hard for students to hear when spoken at normal speed. Don't be surprised if your students make a lot of mistakes in this exercise. They are probably more used to seeing these forms in writing than listening for them.

ANSWERS:
1. A: Will you be
    B: I will . . . I'll . . . be
2. A: are
    B: is . . . are
3. A: Was
    B: were . . . was
    A: Was he
    B: he wasn't . . . was

4. A: We're going to be
    B: We're not going to be . . . is
    A: isn't . . . is
    B: We won't be

☐ EXERCISE 37, p. 320.   Review. (Chapter 10)

TEACHING SUGGESTION: Some students will be able to make longer lists than others. You might suggest a minimum of three predictions and a maximum of six.

☐ EXERCISE 38, p. 320.   Review: small groups. (Chapter 10)

This is a fun "fortune-telling" exercise.

TEACHING SUGGESTION: Your students don't know each other well, but they do have impressions of one another. Tell them to use their powers of observation and intuition to predict the future — to pretend to be fortune tellers. Perhaps they want to read one another's palms. The exercise should be light-hearted and fun.

EXPANSION: Follow this exercise with a written assignment: students predict what is going to happen in their own lives in the next 50 years. When you return their papers, tell them to save these compositions and look at them again when they are past 60.

☐ EXERCISE 39, p. 320.   Review: small groups. (Chapter 10)

This exercise can be written or oral.

TEACHING SUGGESTIONS: You can raise students' interest in this exercise by the way you introduce it. Tell them about the mysterious letter and have them decide how much money it contains. Then ask for suggestions about what they would do with the money. After a short discussion, tell them to read about all six letters and choose one to describe. Tell them how long their description should be (perhaps three to six sentences). Then break the class into groups so they can share their descriptions.

☐ EXERCISE 40, p. 321.   Chapter review: error analysis. (Chapters 8 → 10)

ANSWERS: **1.** Is Ivan <u>going to go</u> to work tomorrow? OR <u>Will Ivan go</u> to work tomorrow?   **2.** When <u>will you</u> call me?   **3.** Will Tom ~~to~~ meet us for dinner tomorrow?   **4.** We went to a movie <u>last</u> night.   **5.** Did you <u>find</u> your keys?   **6.** What time <u>are you</u> going to come tomorrow?   **7.** My sister is going to meet me at the airport. My brother won't ~~to~~ be there.   **8.** Mr. Wong will <u>sell</u> his business and <u>retire</u> next year.   **9.** <u>Will you be</u> in Venezuela next year?   **10.** I'm going to return home in a couple of <u>months</u>.   **11.** I saw Jim three <u>days</u> ago.   **12.** A thief <u>stole</u> my bicycle.

☐ EXERCISE 41, p. 321.   Review: verb forms. (Chapter 10)

This exercise can be done in class or as homework.

TEACHING SUGGESTION: You might ask students to correct their work in pairs.

NOTE: In the example, the main verb is *have.* In British English, this question is sometimes "Have you a bicycle?" and the answer is "Yes, I have." But in American English, the auxiliary *do* is required in both the question and the short answer: "Do you have a bicycle?" Answer: "Yes, I do."

ANSWERS:

2. A: Did you walk
   B: didn't . . . rode
3. A: do you usually study . . .
      Do you go
   B: don't like
4. A: Will you be / Are you going to be
   B: will / am . . . will not be /
      won't be / am not going to be
5. A: Do whales breathe
   B: do
   A: Does a whale have
   B: does
   A: Is a whale
   B: isn't . . . is

6. A: Did Yuko call
   B: did . . . talked
   A: Did she tell
   B: didn't . . . didn't say
   A: was . . . ran . . . didn't
      want . . . tried . . . ran
   B: Is he
   A: isn't . . . is

□ **EXERCISE 42, p. 324.   Let's talk: small groups. (Chapter 10)**

Students have to use verb forms, tenses, and time words together correctly. You could assign this as homework or use it as a quiz.

TEACHING SUGGESTION: Most sentences should include *because*. Give an example for each speaker (A, B, and C):

<u>Picture 1</u>

SPEAKER A: Alex takes the train to work because he lives far away.

SPEAKER B: Alex is going to prepare for work on the train because he has a busy day tomorrow.

SPEAKER C: Alex prepared his work on the train because he didn't have time the night before.

EXPANSION: Students could write about one of the illustrations in a paragraph of four to six sentences.

CHAPTER 11
Expressing Future Time, Part 2

Overview

The chapter opens by contrasting *may, might,* and *maybe* with *will.* Sections on clauses with *before, after, when,* and *if* follow. There is an explanation of how these clauses are used to express habitual present actions. The use of *do* as a main verb is taught in the present, past, and future tenses. The chapter concludes by providing a variety of exercises on all of the verb forms introduced in the student book thus far.

CHART 11-1: *MAY/MIGHT* vs. *WILL*

• *May, might,* and *will* are some of the many modal auxiliaries in English. By focusing on just these few, learners should not become confused. Modals add special qualities (such as possibility, necessity, or advisability) to the meaning of main verbs.

• Stress that *might* and *may* have the same meaning here. Sometimes students have been taught that *might* is the past tense of *may. Might* is used this way only in noun clauses introduced by a past tense verb (e.g., *He said, "I may come"* can become *He said he might come* in reported speech). *May* has additional meanings that are not presented in this lesson.

• For an explanation of *may be* (verb) and *maybe* (adverb), see Chart 11-2.

• WORKBOOK: For additional exercises based on Chart 11-1, see *Workbook* Practices 1 and 2.

☐ EXERCISE 1, p. 325.   Sentence practice. (Chart 11-1)

These modals add meaning to the main verbs. They express the speaker's opinion as to degree of certainty or uncertainty.

TEACHING SUGGESTIONS: Students should complete these sentences with real information. Item 13 is included more as a good topic for spontaneous classroom discussion involving the target structures than as a clear example of the use of *will* vs. *may/might.* Downplay the grammar and engage the class in expressing their opinions about the possibility of beings in the universe besides ourselves.

☐ EXERCISE 2, p. 326.   Let's write and talk. (Chart 11-1)

TEACHING SUGGESTIONS: Have students use their own paper to complete this exercise. The blanks in the student book are purposely too small. When the students are done, they will have two complete paragraphs — one about past activities and the other about future activities. They should write their own paragraphs but share them with partners when they're finished.

☐ **EXERCISE 3, p. 327.   Let's talk: pairwork. (Chart 11-1)**

> *TEACHING SUGGESTION:* Before students begin this pairwork activity, have them think about a specific person for the people in the list (e.g., *a famous athlete* = Tiger Woods). They can then complete their sentences using the list either in order or at random.

CHART 11-2:   *MAYBE* (ONE WORD) vs. *MAY BE* (TWO WORDS)
• The historical development of English has produced these two forms with similar meanings. *Maybe* is an adverb written as a single word and placed only at the beginning of a sentence. *May be* (two words) = a modal auxiliary + a main verb.   • In speaking, *maybe* is stressed on the first syllable: /<u>may</u>bi/. *May be* is longer with two equally stressed syllables.   • WORKBOOK: For additional exercises based on Chart 11-2, see *Workbook* Practices 3–7.

☐ **EXERCISE 4, p. 328.   Sentence practice. (Chart 11-2)**

Point out that items 1 and 2 have <u>exactly</u> the same meaning whereas items 4 and 5 have <u>almost</u> the same meaning.

> *ANSWERS:*   **3.** may go = *a verb;* **may** *is part of the verb*   **4.** Maybe = *an adverb*
> **5.** may like = *a verb;* **may** *is part of the verb*   **6.** may be = *a verb;* **may** *is part of the verb;* Maybe = *an adverb*

☐ **EXERCISE 5, p. 328.   Sentence practice. (Chart 11-2)**

Students should practice pronouncing these two forms. (See the notes in Chart 11-2.)

> *ANSWERS:*   **3.** may be   **4.** may be   **5.** Maybe   **6.** may be . . . Maybe

---

☐ **EXERCISE 6, p. 329.   Listening. (Chart 11-2)**

Maybe + *will* can be hard to hear, especially in the contracted form. Review the pronunciation of these forms before playing the examples and continuing with the exercise.

> *ANSWERS:*   **1.** may + verb   **2.** may + verb   **3.** maybe   **4.** may + verb
> **5.** Maybe   **6.** Maybe   **7.** may + verb   **8.** Maybe

---

☐ **EXERCISE 7, p. 329.   Sentence practice. (Chart 11-2)**

> *TEACHING SUGGESTION:* Students can give the answers orally in class (perhaps with a partner) and write them later for homework.

> *ANSWERS:*   **2.** Maybe the teacher will give a test. The teacher may give a test.
> **3.** Janet may be home early. Janet might be home early.   **4.** She may be late. Maybe she will be late.   **5.** Maybe it will rain tomorrow. It might rain tomorrow.

□ EXERCISE 8, p. 330. Sentence practice. (Chart 11-2)

The adverb *maybe* can be a complete short answer, as in item 1. *May/might* must follow a subject in a short answer: *I don't know. I might.*

Items 2 and 3 (as well as 4 and 5) show the use of different forms with the same meanings.

ANSWERS: **3.** Maybe   **4.** may/might   **5.** Maybe   **6.** Maybe
7. may/might   **8.** Maybe . . . may/might   **9.** Maybe . . . maybe . . . may/might . . . may/might

□ EXERCISE 9, p. 331. Let's talk. (Charts 11-1 and 11-2)

TEACHING SUGGESTION: Keep the pace moving from one student to another, giving them just enough time to think of a truthful answer.

□ EXERCISE 10, p. 331. Let's talk: pairwork. (Charts 11-1 and 11-2)

TEACHING SUGGESTION: Have students share a few of their partner's answers with the class.

□ EXERCISE 11, p. 332. Listening. (Chart 11-2)

The contracted form of *will* might be hard to hear. Students may need to listen to the sentences two or more times.

ANSWERS: **2.** b   **3.** a   **4.** a   **5.** a   **6.** b

□ EXERCISE 12, p. 332. Let's talk: class activity. (Chart 11-2)

This is intended to be a fun and challenging exercise. Don't rush through it. Slowly and gently encourage your students to express their opinions.

You could use this as a quiz for grading or simply for checking the progress of the class.

□ EXERCISE 13, p. 333. Let's talk: pairwork. (Chart 11-2)

EXPANSION: Ask students to add some of their own activities not listed in the chart, perhaps three to five, that they can write on the board to share with the class.

CHART 11-3: FUTURE TIME CLAUSES WITH *BEFORE, AFTER,* AND *WHEN*

• This feature of English seems completely illogical — a future time clause does not permit the use of *will* or *be going to* with its verb.

• Emphasize that both examples below sentence (a) are incorrect. Make sure the students understand which parts of the sentences are wrong. These examples represent extremely common (and logical) errors made by all levels of learners.

   NOTE: When corrected, both sentences should read: *Before Ann **goes** to work tomorrow, she will eat breakfast.*

• WORKBOOK: For additional exercises based on Chart 11-3, see *Workbook* Practices 8–10.

□ **EXERCISE 14, p. 334.   Sentence practice. (Chart 11-3)**

TEACHING SUGGESTION: After students identify the time clauses, you could review word order in sentences with time clauses and the use of commas, as presented in Chart 9-7, page 273, in the student book. Change the positions of the adverb clauses (i.e., time clauses) and note the difference in punctuation of the new sentence.

> *ANSWERS (time clauses):* **2.** After I get home tonight   **3.** before he leaves the office today   **4.** when I go to the grocery store tomorrow   **5.** Before I go to bed tonight   **6.** after I graduate next year

□ **EXERCISE 15, p. 334.   Sentence practice. (Chart 11-3)**

This exercise forces students to pay attention to the differences in verb forms in the main clause and the future time clause. Give them time to see and discuss these differences.

> *ANSWERS:* **2.** am going to buy / will buy . . . go   **3.** finish . . . am going to take / will take   **4.** see . . . am going to ask / will ask   **5.** go . . . am going to meet / will meet   **6.** is going to change / will change . . . works

□ **EXERCISE 16, p. 335.   Let's talk: class activity. (Chart 11-3)**

TEACHING SUGGESTIONS: You should lead this exercise as a conversation. Keep a lively pace, but pay attention to the students' verb forms, especially in future time clauses. You might want to photocopy the exercise so you don't have to hold the heavy student book as you interact with your class.

CHART 11-4:   CLAUSES WITH *IF*

- An *if*-clause states a condition, and its main clause states the effect or result of that condition.

- Point out the use of commas, which is the same for other adverb clauses. (See the footnote below Chart 9-7, p. 273, in the student book.)

- In (c) and (d) students learn that *if*-clauses are like future time clauses — they do not permit the use of *will* or *be going to.*

- WORKBOOK: For additional exercises based on Chart 11-4, see *Workbook* Practices 11–13.

□ **EXERCISE 17, p. 336.   Sentence practice. (Chart 11-4)**

TEACHING SUGGESTION: Give students time to think about verb tenses, singular/plural forms, helping verbs, etc., before they answer. This exercise is intended to clarify the information in Chart 11-4 and let you know if your students have understood it. In this way, this exercise is typical of every other exercise that immediately follows a chart. It can be done in class or as homework.

NOTE: The body of water illustrated on page 337 of the student book is a large lake or freshwater inland sea, not an ocean; hence, the sign about not drinking the water. The purpose of the illustration is to generate a brief, spontaneous discussion with *if*-clauses about what will happen to our world if we continue to pollute it.

ANSWERS: **2.** is ... am going to go / will go   **3.** am not going to stay / will not stay ... is   **4.** don't feel ... am not going to go / will not go   **5.** is going to stay / will stay ... doesn't feel   **6.** am going to stay / will stay ... go   **7.** are ... am going to go / will go   **8.** continue ... are going to suffer / will suffer

☐ **EXERCISE 18, p. 337.   Let's talk: pairwork. (Chart 11-4)**

Make sure students use the *if*-clause in their answers.

☐ **EXERCISE 19, p. 338.   Listening. (Chart 11-4)**

TEACHING SUGGESTION: Give students plenty of time to respond to each question. After they complete all four questions, ask for volunteers to write their answers on the board.

☐ **EXERCISE 20, p. 338.   Let's talk: pairwork. (Chart 11-4)**

Both students should fill out the calendar in their books on page 339. Then one student plays Partner B and asks Partner A questions based on Partner A's datebook entries. Afterward, partners switch roles and continue the exercise.

TEACHING SUGGESTIONS: Lead everyone carefully through the instructions; then walk around as students work. Clarify the instructions as needed so that every student produces a written paragraph based on an interview with his/her partner. If time permits, some of the paragraphs can be shared with the class.

CHART 11-5:   EXPRESSING HABITUAL PRESENT WITH TIME CLAUSES AND *IF*-CLAUSES

• *Habitual* means "repeated frequently as part of a routine." In words that beginning students understand, you could say that *habitual* means "something you do again and again and again" or "something you usually do Monday, Tuesday, Wednesday, Thursday, Friday, Saturday, and Sunday."

• Lead students through the examples so they see the differences between (a) and (b) and between (c) and (d). This idea will help them understand the idea of habitual activity.

• In (d), it may be helpful to add the word *always* or *usually* before *wear*.

• The grammar of present vs. future verb forms in the result clause of a factual conditional sentence may be too difficult for students at this level. Use your own judgment as to how much emphasis you place on this chart. Keep in mind that much of the grammar in this text is revisited in other texts in the *Azar* series. If your students don't understand this grammar right now, they'll have another chance in other texts.

• WORKBOOK: For additional exercises based on Chart 11-5, see *Workbook* Practices 14–17.

☐ **EXERCISE 21, p. 340.   Sentence practice. (Chart 11-5)**

TEACHING SUGGESTION: You might lead the class in doing the first three items. Assign the others for your students to finish in class or for homework.

ANSWERS: **1.** go . . . usually stay **2.** go . . . am going to stay / will stay **3.** go . . . am going to have / will have **4.** go . . . usually have **5.** am . . . usually stay . . . go **6.** am . . . am going to stay / will stay . . . (am going to/will) go **7.** get . . . usually sit . . . read **8.** get . . . am going to sit / will sit . . . (am going to/will) read **9.** often yawn . . . stretch . . . wake **10.** walks . . . is **11.** go . . . am going to stay / will stay . . . leave . . . am going to go / will go **12.** goes . . . is . . . likes . . . takes . . . is

☐ EXERCISE 22, p. 341.   Let's talk: class activity. (Chart 11-5)

This exercise suggests topics for teacher-student interaction; it's not intended as a script to be read verbatim. The idea is to get students talking about their lives and interests — using present and future time clauses.

☐ EXERCISE 23, p. 341.   Sentence practice. (Chart 11-5)

TEACHING SUGGESTION: This exercise can be done in class or as homework. If you want to collect it, ask students to write their answers on a separate piece of paper.

EXPANSION: Make a worksheet that contains your students' most common errors. The next day, give students the worksheet to correct in class.

☐ EXERCISE 24, p. 342.   Listening. (Charts 11-3 → 11-5)

This exercise reviews *before*, *after*, *when* and *if* with future and habitual present time clauses. Students have to differentiate between the two clauses in order to choose the correct completion.

ANSWERS: **2.** I'll get a good night's sleep. **3.** I do my homework. **4.** I'll go shopping. **5.** I exercise. **6.** I'll call my parents. **7.** I'll be happy. **8.** I'll know a lot of grammar.

CHART 11-6: USING *WHAT* + A FORM OF *DO*

• Questions with *what* + a form of *do* are common and useful, especially in everyday conversation.

• Examples (a) and (c) show the use of *do* as both main verb and helping (auxiliary) verb.

• WORKBOOK: For additional exercises based on Chart 11-6, see *Workbook* Practices 18 and 19.

☐ EXERCISE 25, p. 343.   Question practice. (Chart 11-6)

This exercise gives learners practice in using the verb *do* in the present, past, and future.

TEACHING SUGGESTIONS: Give students time to work out the verb tense, the word order, and the singular or plural forms. If done in class, they could work in pairs and change roles after item 6. This exercise could also be assigned as homework.

ANSWERS:

2. A: did you do
   B: came
3. A: are you going to do /
      will you do
   B: am going to come /
      will come
4. A: did you do
   B: watched
5. A: do you do
   B: watch
6. A: are you going to do /
      will you do
   B: am going to watch /
      will watch

7. A: are you doing
   B: am doing
8. A: does Maria do
   B: goes
9. A: are the students doing
   B: are working
10. A: are they going to do /
       will they do
    B: are going to take /
       will take
11. A: did Boris do
    B: went
12. A: does the teacher do
    B: puts . . . looks . . . says

☐ EXERCISE 26, p. 344.   Let's talk: pairwork. (Chart 11-6)

   EXPANSION: For homework, you could have students write the questions they asked their partners. This will help them pay attention to the verb tenses used with various time words.

☐ EXERCISE 27, p. 344.   Review: verb forms. (Chapters 1 → 11)

   Some of these items contain idioms and cultural information that may need to be discussed.

ANSWERS:

1. am going to skip /
   will skip
2. took . . . flew
3. usually walk . . . take
4. A: stole
   B: is
5. A: did you meet
   B: met
6. A: did the movie begin . . .
      Were you
   B: made
7. A: lost
   B: forgot . . . gave . . . lost
      . . . stole . . . didn't have

8. A: Are you going to stay /
      Will you stay
   B: am going to take / will
      take . . . am going to visit /
      will visit
   A: are you going to be /
      will you be
9. A: are you wearing
   B: broke . . . stepped
10. A: Did you see
    B: spoke . . . called
11. B: isn't . . . left
    A: Is she going to be /
       Will she be . . . did she go
    B: went

☐ EXERCISE 28, p. 347.   Listening. (Chapter 11)

   This exercise may be challenging for your students. Once again, they have to supply longer portions of the sentence as they learn to form thought groups rather than listen to discourse as individual, separate words.

☐ **EXERCISE 29, p. 347.   Review. (Chapter 11)**

> *TEACHING SUGGESTION:* It's a good idea to lead the class through a discussion of these items because some of them contain adverbs and other signals that learners often overlook.

ANSWERS: **2.** B   **3.** C   **4.** B   **5.** A   **6.** B   **7.** C   **8.** C   **9.** A
10. D

☐ **EXERCISE 30, p. 348.   Chapter review: error analysis. (Chapter 11)**

ANSWERS: **1.** If it <u>is</u> cold tomorrow morning, my car won't start.   **2.** We <u>may be</u> late for the concert tonight.   **3.** What time <u>are you</u> going to come tomorrow?
4. Fatima will call us tonight when she <u>arrives</u> home safely.   **5.** Emily <s>may</s> will be at the party. OR <u>Maybe</u> Emily will be at the party.   **6.** When <u>I</u> see you tomorrow, I'll return your book to you.   **7.** I may <u>not</u> be in class tomorrow.   **8.** Ahmed puts his books on his desk when he <u>walks</u> into his apartment. OR Ahmed <u>put</u> his books on his desk when he <u>walked</u> into his apartment.   **9.** I'll see my parents when I <u>return</u> home for a visit next July.   **10.** What do you <u>do</u> all day at work?

☐ **EXERCISE 31, p. 349.   Review. (Chapter 11)**

> *TEACHING SUGGESTIONS:* This is a long exercise in the form of a story. It's divided into four parts for easier assignment. You may want to have the class complete the first part together, have pairs or small groups do the second part, and assign the last two for homework. Be sure to check the spelling of some of the more problematic verb forms.

PART I ANSWERS: **1.** are   **2.** are staying   **3.** like   **4.** always makes
5. tells   **6.** go   **7.** went   **8.** asked   **9.** agreed   **10.** put   **11.** brushed
12. sat

PART II ANSWERS: **13.** are you going to tell / will you tell   **14.** begin   **15.** am going to give / will give   **16.** love   **17.** am going to tell / will tell   **18.** was
19. was   **20.** saw   **21.** was   **22.** ran   **23.** stayed   **24.** was   **25.** got
26. stayed   **27.** found   **28.** needed   **29.** to eat   **30.** put   **31.** didn't smell   **32.** didn't see   **33.** hopped   **34.** found   **35.** saw   **36.** looked

PART III ANSWERS: **37.** heard   **38.** didn't see   **39.** decided   **40.** wanted
41. to rest   **42.** said   **43.** heard   **44.** spotted   **45.** flew   **46.** picked
47. didn't know   **48.** ate

☐ EXERCISE 32, p. 353.   Let's talk: small groups. (Chapter 11)

As a follow-up to Exercise 31, this exercise offers students the chance to test their reading comprehension and encourages free discussion.

Discuss the moral of the story with your students. Do our fears bring about our own misfortunes? Do we call down bad luck on ourselves?

NOTE: This exercise was misnumbered in the original printing of the student book. It will be corrected in subsequent printings.

CHAPTER *12*
Modals, Part 1: Expressing Ability

Overview

English has many ways to express ability. This chapter begins with the most common, *can/can't,* and adds a brief study of their pronunciations. Less familiar in grammar books (but very useful) is a short section on the phrase *know how to. Could* is introduced as the past tense form of *can,* followed by the past and present of *be able to.* Two modifiers that often accompany statements of ability, *very* and *too,* are presented next. Meanings of the words *two, too,* and *to* are then explained. The chapter ends with more practice with the prepositions of place — *at* and *in.*

☐ **EXERCISE 1, p. 354.   Let's talk: class activity.**

This is a preview exercise to check your students' understanding of *can.* If this exercise proves to be too easy, you can move quickly through this section.

CHART 12-1:   USING *CAN*

• Lead students through the examples, allowing them to notice and explain the meanings and important features.

• In listening to English speakers, learners often misunderstand the words *can* and *can't.* This is usually because of the pronunciation. In a short answer, *can* is pronounced /kæn/, as expected. However, in a statement or question, *can* is pronounced with no stress and almost no vowel sound: /kn/ or /kən/.
   The negative form, *can't,* is pronounced with more stress but almost no final "t" sound: /kæn/. The final /n/ sound is very short, and many native speakers make a glottal stop here. A glottal stop is formed when the vocal chords close completely for a moment, stopping the air. This is the sound you hear in the negative expression "uh-uh."

• WORKBOOK: For additional exercises based on Chart 12-1, see *Workbook* Practices 1–3.

☐ **EXERCISE 2, p. 355.   Sentence practice. (Chart 12-1)**

This exercise can be done orally in class. You may want students to write the sentences for homework. Remind your class not to stress the word *can* but to stress *can't.* Thus, item 1 will have stresses on *bird* and *fly,* and item 2 will have three stresses: *cow, can't,* and *fly.*

☐ EXERCISE 3, p. 355.   Let's talk: class activity. (Chart 12-1)

This exercise can be fun if students tell the truth about themselves. It also introduces some new vocabulary, so it's good for the whole class to discuss the items together. In their answers, make sure no one uses an infinitive with *to* after *can*. Discuss new vocabulary.

In item 1, *whistle* = make music by blowing air through the lips.
In item 6, *lift* = raise up in your arms.
In item 7, *stick-shift car* = an automobile that has a lever for changing (shifting) gears as the car goes faster or slower.
In item 10, *float* = lie on the water without moving arms or legs.
In item 11, *ski* = move over snow or water while standing on flat skis.
In item 12, *arithmetic* = basic adding, subtracting, multiplying, and dividing of numbers.
In item 14, *sew* = use a needle and thread.
In item 15, *wiggle* = move rapidly back and forth.
In item 16, *chopsticks* = two round sticks of wood held in the hand and used for putting food into one's mouth.

☐ EXERCISE 4, p. 356.   Game: small group activity. (Chart 12-1)

TEACHING SUGGESTION: You may need to go over some vocabulary before students begin this task. If you have pictures of the animals mentioned in the exercise, bring them to class.

EXPANSION: You might ask each group of students to create a few new sentences based on animal facts. Have them present the sentences for the other groups to figure out.

ANSWERS: **1.** Yes. [Ostriches and penguins can't fly.]   **2.** No.   **3.** Yes. [They are very good swimmers.]   **4.** Yes. [They change colors when they are excited.]
5. No. [They jump.]   **6.** No. [It lives there until it grows up.]   **7.** Yes. [The Australian walking fish can climb trees.]   **8.** No. [Sometimes they stand for weeks.]   **9.** No. [Some turtles can live for 200 or more years.]   **10.** Yes. [They can hold their breath for a long time.]

CHART 12-2:   PRONUNCIATION OF *CAN* AND *CAN'T*

- See Chart 12-2, p. 356, in the student book for the pronunciation of *can* and *can't*.

- WORKBOOK: There are no practices in the *Workbook* based on Chart 12-2.

☐ EXERCISE 5, p. 356.   Listening. (Chart 12-2)

Hearing the difference between *can* and *can't* may be difficult for your students. Model both pronunciations for your class slowly; then play the audio example several times. If your class is still having trouble hearing the difference, you may want to read the sentences slowly before playing the audio.

ANSWERS: **2.** can't   **3.** can't   **4.** can   **5.** can't   **6.** can't   **7.** can
8. can't   **9.** can't   **10.** can

☐ EXERCISE 6, p. 357.   Listening. (Chart 12-2)

TEACHING SUGGESTIONS: Ask students to read the want ad; then ask them to call out the skills John will need to get the job. Write them on the board and then play the audio.

After students have circled the answer in their books *(yes* or *no),* check the skills list with them. Ask the class, "What can John do?" and check off the skills John has that would get him the job. Then discuss what John can't do, crossing out the skills John doesn't have. Finally, ask students again if John is a good person for the hotel job.

For follow-up practice, ask students to make sentences with *can* and *can't* to describe John's skills.

ANSWER: No. John would <u>not</u> be a good person for the hotel job.
[**Positives**: good computer and typing skills, friendly phone voice, can work on Saturdays and Sundays. **Negatives**: speaks poor English, can't help hotel guests with their suitcases.]

CHART 12-3: USING *CAN:* QUESTIONS

• Ask students to compare these examples with those using *will* in Chart 10-7, p. 312, in the student book. They should be able to tell you the similarities in word order.

• *Can* refers either to the present or to the future. There is no difference in form. The context of the sentence or conversation gives the necessary information about the time.

• WORKBOOK: For additional exercises based on Chart 12-3, see *Workbook* Practices 4 and 5.

□ EXERCISE 7, p. 357. Question practice. (Chart 12-3)

This exercise can be done in class or assigned as homework. Remind students to pronounce *can* with no stress and almost no vowel sound.

NOTE: The words in parentheses should not be spoken; they only provide information for the response.

ANSWERS:

3. A: Can Jim play the piano?
   B: No, he can't.
4. A: Can you whistle?
   B: Yes, I can.
5. A: Can you go shopping with me this afternoon?
   B: Yes, I can.
6. A: Can Carmen ride a bicycle?
   B: No, she can't.
7. A: Can elephants swim?
   B: Yes, they can.

8. A: Can the students finish this exercise quickly?
   B: Yes, they can.
9. A: Can the doctor see me tomorrow?
   B: Yes, he/she can.
10. A: Can you stand on your head?
    B: Yes, I can.
11. A: Can you have pets in the dormitory?
    B: No, we can't.

□ EXERCISE 8, p. 358. Let's talk: pairwork. (Chart 12-3)

Walk around the room, helping pairs as necessary.

□ EXERCISE 9, p. 359. Let's talk: pairwork. (Chart 12-3)

In this exercise, students are combining repetitive pattern practice with the communication of real information to a classmate.

Modals, Part 1: Expressing Ability **135**

TEACHING SUGGESTION: Lead the class through the example; then let them work in pairs, changing roles after item 9. Discuss new vocabulary.

In items 2, 4, 12, 14, and 15, *get* = buy, obtain.

In item 3, *a fan* = an electric fan that sits on a floor or desktop to move air and cool a room's temperature.

In item 10, *a hammer* = a metal tool for pounding nails into a hard substance (wood or plaster) in order to fasten something else to it.

In item 11, *a tiger* = a big, powerful, brown and black-striped cat from Asia.

In item 15, *a sandwich* /sændwɪc/ = (usually) some meat, cheese, or fresh greens between two slices of bread.

In item 16, *cash a check* = get money from a bank or a shop by writing a check.

In item 17, *a DVD* = a "digital versatile disk"; a disk containing a movie or other video material, usually for home entertainment.

In item 18, *cold medicine* = medicine taken to treat the symptoms of a head or chest cold.

☐ **EXERCISE 10, p. 360.   Listening. (Chart 12-3)**

TEACHING SUGGESTIONS: Play the audio for the first conversation and ask students to write the words they hear. Then review the correct answers with the class. Afterward, play the other two conversations and have students complete the answers on their own.

NOTE: You might want to play the audio twice before you go over the answers with the class.

EXPANSION: You could ask different pairs of students to take the parts of Speakers A and B and read their completed conversations aloud.

> *ANSWERS:*
> **1.** B: Can I
>   A: He can't come . . .
>   Can I . . . He can
>
> **2.** A: Can you help
>   B: I can try
>   A: we can do
>
> **3.** A: I can't hear . . .
>   Can you
>   B: I can't . . . can't
>   A: Can you do

CHART 12-4:   USING *KNOW HOW TO*
• Using *Do you know how to* to express ability in a question is much more common than using *can*.
• The basic pattern for using the helping verb *do* in questions is presented in Chart 3-10, p. 74, in the student book.
• WORKBOOK: For additional exercises based on Chart 12-4, see *Workbook* Practices 6 and 7.

☐ **EXERCISE 11, p. 360.   Let's talk: pairwork. (Chart 12-4)**

Lead the class through the example; then let them work in pairs, changing roles after item 8. Pairs that finish early can switch roles so that Partner A becomes Partner B and vice-versa. Discuss new vocabulary.

In items 4, 10, and 13, *get to* (a place) = find your way there.

In item 12, *a screwdriver* = a slender metal tool for turning screws into wood or metal in order to fasten two things together.

In item 16, *the square root of* (a number) = a second number that, multiplied by itself, produces the original number (e.g., the square root of 9 is 3 because $3 \times 3 = 9$, or $3^2 = 9$). Note: The symbol for *the square root of* is called a "radical."

☐ EXERCISE 12, p. 361.   Let's talk: find someone who . . . . (Chart 12-4)

> *TEACHING SUGGESTION:* Students should answer the questions truthfully. When they report their answers, have them use complete sentences with *know how to* and *don't know how to.*

☐ EXERCISE 13, p. 362.   Let's write: small groups. (Chart 12-4)

> This should be a fun, relaxed communicative practice of the target structure *know how to.* Some of the answers will be funny, and others will surprise everyone in the class. Keep the tone light, especially when you get to item 8!

CHART 12-5:   USING *COULD:* PAST OF *CAN*

- This is only one of many meanings for the word *could.* *Could* is a complicated word; in fact, all of the modals are complicated words, with nuances and idiomatic usages that do not lend themselves to easy explanations.

- When *could* is used to mean "past ability," it is usually used in the negative. Other expressions are more commonly used to express affirmative past ability (e.g., *managed to* or *was/were able to):*

> *I managed to finish my homework before midnight last night.*
> *Fred was able to fix my radio for me.*

For this reason, Exercises 15 and 16 focus on negative *could.* It's good to avoid the affirmative *could* for ability at this stage in the learners' experience.

- It's important to show how the time/tense relationship is established in each pair of examples. A period of time in the past must be established (e.g., *last month, yesterday,* or another verb in the past tense) so that the word *could* can be used appropriately.

- WORKBOOK: For additional exercises based on Chart 12-5, see *Workbook* Practices 8–11.

☐ EXERCISE 14, p. 362.   Let's talk: pairwork. (Chart 12-5)

> Students practice *could* while revisiting their pasts. Open up the discussion to other things they could or couldn't do as children.

☐ EXERCISE 15, p. 363.   Sentence practice. (Chart 12-5)

> This exercise can be done in class or assigned as homework. Students are gaining experience with *because*-clauses as well as the target structure of *couldn't.* This exercise prepares learners for Exercise 16, in which they have to make up their own *because*-clauses.

> *ANSWERS:*   **2.** couldn't call you   **3.** couldn't watch TV   **4.** couldn't light the candles   **5.** couldn't come to class   **6.** couldn't listen to music   **7.** couldn't wash his clothes   **8.** couldn't go swimming   **9.** couldn't get into my car   **10.** couldn't go to the movie

☐ EXERCISE 16, p. 363.   Sentence practice. (Chart 12-5)

> TEACHING SUGGESTION: You might have students work in pairs to create sentences; then ask for volunteers to write them on the board.

☐ EXERCISE 17, p. 364.   Let's talk: class activity. (Chart 12-5)

> This is a teacher-led activity.

> TEACHING SUGGESTION: Give students enough time to think of good responses. You may want them to work in small groups and come up with three or four responses for each item.

☐ EXERCISE 18, p. 364.   Review: error analysis. (Charts 12-1 → 12-5)

> TEACHING SUGGESTION: Students can work individually or with partners. You might make it a contest to see who can find and correct all the mistakes first.

> ANSWERS: 1. Could you ~~to~~ drive a car when you were thirteen years old?   2. If your brother goes to the graduation party, he can <u>meet</u> my sister.   3. I couldn't <u>open</u> the door because I didn't have a key.   4. Please turn up the radio. I can't ~~to~~ hear it.
> 5. When Ernesto arrived at the airport last Tuesday, he <u>couldn't</u> find the right gate.
> 6. Mr. Lo was born in Hong Kong, but now he lives in Canada. He <u>could not</u> understand spoken English before he moved to Canada, but now he <u>speaks</u> and <u>understands</u> English very well.

CHART 12-6:   USING *BE ABLE TO*

- The modal *can* has the same form for present and future. *Be able to* has different forms for the tenses.

- WORKBOOK: For additional exercises based on Chart 12-6, see *Workbook* Practices 12–15.

☐ EXERCISE 19, p. 365.   Sentence practice. (Chart 12-6)

> You could work through a few of the items in class and assign the rest as homework. This exercise asks students to see the relationship between *can/could* and *be able to*. Students need to pay special attention to the tense forms of *be* used in the new sentences.

> ANSWERS: 3. Mark is bilingual. He is able to speak two languages.   4. Sue will be able to get her own apartment next year.   5. Animals aren't able to speak.   6. Are you able to touch your toes without bending your knees?   7. Jack wasn't able to describe the thief.   8. Were you able to do the homework?   9. I wasn't able to sleep last night because my apartment was too hot.   10. My roommate is able to speak four languages. He's multilingual.   11. I'm sorry that I wasn't able to call you last night.   12. I'm sorry, but I won't be able to come to your party next week.
> 13. Will we be able to take vacations on the moon in the 22nd century?

☐ EXERCISE 20, p. 366.   Sentence practice. (Chart 12-6)

> Encourage students to use their imagination to make interesting sentences. Perhaps they could work in pairs; afterward, you could ask each pair to tell the class their most interesting answers.

□ EXERCISE 21, p. 367. Listening review: CAN / BE ABLE TO / KNOW HOW TO.
(Charts 12-1 → 12-6)

TEACHING SUGGESTIONS: Play the audio and ask students to complete the exercise sentence by sentence. You could go over the answers after each conversation, or try this option: Divide the class into groups. Ask each group to discuss their answers and choose the correct ones. Then choose two members of a group to read a dialogue to the class. Correct their answers as necessary.

ANSWERS:

1. A: Were you able to talk
   B: I couldn't . . . can try
2. A: Do you know how to make
   B: can make
   A: Can you teach
   B: I can
3. A: Are you able to understand
   B: couldn't understand . . .
   can understand
   A: can't understand

4. A: will you be able to
   B: wasn't able to . . . 'll try . . .
   I will be able to
5. B: I can
   A: can see . . . Can you come
   B: I can . . . don't know

CHART 12-7: USING *VERY* AND *TOO* + ADJECTIVE

• The words *very* and *too* are often called "intensifiers." They give a stronger meaning to the adjectives that follow them.

• It is difficult for some learners to remember that the intensifier *too* gives a negative meaning to the adjective. You might demonstrate the natural tendency for a speaker to frown and shake his or her head from side to side negatively when using *too* in this way.

• The drawings illustrate the meanings of examples (a) and (b).

• WORKBOOK: For additional exercises based on Chart 12-7, see *Workbook* Practices 16–18.

□ EXERCISE 22, p. 368. Class activity. (Chart 12-7)

TEACHING SUGGESTION: Do this exercise in class with your students. Ask for volunteers to give the answers orally. Write each pair of answers on the board.

ANSWERS: **1.** The soup is too hot. Jack can't eat it. The soup is very hot, but Ricardo can eat it. **2.** The coat is very small, but Tom can wear it. The coat is too small. Susan can't wear it. **3.** The shoes are too tight. Marika can't wear them. The shoes are very tight, but Mai can wear them. **4.** The problem is too hard. Robert can't do it. The problem is very hard, but Talal can do it.

□ EXERCISE 23, p. 370. Sentence practice. (Chart 12-7)

This exercise gives practice with the negative meaning of *too* + adjective. If done in class, give students a few minutes to work out the answers; then lead the class through all the items.

ANSWERS: **1.** eat it.   **2.** buy it.   **3.** go swimming.   **4.** take a break.
5. do his homework.   **6.** reach the cookie jar.   **7.** sleep.   **8.** lift it.

☐ EXERCISE 24, p. 371.   Sentence practice. (Chart 12-7)

This exercise can be done in class or assigned as homework.

ANSWERS: **1.** too heavy.   **2.** too young.   **3.** too noisy.   **4.** too cold.
5. too tired.   **6.** too expensive.   **7.** too small.   **8.** too tall.

☐ EXERCISE 25, p. 371.   Sentence practice. (Chart 12-7)

This exercise can be done in class or assigned as homework. After Exercises 23 and 24, learners should know that *too* before an adjective implies a negative result. In this exercise, they must decide whether *too* or *very* is correct. Items 11 and 12 provide a good contrast in meaning.

ANSWERS: **3.** too   **4.** very . . . very   **5.** too   **6.** very   **7.** very   **8.** too
9. too   **10.** very   **11.** very   **12.** too   **13.** too   **14.** very   **15.** too
16. very   **17.** too   **18.** too

CHART 12-8:   USING *TWO, TOO,* AND *TO*

• Point out the positions of *too* in examples (b) and (c). When *too* means "also," the word is usually at the end of the sentence or clause. (In formal speech, you might hear "I too saw the movie"; however, *also* is more common in that particular word order: "I also saw the movie.")

• In speaking, the word *to* is not stressed. It may sound more like /tə/. The words *two* and *too* are stressed (spoken with a higher pitch and more sound).

• WORKBOOK: For additional exercises based on Chart 12-8, see *Workbook* Practices 19 and 20.

☐ EXERCISE 26, p. 373.   Sentence practice. (Chart 12-8)

This exercise can be done in class.

TEACHING SUGGESTIONS: It's impossible to tell which word students are saying when they read their answers to this exercise aloud, so you might have them spell the words. Or, pass out index cards and have them write one word on each of three cards in large letters: TOO, TWO, and TO. You could ask all students to hold up the correct answer card so that you can scan the room and quickly check their answers.

ANSWERS: **2.** two   **3.** too . . . too . . . to   **4.** to . . . to . . . to . . . too
5. to . . . to . . . too   **6.** to . . . to   **7.** to . . . to   **8.** too   **9.** too . . . to . . . to
10. two . . . to . . . two . . . too

CHART 12-9: MORE ABOUT PREPOSITIONS: *AT* AND *IN* FOR PLACE

• These are idiomatic uses for *at* and *in*. They must be memorized because there is no clear logic to predict their forms.

• In (a) no article *(a/an/the)* is used. However, with other nouns an article is usually necessary: *at the office, sitting at a table, working at his desk.*

• In example (d) you might point out that proper nouns (names) do not usually have an article *(a/an/the)* in English. In example (c) *the* is used to identify a unique or specific room. (See Charts 7-6 and 7-7, pp. 199 and 203, in the student book.)

• The difference between *at* and *in* is not easy to understand, so take some time to discuss (e) and (f) with your class.

• Perhaps review prepositions of place in Charts 1-7, 5-7, and 5-8, pp. 18, 134, and 135, in the student book.

• WORKBOOK: For additional exercises based on Chart 12-9, see *Workbook* Practices 21 and 22.

□ EXERCISE 27, p. 375.   Sentence practice. (Chart 12-9)

This exercise can be done in class or assigned as homework. Call attention to the footnote for item 1, and make sure students understand that *at* is <u>not</u> correct in item 2.

> *ANSWERS:*   3. at   4. in   5. in . . . at   6. in . . . in   7. in   8. in
> 9. at . . . at   10. in   11. in   12. in   13. at   14. in . . . in   15. in
> 16. at   17. at   18. At   19. in   20. in

□ EXERCISE 28, p. 376.   Let's talk: class activity. (Chart 12-9)

This exercise is teacher-led; it is a quick check of students' use of *at* and *in.*

□ EXERCISE 29, p. 377.   Let's talk: pairwork. (Chart 12-9)

Ask pairs to share some of their partner's answers with the class.

□ EXERCISE 30, p. 377.   Review: let's talk. (Chapter 12)

TEACHING SUGGESTIONS: Divide the class into small groups. Everyone should contribute to the group's answers, and one person should write them down. The same person (or another) can report to the class. After all groups have finished the exercise, go through the items, eliciting at least two different responses for each. Ask students to give only the most interesting responses that do not duplicate those of another group. Discuss new vocabulary.

In item 8, *illiterate* = unable to read or write at all or beyond a very basic level.

□ EXERCISE 31, p. 378.   Chapter review: error analysis. (Chapter 12)

TEACHING SUGGESTION: Use this exercise as a game. Divide the class into small groups. Call out any item number (not in order). Have students work together to figure out the answer. The first group to give the correct sentence (orally or written on the board) gets a point.

ANSWERS: **1.** We will ~~can~~ go to the museum tomorrow afternoon.   OR   We ~~will~~ can go to the museum tomorrow afternoon.   **2.** We can't count all of the stars in the universe. There are <u>too</u> many.   **3.** Can you ~~to~~ stand on your head?   **4.** I saw a beautiful vase at a store yesterday, but I couldn't <u>buy</u> it.   **5.** The shirt is <u>very</u> small. I can wear it.   OR   The shirt is too small. I <u>can't</u> wear it.   **6.** Sam <u>knows</u> how to count to 1000 in English.   **7.** When I was on vacation, I <u>could</u> swim every day.   **8.** When we lived <u>in</u> Tokyo, we took the subway every day.   **9.** Honeybees <u>are</u> not able to live in very cold climates.   **10.** Where <u>can we</u> go in the city for an inexpensive meal?   **11.** James can <u>read</u> newspapers in five languages.   **12.** Sorry. I <u>wasn't</u> able to get tickets for the concert.   **13.** I can't finish my homework because I'm <u>too</u> tired.

CHAPTER 13
Modals, Part 2: Advice, Necessity, Requests, Suggestions

Overview

English uses the verb system in complex ways. Some verbs have special meanings that give force to a sentence, such as giving advice *(should)*, requiring necessary action *(have to, must)*, making a request *(could, would)*, or making a suggestion *(let's)*. This chapter introduces all of these and revisits those presented in the previous chapter. *Could, can,* and *may* have already been introduced with other meanings. They now return in polite questions and requests. Another structure introduced in this chapter is imperative sentences, also called "commands."

CHART 13-1: USING *SHOULD*

- This chapter adds *should, let's, have to,* and *must* to the modals and similar expressions already presented in the text: *will, be going to, can, could, be able to, may,* and *might.*

- The text presents only present/future *should.* The past form is *should have* + past participle: *I should have finished my homework.* You may not want to mention the past form to your class since it involves past participles, which aren't taught at this level.

- Ask the class what they notice about the examples before looking at the right side of this chart. You might use this approach throughout the chapter.

- WORKBOOK: For additional exercises based on Chart 13-1, see *Workbook* Practices 1–4.

☐ EXERCISE 1, p. 379. Sentence practice. (Chart 13-1)

> *TEACHING SUGGESTIONS:* Discuss the meaning of the sentences. Encourage students to use their own words to complete the sentences as well as to find the proper completion from the list. You could work through a few of the items with your class and assign the rest as homework. Discuss new vocabulary in the list.
>
> *the manager* = the person in charge of running a rental building (repairs and renters).
> *the immigration office* = the government office that issues visas and passports.
> *take a nap* = sleep for a short time during the day.

> ANSWERS: **2.** You should go to bed and take a nap.   **3.** You should go to the bank.
> **4.** You should see a dentist.   **5.** You should study harder.   **6.** You should call the
> manager.   **7.** You should go to the immigration office.   **8.** You should buy a new
> pair of shoes.

☐ **EXERCISE 2, p. 380.   Let's talk: small groups. (Chart 13-1)**

Answers will vary; in fact, interesting cultural issues may arise. Allow enough time for students to discuss the reasons for their answers.

☐ **EXERCISE 3, p. 381.   Sentence practice. (Chart 13-1)**

This exercise checks how well students understand the meaning of *should* and *shouldn't* in typical contexts. It can be done in class or assigned as homework. Discuss new vocabulary.

In item 10, *jaywalk* = cross a street at a place other than at a marked crossing, or walk against the traffic light.

EXPANSION: Give students a chance to discuss their opinions, either as a class or in small groups.

ANSWERS: **3.** shouldn't   **4.** should   **5.** shouldn't   **6.** shouldn't
7. should   **8.** shouldn't   **9.** shouldn't   **10.** should . . . shouldn't
11. should   **12.** shouldn't   **13.** should   **14.** shouldn't

☐ **EXERCISE 4, p. 382.   Let's talk: small groups. (Chart 13-1)**

Divide the class into groups of three or four students each.

TEACHING SUGGESTION: Each student in a group reads one item, and the others give advice. Encourage them to be helpful. Discuss new vocabulary.

In item 3, *a newcomer* = someone who has come to live in a place for the first time.

☐ **EXERCISE 5, p. 383.   Listening. (Chart 13-1)**

TEACHING SUGGESTION: Play the audio twice. The first time, students circle *should* or *shouldn't*. The second time, they decide if they agree *(yes)* or disagree *(no)* with the sentences they hear. Some of their answers may lead to interesting cultural discussions.

ANSWERS: **1.** should   **2.** should   **3.** shouldn't   **4.** should   **5.** should
6. shouldn't   **7.** should   **8.** shouldn't

☐ **EXERCISE 6, p. 383.   Writing. (Chart 13-1)**

The questions are only suggestions; they do not have to be answered in the exact order given here. The writers should respond to the topic with natural sentences that make an interesting paragraph.

NOTE: Students don't need to use *should/shouldn't* in every sentence.

CHART 13-2:   USING *HAVE* + INFINITIVE *(HAVE TO / HAS TO)*

• *Have to* is common and useful. Most of your students are probably already familiar with it.

• This modal verb has a special pronunciation:
  have to = /hæftə/
  has to = /hæstə/

• WORKBOOK: For additional exercises based on Chart 13-2, see *Workbook* Practices 5–10.

☐ **EXERCISE 7, p. 384. Let's talk: class activity. (Chart 13-2)**

This is a teacher-led activity.

TEACHING SUGGESTIONS: Tell students to use the same verb in their responses that is used in the question. This means that not every answer will use *has/have to* (which is at times contrasted with *want to*). Keep the pace natural, and show interest in students' answers. Add a comment if you wish. If time is short, you may want to omit some items.

☐ **EXERCISE 8, p. 384. Let's talk: class activity. (Chart 13-2)**

TEACHING SUGGESTION: Lead students through the example before they close their books. Give them time to think before they respond. Practicing *because*-clauses is just as important as practicing *have to* in this exercise.

☐ **EXERCISE 9, p. 385. Sentence practice. (Chart 13-2)**

This exercise reviews the various forms of *have to:* singular, plural, past, negative, and question. You may want to work through a few of the items in class and assign the rest as homework.

> *ANSWERS:*
>
> 2. A: do you have to go
>   B: I have to find
> 3. A: does Sue have to leave for
>   B: She has to be
> 4. B: I had to buy
>   A: did you have to buy
> 5. I have to go . . . I have to get
>
> 6. she had to study
> 7. do you have to be
> 8. Does Tom have to find
> 9. A: Yoko doesn't have to take
>   B: Do you have to take
> 10. He had to stay . . . He had to finish

☐ **EXERCISE 10, p. 386. Listening. (Chart 13-2)**

TEACHING SUGGESTION: Model "hafta" and "hasta" for students before playing the audio. Remind students that they do not need to speak this way; it is more important that they simply understand these words in common speech.

> *ANSWERS:* **2.** have to **3.** have to **4.** has to **5.** have to **6.** have to
> **7.** have to **8.** has to **9.** has to **10.** have to

CHART 13-3: USING *MUST*

• Point out that *have to* occurs with much greater frequency than *must* in everyday usage.

• *Must* is much stronger than *have to,* but the meaning is essentially the same in the affirmative. Indeed, the past form of *must* (meaning "necessity" as it does in this chart) is *had to.* You may want to mention this to your students.

• In the negative, the meanings of *must* and *have to* are different, as pointed out in examples (d) and (e).

• The differences between *must* and *should* are sometimes difficult to explain. Expand upon the contrastive examples in the chart to give students a clear understanding of the differences in meaning.

• WORKBOOK: For additional exercises based on Chart 13-3, see *Workbook* Practices 11–13.

☐ EXERCISE 11, p. 388.   Sentence practice. (Chart 13-3)

This exercise gives further examples of typical uses of *must*. You may want to work through it with your class.

TEACHING SUGGESTIONS: Some students may be tempted to use *should*. Point out that even though *should* is grammatically correct, its meaning isn't strong enough; thus, *must* is required. Discuss new vocabulary in the list.

Close the door behind you. = As you go out of the room, you should close the door.
a library card = a card that permits you to borrow books from a library.
an income tax = payment to the government of a percentage of the money that you earn in one year.
a tablet = medicine in the form of a pill.

ANSWERS: **2.** must stop.   **3.** must have a library card.   **4.** must pay an income tax.   **5.** must study harder.   **6.** must listen to English on the radio and TV. OR must make new friends who speak English. OR must read English newspapers and magazines. OR must speak English outside of class every day. OR must study harder. OR must talk to myself in English.   **7.** must have a passport.   **8.** must go to medical school.   **9.** must close the door behind you.   **10.** must take one tablet every six hours.

☐ EXERCISE 12, p. 389.   Sentence practice. (Chart 13-3)

TEACHING SUGGESTION: You may want students to brainstorm in small groups before they give their answers. These questions might produce some interesting responses and discussion. Encourage students to use *must* or *have to.*

☐ EXERCISE 13, p. 389.   Sentence practice. (Chart 13-3)

This exercise could be used as a quiz. Students need to pay attention to the difference between *must* and *have to* in the negative as well as their singular and plural forms.

ANSWERS: **2.** B   **3.** B   **4.** A   **5.** C   **6.** A   **7.** B   **8.** A

☐ EXERCISE 14, p. 390.   Let's talk: small groups. (Chart 13-3)

You may find that students come up with differences in the *should* and *have to* responses, and interesting discussions could arise.

☐ EXERCISE 15, p. 390.   Listening. (Chart 13-3)

Although this looks like a simple exercise, different laws and customs could trigger a lively discussion when you go over the answers in class.

ANSWERS: (Answers may vary.)

CHART 13-4: POLITE QUESTIONS: *MAY I, COULD I,* AND *CAN I*

- This chart explains the language functions of asking and giving permission.

- You may wish to discuss the notion of politeness and informality. The ranges and uses of such forms are different in many cultures; discussing them can be very interesting and useful to students of English.

- Some people consider requests with *Can I* to be informal or too direct. Many people use *Can I* in most situations, adding *please* to be more polite.

- WORKBOOK: For additional exercises based on Chart 13-4, see *Workbook* Practice 14.

☐ EXERCISE 16, p. 391. Let's talk: pairwork. (Chart 13-4)

TEACHING SUGGESTION: The pictures give a different kind of cue — visual instead of written. Students can work in pairs to construct the dialogues. You might ask them to stand up and perform the parts in the pictures.

SAMPLE DIALOGUES: (top to bottom)

May I please have another cup of coffee? Certainly.
Can I have this apple? Yes.
Could I make an appointment to see you outside of class? Of course.
May I come in? Yes, of course.

☐ EXERCISE 17, p. 392. Let's talk: pairwork. (Chart 13-4)

TEACHING SUGGESTIONS: Lead students through the example. Indicate who you are talking <u>to</u> and who you are talking <u>about</u>. Divide the class into pairs; then move around the classroom listening to your students' conversations.

CHART 13-5: POLITE QUESTIONS: *COULD YOU* AND *WOULD YOU*

- The word *please* is optional but frequently used in such requests. (Some learners feel that speakers of English use *please* and *thank you* too much!)

- *I'd be glad to* = I would be happy to do what you asked.

- *Could you* is used more often than *Would you* in requests.

- WORKBOOK: For additional exercises based on Chart 13-5, see *Workbook* Practice 15.

☐ EXERCISE 18, p. 393. Let's talk: pairwork. (Chart 13-5)

Note that *sir* in item 1 is used only in speaking to a male person; for females the polite word, although not often used, is *ma'am* /mæm/ or *miss* /mɪs/.

In item 2, *Excuse me?* is spoken with rising intonation as is the word *Pardon?*. These questions are different in meaning from the sentences *Excuse me, sir* in item 1 and *Pardon me, sir,* which are ways to catch someone's attention.

1. A: Excuse me, sir. Could you please open the door for me?
   B: Of course. I'd be happy to.
2. A: Would you please shut the window?
   B: Excuse me? I didn't understand what you said.
   A: I said, "Would you please shut the window?"
   [Note: Some students might spontaneously use an infinitive in reported speech: "I asked you to shut the window."]
   B: Certainly. I'd be glad to.

□ EXERCISE 19, p. 394.   Let's talk: pairwork. (Chart 13-5)

> *TEACHING SUGGESTIONS:* Lead the class through the example. Substitute Partner B's name in the parentheses when Partner A speaks. When most pairs are finished, ask for volunteers to perform some of the exchanges.

□ EXERCISE 20, p. 394.   Let's talk: pairwork. (Chart 13-5)

> *TEACHING SUGGESTIONS:* Students can use their imagination here, especially if you ask them to perform their dialogues for the class. Lead them through the examples; then give them time to work out the conversations. In the first example, *(knock, knock)* indicates that the student should make the sound of someone knocking on a door, perhaps by knocking on a desk top with his/her knuckles. Other appropriate sound effects could be added to the dialogues. If you are short on time, assign just one or two dialogues to each pair.

CHART 13-6:   IMPERATIVE SENTENCES

• Imperative sentences make much stronger requests than the polite questions in Charts 13-4 and 13-5, pp. 391 and 393, in the student book. The sound of the speaker's voice can make an imperative either a very strong order or a softer request. Also, as in (i), the use of *please* will soften the imperative. Imperative sentences have several uses. Discuss the different effects of (f)–(i). Students might be able to compare the English variants with how their own language expresses them.

• Point out the negative examples (d) and (e). The meaning of *don't* is "you must not."

• The "understood subject" of an imperative sentence is *you*. The speaker directs an imperative sentence to a second person or persons. Some students may want to use *you*, and they need to know that this is incorrect.

• WORKBOOK: For additional exercises based on Chart 13-6, see *Workbook* Practices 16–19.

□ EXERCISE 21, p. 395.   Sentence practice. (Chart 13-6)

This exercise gives contextualized examples of imperative sentences for you to discuss in class. You might ask students to identify which type of imperative meaning is used in each dialogue — orders, directions, requests, or advice.

In item 1, *wait for me* is probably more of a request than an order; *hurry up* is advice. *Let's,* which is presented in Chart 13-9, p. 402, in the student book, could probably be analyzed as a type of imperative sentence. If students identify it as such, tell them it's actually a type of modal with a meaning close to *shall* when used in a question, such as *Shall we go?*.

IMPERATIVES: **1.** (Wait) . . . (Hurry) . . . Let's   **2.** Hold . . . Drink . . . Breathe . . . Eat [*hiccups* (also spelled: *hiccoughs*) = a series of uncontrollable gulps that the body makes to get air into the lungs. (The speakers are giving Jim some traditional advice on how to cure the hiccups. You might ask your students what techniques they use.)]   **3.** Don't forget   **4.** Walk . . . turn . . . Go . . . turn   **5.** Wait . . . Do (it) . . . Hang (up) . . . Make . . . Put . . . Empty

☐ **EXERCISE 22, p. 396.   Sentence practice. (Chart 13-6)**

Students should be able to offer answers quickly without writing them down. Discuss alternatives. You may want to brainstorm the first one as a class.

SAMPLE COMPLETIONS: **1.** Watch out! / Look out!   **2.** Open wide. / Open your mouth wide, please.   **3.** Stop! Don't eat that dirt!   **4.** Come here. OR Here, boy/girl!

☐ **EXERCISE 23, p. 397.   Let's talk: class activity. (Chart 13-6)**

This is a teacher-led activity. Have different students volunteer responses for each situation. Books should be closed.

SAMPLE RESPONSES: **1.** Study Chart 7-16 before you come to class. (Please) do Exercise 37.   **2.** Hold your breath. Blow into a paper bag.   **3.** Come straight home after school. Put on your jacket.   **4.** Get more exercise. Eat healthful foods. **5.** Use 1 cup of rice and 2 cups of water. Add a little salt to the water. Bring the water to a boil, then turn the heat down. Etc.   **6.** Visit the (. . .). Go downtown and see (. . .). Eat at (. . .).

CHART 13-7: MODAL AUXILIARIES

- The text has been presenting modals throughout. This chart provides a grammar label and explains the term "modal auxiliary" /modəl ɔkzɪlyəri/.

- One common mistake for learners is adding the word *to* after every modal auxiliary (e.g., *★He can to play the piano. You must to be careful.*). This chart shows clearly that only a few expressions require *to*. (The expressions in example (b) are called "modal auxiliaries" by some; others call them "periphrastic modals." This text calls them "similar expressions.")

- WORKBOOK: For additional exercises based on Chart 13-7, see *Workbook* Practice 20.

☐ **EXERCISE 24, p. 398.   Sentence practice. (Chart 13-7)**

This exercise helps learners focus on the use of *to*.

> *TEACHING SUGGESTION:* You might lead students through the exercise, asking them to read an item and raise their right hands if they think *to* is required. This helps them use caution and judgment before automatically including *to* in a sentence. Exercises like this are intended to encourage students' self-monitoring; these structures are often the source of common and frequent errors.

ANSWERS: **3.** X   **4.** to   **5.** X   **6.** X   **7.** to   **8.** X   **9.** X   **10.** X **11.** X   **12.** X   **13.** to   **14.** X

CHART 13-8: SUMMARY CHART: MODAL AUXILIARIES AND SIMILAR EXPRESSIONS

• By now, students should know the meaning of each auxiliary in this chart. They should be impressed by how much they already know about modal auxiliaries in English!

• This is by no means an exhaustive presentation of these auxiliaries. There are other meanings and uses of many of these expressions; students will expand their understanding of modals in subsequent texts in this grammar series.

• WORKBOOK: For additional exercises based on Chart 13-8, see *Workbook* Practice 21.

□ EXERCISE 25, p. 400. Let's talk: small groups. (Chart 13-8)

> *TEACHING SUGGESTION:* Lead the class through the example; then divide students into small groups to continue. Give them a time limit for completing the exercise. Ask for volunteers to share answers. Groups that finish sooner can continue to the next exercise.

□ EXERCISE 26, p. 400. Sentence practice. (Chart 13-8)

> This exercise is a review of singular/plural, verb tenses, and some modal auxiliaries. You might want to use it as a quiz.

> *ANSWERS:* **2.** C **3.** C **4.** C **5.** A **6.** C **7.** C **8.** A **9.** B **10.** B

□ EXERCISE 27, p. 401. Listening. (Chart 13-8)

> This exercise may be difficult for students. Play each sentence at least twice, and leave enough time for your students to examine each option. When going over the answers, be prepared to explain the meanings of the incorrect options as well as those that are correct.

> *ANSWERS:* **2.** b **3.** a **4.** b **5.** c **6.** b **7.** b **8.** c

CHART 13-9: USING *LET'S*

• Often a suggestion with *let's (let us)* is followed by a tag question.
   Very formal: *Let's go, shall we?*
   More usual: *Let's go, okay?*

• Another verb *let/lets* means "to permit or allow something." This verb is never the first word in a sentence, and it never has an apostrophe. For example:
   Mrs. Smith lets her children stay up late on Saturday night.

• WORKBOOK: For additional exercises based on Chart 13-9, see *Workbook* Practice 22.

□ EXERCISE 28, p. 402.   Sentence practice. (Chart 13-9)

TEACHING SUGGESTIONS: For each item, talk to one student as if you were having a conversation. Encourage students to respond with some expression of interest or feeling, as they would in a conversation with a friend. Preview the vocabulary in the list.

go dancing (note that no preposition is used)
a seafood restaurant = one that specializes in fish and other seafood.
the zoo /zu/ = an animal park.

EXPANSION: Have students work in pairs, completing the conversations again but using words not in the list.

SAMPLE COMPLETIONS: **2.** Let's go to Florida.   **3.** Let's go to a seafood restaurant.   **4.** Let's go to the zoo.   **5.** Let's go to a movie.   **6.** Let's walk.   **7.** Let's eat.   **8.** Let's go dancing.   **9.** Let's get a cup of coffee.

□ EXERCISE 29, p. 403.   Let's talk: pairwork. (Chart 13-9)

Lead the class through the instructions and the example. Tell them to substitute their own words for the words in parentheses.

□ EXERCISE 30, p. 404.   Review: Chapters 12 and 13.

TEACHING SUGGESTION: You may want to use this exercise as a game. See Chapter 12, Exercise 31, of this *Teacher's Guide* for further information.

ANSWERS: **1.** Would you please ~~to~~ help me?   **2.** I will ~~can~~ go to the meeting tomorrow. OR I ~~will~~ can go to the meeting tomorrow.   **3.** My brother wasn't able to call me last night.   **4.** Ken should write us a letter.   **5.** I had to go to the store yesterday.   **6.** Susie! You must not ~~to~~ play with matches!   **7.** Would / Could / Can you please hand me that book?   **8.** Ann couldn't answer my question.
9. Shelley can't go to the concert tomorrow.   **10.** Let's go to a movie tonight.
11. Don't ~~to~~ interrupt. It's not polite.   **12.** Can you ~~to~~ stand on your head?
13. I saw a beautiful dress at a store yesterday, but I couldn't buy it.   **14.** Close the door, please. Thank you.   **15.** May I please ~~to~~ borrow your dictionary? Thank you.

CHAPTER 14
Nouns and Modifiers

Overview

This chapter deals with many ways to modify a noun. It begins with the terminology "adjective" and "noun"; then it shows that a noun can modify another noun. Students learn the order of nouns and their modifiers, some of which come before and some of which follow the noun. Next, students practice using multiple modifiers and learn some new vocabulary. This is followed by practice with phrases of quantity that modify nouns. Students then study how to solve subject-verb agreement problems that arise when they use these phrases. Indefinite pronouns and the use of *every* follow. Finally, students are introduced to the way adjectives are used with linking verbs and how common adverbs are contrasted with adjectives.

☐ EXERCISE 1, p. 405.   Noun and adjective practice.

This exercise is a quick review of what students already know about nouns and adjectives. It can be done in class. Its purpose is to check on students' understanding of the grammar terms "noun" and "adjective" before proceeding with the chapter.

ANSWERS: **3.** ADJ   **4.** NOUN   **5.** NOUN   **6.** NOUN   **7.** ADJ   **8.** NOUN   **9.** ADJ   **10.** NOUN   **11.** ADJ   **12.** NOUN

CHART 14-1: MODIFYING NOUNS WITH ADJECTIVES AND NOUNS

• The word *modify* is explained in Chart 6-2, p. 161, in the student book.

• One unusual feature of English is that a noun can modify another noun. These nouns are called "noun adjuncts" and do not add any letters or sounds. Call attention to the incorrect example in (c) where the modifier has been given a plural form. Making a noun adjunct plural is a common error. (The explanation in the text says that a modifying noun is *always* singular. The authors should, and indeed do, know better than to use *always* or *never* when explaining English grammar! There are exceptions, of course, one of which is *sports* in *a sports car, a sports jacket,* etc.)

• The order of modifiers is shown in Chart 14-2, p. 410, in the student book.

• WORKBOOK: For additional exercises based on Chart 14-1, see *Workbook* Practices 1–6.

□ **EXERCISE 2, p. 406.   Sentence practice. (Chart 14-1)**

Whether students do this exercise in class or as homework, they may encounter new vocabulary, so check students' comprehension as you review the answers.

ANSWERS:

	ADJ		**NOUN**
2.	wise	→	woman
3.	native	→	language
4.	busy	→	waitress
	empty	→	cup
5.	young	→	man
	heavy	→	suitcase
6.	uncomfortable	→	chair
7.	international	→	news
	front	→	page
8.	wonderful	→	man

□ **EXERCISE 3, p. 406.   Sentence practice. (Chart 14-1)**

Nouns modifying other nouns (noun adjuncts) are a common feature in English. Exercises 3–7 give plenty of practice with these modifiers. Exercise 3 can be done in class or assigned as homework.

In a related structure, a noun adjunct is attached to the noun it modifies, resulting in a compound noun (e.g., *bookstore, textbook, moonlight, mailman)*. The student book does not deal with compound nouns, but you may choose to mention this phenomenon. If students want to know if a word such as *bookstore* is one word or two words, they simply need to consult their dictionaries.

The following examples are fun — but they can be confusing.
Chocolate milk is a delicious drink. (Chocolate modifies *milk.)*
Milk chocolate is a delicious kind of candy. (Milk modifies *chocolate.)*

ANSWERS:

	ADJ		**NOUN**
2.	new	→	CDs
	music	→	store
3.	train	→	station
4.	Vegetable	→	soup
5.	movie	→	theater
	furniture	→	store
6.	lunch	→	menu
7.	traffic	→	light
8.	business	→	card

□ **EXERCISE 4, p. 406.   Listening. (Chart 14-1)**

You may need to play the audio more than once.

EXPANSION: Write some of the nouns on the board: *chicken, car,* etc. Ask students to brainstorm other noun-adjective or noun-noun combinations with the given words.

ANSWERS: 1. ADJ   2. NOUN   3. NOUN   4. ADJ   5. ADJ   6. NOUN
7. ADJ   8. ADJ   9. NOUN   10. ADJ

☐ **EXERCISE 5, p. 407. Sentence practice. (Chart 14-1)**

You may want to do this exercise orally in class and then have students write it as homework. Point out that the modifier is not plural even though the noun it modifies may be plural. Also, the modifier is usually spoken with more stress (higher pitch) than the noun.

In item 1, *vases* = AmE /vesəz/; BrE /vazəz/.

ANSWERS: **3.** a newspaper story. **4.** hotel rooms. **5.** an office worker.
6. a price tag. **7.** a computer room. **8.** airplane seats. **9.** a park bench.
10. bean soup.

☐ **EXERCISE 6, p. 407. Let's talk: small groups. (Chart 14-1)**

In item 5, the noun *official* is spoken with more stress. In all other items, it is the modifier that is spoken with more stress.

ANSWERS: **2.** store. **3.** class. **4.** race. **5.** official. **6.** soup.
7. program. **8.** trip. **9.** keys. **10.** tickets. **11.** room. **12.** number.

☐ **EXERCISE 7, p. 409. Sentence practice. (Chart 14-1)**

You could work through a few of the items in class and assign the rest as homework. This exercise helps students learn to differentiate between noun-noun combinations and adjectives. Point out that the adjective precedes both nouns.

ANSWERS: **2.** good television program. **3.** dangerous mountain road. **4.** bad automobile accident. **5.** interesting magazine article. **6.** delicious vegetable soup.
7. funny birthday card. **8.** narrow airplane seats.

CHART 14-2: WORD ORDER OF ADJECTIVES

• When more than one adjective modifies a noun, English prefers a specific sequence. This chart and the following exercises introduce that sequence.

• In the authors' experience, the word order of adjectives is not a major problem for students in their spontaneous usage, but the teaching of this word order can sometimes force errors. The authors are not sure how to avoid this, other than to treat this unit as "information you can reference" as opposed to "information you must memorize."

• The term "opinion adjective" is used in this textbook. Other grammar books may use other terms for this, such as "descriptive" or "evaluative" adjective. The point to learn is that such adjectives express the speaker's/writer's opinion. *Beautiful* is an opinion; *red* is not.

• Adjectives can be divided into eighteen or more categories, but the six in this chart are the most useful to learn.

• Note that commas are not used between adjectives in different categories. However, more than one adjective in a category can modify a noun; in that case, commas are necessary between the adjectives within that same category, e.g., *She bought a beautiful, expensive old glass vase.*

• WORKBOOK: For additional exercises based on Chart 14-2, see *Workbook* Practices 7 and 8.

□ **EXERCISE 8, p. 410. Adjective practice. (Chart 14-2)**

You may want to work through a few of the items in class and assign the rest as homework.

TEACHING SUGGESTIONS: If done in class, give students enough time to work out their answers; then have them check their answers with a partner and discuss any questions that arise. Remind them that nationalities begin with a capital letter. It's a good idea for everyone to say these phrases aloud; you may want to lead the class in choral repetition of the answers.

ANSWERS: **2.** delicious Thai   **3.** small red   **4.** big old brown   **5.** narrow dirt **6.** serious young   **7.** beautiful long black   **8.** famous old Chinese   **9.** thin brown leather   **10.** wonderful old Native American

□ **EXERCISE 9, p. 411. Sentence practice. (Chart 14-2)**

This exercise can be done in class or assigned as homework. The choice of *a* or *an* in items 4, 5, 7, and 8 depends on the first sound of the word following the article.

ANSWERS: **2.** Asian   **3.** leather   **4.** an unhappy   **5.** a soft   **6.** brick **7.** an important   **8.** a polite   **9.** coffee   **10.** Canadian

□ **EXERCISE 10, p. 412. Sentence practice. (Chart 14-2)**

You may want your class to work in small groups. Students can use their imagination to add interesting words to these items. The sample completions here are only some possibilities. Your students may think of other answers that are just as good.

The choice of *a* or *an* in items 2, 6, and 9 depends on the first sound of the word following the article.

□ **EXERCISE 11, p. 413. Sentence practice. (Chart 14-2)**

This is a review of structures taught thus far in Chapter 14. You may want to do a few items in class and assign the rest as homework. Remind students that some sentences have no mistakes. Ask for volunteers to write the sentence corrections on the board.

In item 1, *wood* could also be the adjective form *wooden*.

ANSWERS: **3.** famous Chinese landmark   **4.** an honest young man   **5.** an interesting newspaper article   **6.** *(no change)*   **7.** cold mountain stream **8.** favorite Italian food   **9.** *(no change)*   **10.** comfortable old brown leather shoes **11.** tiny black insects   **12.** brown cardboard box   **13.** *(no change)* **14.** handsome middle-aged man . . . short brown hair   **15.** an expensive hotel room

□ **EXERCISE 12, p. 414. Let's talk: pairwork. (Chart 14-2)**

Divide the class into pairs.

TEACHING SUGGESTIONS: Go through the examples first. Remind partners to switch A and B roles after item 20 and to work quickly. Students should be pleasantly surprised by how easily they can think of typical completions, e.g., *a kitchen table, a kitchen knife, a kitchen door.*

TEACHING SUGGESTION: Be prepared to explain why the uncircled words do not work for each sentence.

> ANSWERS: **1.** cake   **2.** keys   **3.** jeans; shoes   **4.** test   **5.** games
> **6.** article; story

CHART 14-3: EXPRESSIONS OF QUANTITY: *ALL OF, MOST OF, SOME OF, ALMOST ALL OF*

• Use the illustration in the chart to discuss the expressions used in (a)–(d).

   NOTE: In the picture, Rita is the mother, Mike is the father, Susie is their daughter, and Matt is their son. Tell the class (for the purpose of discussion) that Matt's plate is clean except for the small amount of food they see to his left.

• Example (d) illustrates a common mistake made by learners: confusing *most of* with *almost all of.* The phrase **almost of* is not possible.

• In this chapter, the phrase *all of* is learned and practiced. Speakers often omit *of* after the word *all: She ate all (of) her food.* It is not possible to omit *of* after the words *most* or *some,* so it is a good idea to teach the preposition *of* with all three of these quantity words at this level.

• WORKBOOK: For additional exercises based on Chart 14-3, see *Workbook* Practice 9.

☐ EXERCISE 14, p. 416. Sentence practice. (Chart 14-3)

Do this exercise in class with your students. They may prefer to work in small groups before giving their answers.

   Items 1–5 use the words *odd* and *even* to describe numbers. Students should find this a useful concept.

   Items 6–9 use present progressive *(are flying)* to describe the action in a picture.

   Items 10–13 should reflect the situation in your class.

> ANSWERS: **2.** All of   **3.** Most of   **4.** Some of   **5.** Almost all of
> **6.** Almost all of   **7.** Most of   **8.** All of   **9.** Some of   **10.–13.** *(free response)*

CHART 14-4: EXPRESSIONS OF QUANTITY: SUBJECT-VERB AGREEMENT

• Not all expressions of quantity follow the subject-verb agreement rule, as the next charts explain.

• WORKBOOK: For additional exercises based on Chart 14-4, see *Workbook* Practices 10 and 11.

□ EXERCISE 15, p. 417.   Sentence practice. (Chart 14-4)

You may want to work through a few of the items in class, and assign the rest as homework.

TEACHING SUGGESTION: The drawing in item 8 illustrates a common saying: "An optimist sees the glass and says it is half full, but a pessimist sees the same glass and says it is half empty." Point out that this shows opposite ways of interpreting the same information.

In items 5 and 6, point out that *word* is a count noun, but *vocabulary* is a noncount noun.

ANSWERS: **2.** are   **3.** was   **4.** were   **5.** are   **6.** is   **7.** are . . . are   **8.** is   **9.** is   **10.** are   **11.** arrive   **12.** arrives

□ EXERCISE 16, p. 418.   Listening. (Chart 14-4)

TEACHING SUGGESTION: If necessary, review the range of percentages with the class: 100% = *all of* and 40% = *some of*.

ANSWERS: **1.** 100%   **2.** 30%   **3.** 50%   **4.** 90%   **5.** 70%   **6.** 85%

CHART 14-5:   EXPRESSIONS OF QUANTITY: *ONE OF, NONE OF*

• Using *one of* causes students a lot of singular-plural agreement problems. Common errors:
  ★One of my friend is coming. One of my friends are coming.

• You could make a circle on the board and draw several smaller circles inside it. The small circles represent *your friends* in example (a). Label one of the circles to represent *Sam.* Point to the filled-in circle as you explain example (a).

• The footnote below Chart 14-5, p. 419, in the student book, explains the usage of examples (c) and (d).

• WORKBOOK: For additional exercises based on Chart 14-5, see *Workbook* Practices 12–16.

□ EXERCISE 17, p. 419.   Sentence practice. (Chart 14-5)

Students may work in pairs or do this exercise as homework.

TEACHING SUGGESTION: When you lead your class through the answers, check to see or hear that the *-s* is added where it's required.

ANSWERS: **2.** (. . .) is one of my classmates.   **3.** One of my books is red.
4. One of my books has a green cover.   **5.** (. . .) is one of my favorite places in the world.   **6.** One of the students in my class always comes late.   **7.** (. . .) is one of my best friends.   **8.** One of my friends lives in (. . .) .   **9.** (. . .) is one of the best programs on TV.   **10.** (. . .) is one of the most famous people in the world.
11. One of my biggest problems is my inability to understand spoken English.
12. (. . .) is one of the leading newspapers in (. . .).   **13.** None of the students in my class speaks/speak (. . .).   **14.** None of the furniture in this room is soft and comfortable.

☐ EXERCISE 18, p. 420.   Let's talk. (Chart 14-5)

Students should write their answers and then compare them with their classmates' answers. The freedom to use their own ideas can produce interesting responses.

☐ EXERCISE 19, p. 421.   Sentence practice. (Chart 14-5)

Work through a few of the items in class and assign the rest as homework. The map belongs with item 9.

ANSWERS: 2. are   3. is   4. are   5. is   6. is   7. have   8. has
9. live   10. lives   11. is/are   12. is

☐ EXERCISE 20, p. 421.   Sentence practice. (Chart 14-5)

Work through a few of the items in class and assign the rest as homework.

ANSWERS: 2. are   3. is   4. are   5. is   6. are   7. is   8. is
9. are   10. is

☐ EXERCISE 21, p. 422.   Listening. (Chart 14-5)

Students need to pay attention to the quantity words as well as the word *of* and any plural noun endings.

ANSWERS: 1. Some of the homework   2. One of the books   3. None of the
children   4. All of the students   5. Half of the class   6. Almost all of the food
7. A lot of the exercises   8. Most of the movie

☐ EXERCISE 22, p. 422.   Listening review. (Chart 14-5)

TEACHING SUGGESTIONS: Before you play the audio, make sure your students know the following words: *mustache, smile, frown, sunglasses,* and *hat*. Point these out in the illustrations. After playing the audio for one item, give students enough time to scan the illustrations and circle their answers before continuing to the next item.

ANSWERS: 1. yes   2. no   3. yes   4. yes   5. no   6. no   7. no
8. yes

☐ EXERCISE 23, p. 423.   Let's talk: class activity. (Chart 14-5)

TEACHING SUGGESTIONS: Tell students that you don't want an exact number in their answers unless the number is very small. They'll spend too much time counting! In items 1, 4, and 5, you can substitute some familiar (or similar) words for those in the parentheses.

CHART 14-6: INDEFINITE PRONOUNS: *NOTHING* AND *NO ONE*

• Learners must understand that there are often two or more correct ways to state an idea. This chart presents one example of this.

• It might be useful to point out that only one "*no*-word" can be used in a correct sentence in English: either *not* or *nothing/no one/nobody,* but not both.

• Strange developments in historical English produced the following: *no* is pronounced /no/ in *no one* and *nobody,* but *nothing* is pronounced /nəθIŋ/.

• In AmE, *no one* is written as two words; in BrE, it is usually hyphenated: *no-one.*

• WORKBOOK: For additional exercises based on Chart 14-6, see *Workbook* Practices 17 and 18.

☐ EXERCISE 24, p. 423. Sentence practice. (Chart 14-6)

Students could work through items 1–9 in class (perhaps in pairs) and do the rest as homework.

ANSWERS: 1. anything   2. nothing   3. anyone   4. no one   5. nothing
6. anything   7. anything   8. nothing   9. nothing   10. anyone   11. No one   12. nothing   13. No one   14. anyone   15. A: anything B: nothing

CHART 14-7: INDEFINITE PRONOUNS: *SOMETHING, SOMEONE, ANYTHING, ANYONE*

• You could also introduce indefinite pronouns with *-body* if you wish: *somebody* and *anybody.*

• Note the parallel uses in Charts 14-6 and 14-7. Point these out to your students.

• WORKBOOK: For additional exercises based on Chart 14-7, see *Workbook* Practices 19–21.

☐ EXERCISE 25, p. 425. Sentence practice. (Chart 14-7)

Students could work through items 1–9 in class (perhaps in pairs) and do the rest as homework. Point out the information in the footnote on p. 425 of the student book: *Someone* and *somebody* have the same meaning; *anyone* and *anybody* have the same meaning.

ANSWERS: 2. something/anything   3. anything   4. something   5. anything
6. something/anything   7. someone   8. anyone   9. someone
10. someone/anyone   11. something   12. anything   13. something/anything
14. someone   15. anyone   16. anything *(also possible:* anyone*)*   17. anyone
18. Someone   19. someone/anyone   20. anything

CHART 14-8: USING *EVERY*

- Learners sometimes ask why *everyone, everybody,* and *everything* are written as one word, but *every day, every person,* etc., are written as two words. This is just a tradition in English. (Note here that *everyday* is spelled as one word when it is used as an adjective: *everyday life, everyday experiences, everyday food,* etc.)

- WORKBOOK: For additional exercises based on Chart 14-8, see *Workbook* Practices 22–24.

☐ EXERCISE 26, p. 426.   Sentence practice.   (Chart 14-8)

Students could work through items 1–8 in class (perhaps in pairs) and do the rest as homework. Items 11–14 are questions.

ANSWERS: **2.** book . . . is   **3.** students are   **4.** student is   **5.** teacher . . . gives   **6.** teachers . . . give   **7.** child . . . likes   **8.** children . . . know   **9.** people . . . are   **10.** wants   **11.** Do . . . students   **12.** Does . . . person   **13.** Do . . . people   **14.** Does   **15.** city . . . has   **16.** students . . . is

☐ EXERCISE 27, p. 427.   Review: error analysis.   (Charts 14-1 → 14-8)

This exercise contains some of the most frequent mistakes that learners make. It is important to review them carefully.

    TEACHING SUGGESTION: You might make this exercise a game. See Chapter 12, Exercise 31, in this *Teacher's Guide* for further information.

ANSWERS: **1.** I work hard every <u>day</u>.   **2.** I live in an apartment with one of my <u>friends</u>.   **3.** We saw a pretty <u>flower</u> garden in the park.   **4.** Almost <u>all</u> of the students are in class today.   **5.** Every <u>person</u> in my class <u>is</u> studying English.   **6.** All of the <u>big cities</u> in North America <u>have</u> traffic problems.   **7.** One of my cars <u>is</u> dark green.   **8.** Nadia drives a <u>small blue</u> car.   **9.** Istanbul is one of my favorite <u>cities</u> in the world.   **10.** Every ~~of~~ <u>student</u> in the class <u>has</u> a grammar book.   **11.** The work will take a long time. We can't finish <u>everything</u> today.   **12.** Everybody in the world <u>wants</u> peace.

CHART 14-9: LINKING VERBS + ADJECTIVES

- This chart introduces a few common linking verbs. Other common linking verbs not presented here are *appear, become, grow, seem,* and *stay.*

- WORKBOOK: For additional exercises based on Chart 14-9, see *Workbook* Practices 25 and 26.

☐ EXERCISE 28, p. 428.   Let's talk: pairwork.   (Chart 14-9)

With a partner, students can take turns responding. In Part I, they might say, "I feel good today" or "I don't feel good today." In Part II, they make truthful sentences about their opinions, such as "Pineapples taste good." In Part III, they express opinions, such as "The floor looks very clean."

☐ **EXERCISE 29, p. 429.   Let's talk. (Chart 14-9)**

Students can work in pairs or small groups.

TEACHING SUGGESTIONS: You might ask for volunteers to portray an emotion to the whole class. Lead them through the example first. This exercise can lead to a lot of laughter.

☐ **EXERCISE 30, p. 429.   Sentence practice. (Chart 14-9)**

Students could work in pairs to complete this exercise. Before they begin, take time to discuss new vocabulary.

In item 1, *terrific* = very wonderful (informal); *it sounds* + adjective = it seems (adjective) to me.

In item 3, *the community theater* = the theater that a small town or neighborhood owns; amateur theatrics.

In item 4, *overpopulation* = too many people living in one area, causing a strain on resources and facilities.

In item 11, *darling* and *honey* = names that lovers or spouses call each other; terms of endearment for children.

In item 12, *I sure do* = Yes, I most certainly smell it (informal); the footnote on p. 430 of the student book explains the meaning of *pyew*.

☐ **EXERCISE 31, p. 430.   Let's talk. (Chart 14-9)**

TEACHING SUGGESTION: You might make this exercise a game. The team with the longest (and most correct) list for each item is the winner.

CHART 14-10:   ADJECTIVES AND ADVERBS

• This chart is an introduction to adverbs of manner. Emphasize that adverbs modify verbs (i.e., give information about verbs), whereas adjectives modify nouns. Students need to understand what an adverb is before they study the comparative and superlative forms of adverbs in the following charts.

• A few adjectives end in *-ly,* for example, *friendly, lovely, kindly* (e.g., *a friendly person, a lovely day, a kindly gentleman*). These adjectives should not be confused with adverbs that end in *-ly.*

• WORKBOOK: For additional exercises based on Chart 14-10, see *Workbook* Practices 27–31. For more exercises on nouns (found in *Workbook* Charts 14-A and 14-B), see *Workbook* Practices 32–35.

☐ **EXERCISE 32, p. 431.   Sentence practice. (Chart 14-10)**

TEACHING SUGGESTION: Discuss the functions of the adjectives and adverbs with your students. Ask them to identify the noun or verb being modified by the completion.

ANSWERS: **3.** clearly   **4.** clear   **5.** careless   **6.** carelessly   **7.** easy
8. easily   **9.** good   **10.** well

☐ EXERCISE 33, p. 432. Sentence practice. (Chart 14-10)

You could work through a few of the items with your class and assign the rest as homework. Spelling is important in this exercise. Review the answers carefully.

> ANSWERS: 1. carefully 2. correct 3. correctly 4. fast 5. quickly
> 6. fast 7. neat 8. neatly 9. hard 10. hard 11. honestly
> 12. slowly 13. quickly 14. careless 15. early 16. early 17. loudly
> 18. slowly . . . clearly

☐ EXERCISE 34, p. 433. Sentence practice. (Chart 14-10)

You may want to work through a few of the items with your class and assign the rest as homework.

This exercise is more difficult than Exercise 33 because it contains linking verbs. If necessary, review linking verbs with the class before assigning the exercise.

> ANSWERS: 1. well 2. fast 3. quickly 4. fast 5. softly 6. hard
> 7. late 8. easily 9. quietly 10. beautiful 11. good 12. good
> 13. fluently

☐ EXERCISE 35, p. 434. Review. (Chapter 14)

This exercise could be used as a quick review quiz to see how much your class has learned in this chapter.

> ANSWERS: 2. B 3. D 4. D 5. C 6. A 7. A 8. B

☐ EXERCISE 36, p. 434. Chapter review: error analysis. (Chapter 14)

You might divide the class into small groups to discuss the corrections that need to be made; then review the answers as a class.

> ANSWERS: 1. Everybody <u>wants</u> to be <u>happy</u>. 2. One of the <u>buildings</u> on Main
> Street is the post office. 3. I didn't see <u>anybody</u> at the mall. OR I <u>saw</u> nobody at the
> mall. 4. At the library, you need to do your work <u>quietly</u>. 5. I walk in the park
> every <u>day</u>. 6. Mr. Jones teaches English very <u>well</u>. 7. The answer looks <u>clear</u>.
> Thank you for explaining it. 8. Every grammar test <u>has</u> a lot of difficult questions.

☐ EXERCISE 37, p. 435. Review: small groups. (Chapter 14)

This is a test of vocabulary for both the student who describes the item and the classmates who have to guess the noun.

TEACHING SUGGESTION: Give everyone in the groups five minutes to think of a noun and the clues before you begin the game.

☐ EXERCISE 38, p. 435. Review. (Chapter 14)

TEACHING SUGGESTION: If all of your students are from the same place, you could bring items to the class. Choose old or unusual items that most young people would not necessarily be familiar with.

CHAPTER 15
Possessives

Overview

This chapter explains the ways possession changes the form of nouns and pronouns. The use of the apostrophe with singular/plural and regular/irregular nouns is outlined. Possessive pronouns are introduced, followed by the possessive question word *whose*. The chapter ends with a contrast of *whose* and *who's*.

CHART 15-1: POSSESSIVE NOUNS

- Apostrophe /əpˈastrəfi/ or /əpˈɔstrəfi/.

- The pronunciation of the possessive *-s* ending follows the same rules as the *-s* ending on nouns and verbs. (See Charts 3-5 and 3-8, pp. 61 and 66, in the student book.)

- WORKBOOK: For additional exercises based on Chart 15-1, see *Workbook* Practices 1–6.

☐ EXERCISE 1, p. 436. Punctuation practice. (Chart 15-1)

You may want to work through items 1–6 with the class and assign the rest as homework.

TEACHING SUGGESTION: Students might check their homework answers with a partner the next day, after which you could review the answers with the class.

> *ANSWERS:* **2.** Bob's   **3.** teachers'   **4.** mother's   **5.** parents' (two people) OR parent's (one person)   **6.** father's   **7.** girl's   **8.** girls'   **9.** Tom's
> **10.** Anita's   **11.** Alex's   **12.** students'   **13.** elephant's   **14.** monkey's
> **15.** Monkeys'

☐ EXERCISE 2, p. 437. Sentence practice. (Chart 15-1)

This exercise should be done in class so the pronunciation of the *-s* ending can be practiced. The pronunciation of names in their English possessive forms may be difficult, but students should follow the usual rules for pronouncing *-s* endings.

NOTE: If a person's name ends in *-s*, there are two possible ways of writing the possessive form: (1) by adding an apostrophe + *-s*, as in *Charles's last name is Smith*, and (2) by adding only an apostrophe, as in *Charles' last name is Smith*.

☐ EXERCISE 3, p. 438.   Let's talk: small groups. (Chart 15-1)

TEACHING SUGGESTION: Ask for volunteers to share some of their answers with the class.
You may want them to write their answers on the board so you can check the placement of
the apostrophes.

☐ EXERCISE 4, p. 438.   Listening. (Chart 15-1)

At this level, many students have trouble hearing the -s ending, whether as a possessive or
other marker. You will probably need to play the audio more than once. If your students
have a lot of trouble with these sentences, you may want to create more exercises of this
type to provide additional practice.

ANSWERS: 1. Bob's   2. Bob   3. teacher's   4. teacher   5. friend
6. friend's   7. manager's   8. cousin

☐ EXERCISE 5, p. 438.   Sentence practice. (Chart 15-1)

TEACHING SUGGESTION: It might be helpful to draw a diagram of family relationships to
review some of the vocabulary needed in this exercise.

PRONUNCIATIONS: niece /nis/; nephew /nɛfyu/

ANSWERS: 2. brother   3. mother   4. children   5. sister   6. mother
7. wife   8. mother . . . father   9. daughter   10. son

☐ EXERCISE 6, p. 439.   Sentence practice. (Chart 15-1)

You may choose to use this as a practice quiz to check students' understanding of possessive
nouns and the correct placement of apostrophes.

ANSWERS: 2. B   3. A   4. B   5. A   6. C   7. B   8. C   9. B
10. A

CHART 15-2: POSSESSIVE: IRREGULAR PLURAL NOUNS

• Punctuation of possessive nouns is very complicated in English. Some of your students may
not be especially interested in these finer points of punctuation.

• Pronunciation of the final -s follows the usual rules. (See Charts 3-5 and 3-8, pp. 61 and 66, in
the student book.)

• WORKBOOK: For additional exercises based on Chart 15-2, see Workbook Practices 7–9.

☐ EXERCISE 7, p. 440.   Sentence practice. (Chart 15-2)

Work through this exercise as a class.

TEACHING SUGGESTION: Ask students for the answers and write the correct possessive
forms on the board.

ANSWERS: **2.** my friend's **3.** my friends' **4.** the child's **5.** the children's
6. the woman's **7.** the women's

☐ **EXERCISE 8, p. 440.   Sentence practice. (Chart 15-2)**

This exercise can be done in class or assigned as homework.

ANSWERS: **2.** girl's **3.** girls' **4.** women's **5.** uncle's **6.** person's
7. people's **8.** Students' **9.** brother's **10.** brothers' **11.** wife's
12. dog's **13.** dogs' **14.** men's **15.** man's . . . woman's **16.** children's

☐ **EXERCISE 9, p. 441.   Punctuation practice. (Chart 15-2)**

TEACHING SUGGESTION: You might want to do this exercise in the form of a game. See Chapter 12, Exercise 31, of this *Teacher's Guide* for further information.

ANSWERS: **2.** Yuko's **3.** classmates' **4.** roommate's **5.** parents' *(two people)* OR parent's *(one person)* **6.** people's **7.** husband's **8.** men's
9. children's **10.** father's **11.** Rosa's **12.** women's

---

CHART 15-3: POSSESSIVE PRONOUNS: *MINE, YOURS, HIS, HERS,*
OURS, THEIRS

• Languages vary in their ways of indicating possession with pronouns. Learners continue to make mistakes with these English forms for a long time.

• You may want to point out that the *-s* on *yours, hers, ours,* and *theirs* does not depend on a singular or plural reference:

        That book is hers. → *Those books are hers.*
  When does your class begin? → *When does yours begin?*

• WORKBOOK: For additional exercises based on Chart 15-3, see *Workbook* Practice 10.

☐ **EXERCISE 10, p. 442.   Sentence practice. (Chart 15-3)**

TEACHING SUGGESTION: This exercise can be confusing. Give students time to think before they respond. You may want to have them give the answers orally in class and write them later as homework.

ANSWERS: **2.** them . . . their . . . theirs **3.** you . . . your . . . yours **4.** her . . . her . . . hers **5.** him . . . his . . . his **6.** us . . . our . . . ours

☐ **EXERCISE 11, p. 443.   Sentence practice. (Chart 15-3)**

Remind students that every answer must be a possessive noun or a possessive pronoun.

    TEACHING SUGGESTION: You might divide the class into pairs and ask partners to take turns completing the items. Partners can check each other's answers.

2. a. ours
   b. theirs
   c. Our
   d. Theirs
3. a. Tom's
   b. Mary's
   c. His
   d. Hers
4. a. mine
   b. yours
   c. Mine . . . my
   d. Yours . . . your
5. a. Jim's
   b. Ours
   c. His
   d. Ours

6. a. my
   b. yours
   c. Mine . . . my
   d. Yours . . . your
7. a. Our
   b. Theirs
   c. Ours
   d. Their
8. a. Ann's
   b. Paul's
   c. Hers . . . her
   d. His . . . his

☐ EXERCISE 12, p. 444. Sentence practice. (Chart 15-3)

TEACHING SUGGESTION: Lead the class in the first two items. Then have students work with partners to read the dialogues as they complete the exercise.

ANSWERS:

2. hers
3. A: your
   B: my . . . Mine
4. yours
5. theirs. Their
6. A: our . . . yours
   B: Ours
7. A: your
   B: his

8. A: your
   B: yours . . . yours
   A: Mine
9. A: your
   B: yours
   A: Yours
   B: hers
   A: My . . . His

CHART 15-4: QUESTIONS WITH *WHOSE*

• In examples (a) and (b), *whose* is like a possessive adjective followed by a noun. In examples (c) and (d), *whose* is like a possessive pronoun.

• Learners often confuse *whose* with *who's (who is* or *who has* when *has* is used as the auxiliary in the present perfect). The illustration in Chart 15-4, p. 446, in the student book shows the difference in these two words.

• The word *whose* is the same for singular and plural references, as in examples (c) and (d).

• WORKBOOK: For additional exercises based on Chart 15-4, see *Workbook* Practices 11–15. For more exercises on personal pronouns and apostrophes (found in *Workbook* Charts 15-A and 15-B), see *Workbook* Practices 16–20.

□ **EXERCISE 13, p. 446. Sentence practice. (Chart 15-4)**

Lead the class through this exercise slowly so that everyone hears the correct answers.
Discuss any questions that arise about singular/plural forms.

ANSWERS: **2.** are those **3.** is this **4.** is that **5.** are those **6.** are these

□ **EXERCISE 14, p. 447. Let's talk: pairwork. (Chart 15-4)**

TEACHING SUGGESTION: After pairs have had time to ask and answer several questions,
ask students to perform a few of their exchanges for the class.

□ **EXERCISE 15, p. 447. Sentence practice. (Chart 15-4)**

This exercise can be done in class or assigned as homework.

TEACHING SUGGESTIONS: If done in class, you or your students can write the correct
answers on the board, or students can hold up index cards that you have passed out. Each
card contains one word: *Whose* or *Who's.*

ANSWERS: **2.** Whose **3.** Who's **4.** Who's **5.** Whose **6.** Who's

□ **EXERCISE 16, p. 447. Listening. (Chart 15-4)**

TEACHING SUGGESTIONS: Do the first two items as a class before asking students to finish
the exercise. Play the audio more than once if necessary. Correct the answers with the class
by writing them on the board.

ANSWERS: **1.** Who's **2.** Whose **3.** Who's **4.** Who's **5.** Whose
6. Whose **7.** Who's **8.** Whose **9.** Whose **10.** Who's

□ **EXERCISE 17, p. 447. Chapter review: error analysis. (Chapter 15)**

Although this exercise is short, it is very challenging. After students have completed it, go
over each sentence carefully so they have a good understanding of the corrections.

ANSWERS: **1.** <u>Who's</u> that woman? **2.** What are those <u>people's</u> names? **3.** Mr.
and Mrs. Swan like <u>their</u> apartment. **4.** The two <u>students</u> study together in the
library every afternoon. **5.** <u>Whose</u> book is this? **6.** Those shoes in the bag are
<u>theirs</u>, not <u>ours</u>. **7.** My <u>father's</u> sister has M.D. and Ph.D. degrees. **8.** Did you
meet your <u>children's</u> teacher? **9.** This is <u>my</u> pillow and that one is <u>yours</u>.

□ **EXERCISE 18, p. 448. Let's talk: review of Chapters 14 and 15.**

This logic puzzle reviews nouns, adjectives, noun-noun combinations, a few quantity
expressions, and possessives. As students work through the puzzle, they will be practicing
these structures without realizing they are doing so; in other words, using English
authentically. At first glance, this task may look difficult, but you will find students very
engaged in trying to figure out the answers.

NOTE: Explain that an "unnecessary clue" is simply additional information — it won't
help students solve the puzzle. It just makes the puzzle more challenging.

The girls' names are: Jill, Julie, Joan, and Jan. Although *Jan* is occasionally a boy's
name, it is not used so here.

Engaged	JACK	JIM	JAKE	JOHN	JILL	JULIE	JOAN	JAN
yes			x					x
no	x	x		x	x	(x)	x	

2. It can't be Joan. She's already married.
3. Clues 3 and 4 work together. It can't be Jill or Jack because they met at Jill's sister's wedding one year ago. The Facts in the student book say that the engaged couple met just five months ago.
4. See Clue 3. So far, the answers are "no" for Julie, Joan, Jill, and Jack. Since there is only one woman left, Jan must be the engaged woman.
5. Clues 5 and 7 work together. Jan's boyfriend is a medical student, so that rules out Jim (a computer-science student).
6. (unnecessary clue)
7. See Clue 5.
8. (unnecessary clue)
9. It can't be John, since Jan doesn't love him. The only man left is Jake. Jan and Jake are the engaged couple.

CHAPTER 16
Making Comparisons

Overview

This chapter describes several ways to combine ideas when making comparisons. The purpose of most comparisons is to form or express a judgment that favors one thing more than another. Thus, both comparison and contrast are introduced in this chapter.

The first section introduces some adjectives with prepositions: *the same as, similar to,* and *different from.* Then the adjectives *like* and *alike* are explained and practiced. Next is a section on the comparative ending *-er* and the modifier *more (than),* followed by the superlative ending *-est* and the modifier *most.* A different kind of contrast is expressed when the conjunction *but* connects two clauses.

The chapter concludes with an examination of some adverbs that are often confusing to second-language learners. These are practiced with various kinds of comparisons. By the end of the review exercises, students should have a good understanding of comparisons and contrasts and how to express them in English.

**CHART 16-1:   COMPARISONS: USING *THE SAME (AS), SIMILAR (TO),*
                AND *DIFFERENT (FROM)***

• It is recommended that you teach *the same* as a phrase so that learners always use the article *the* in this expression. The omission of *the* before *same* is a common error.

• It is also recommended that you teach the prepositions as part of each phrase so that learners think of them as a whole (e.g., *the same as, similar to, different from*).
  Note that the preposition is NOT used when only the adjective follows the verb, as in the first sentence below each picture in Chart 16-1, p. 449, in the student book.

• WORKBOOK: For additional exercises based on Chart 16-1, see *Workbook* Practices 1–3.

☐ EXERCISE 1, p. 449.   Let's talk: class activity. (Chart 16-1)

This can be a teacher-led activity. Students should answer with complete sentences.

NOTE: In a conversation, the answers would probably be "Yes, they are." or "No, they're not." Since this is an exercise (not a conversation), the questions are intended as prompts for using the target structures and the vocabulary.

ANSWERS: **1.** Yes. Pictures A and B are the same.   **2.** No. Pictures A and C aren't the same.   **3.** Yes. Pictures A and C are similar.   **4.** Yes. Pictures A and C are different.   **5.** No. Pictures C and D aren't similar.   **6.** Yes. Pictures C and D are different.

EXERCISE 2, p. 450.   Sentence practice. (Chart 16-1)

You may want to work through a few of these with your class and assign the rest as homework. Tell the class to be sure that each sentence is completed with the following: a preposition, the article *the,* and a singular or plural verb.

A, F, and G are triangles /<u>tray</u>æŋgəlz/ (A and F are equilateral triangles; G is a right triangle). B and D are rectangles /<u>rɛk</u>tæŋgəlz/. E is a square. (Note: a square can be considered a kind of rectangle.) C is a circle /<u>sr</u>kəl/.

ANSWERS: **3.** C is different from D.   **4.** B is the same as D.   **5.** B and D are the same.   **6.** C and D are different.   **7.** A and F are the same.   **8.** F and G are similar.   **9.** F is similar to G.   **10.** G is similar to A and F, but different from C.

□ **EXERCISE 3, p. 450.   Listening. (Chart 16-1)**

TEACHING SUGGESTIONS: Give students enough time to find the pictures in Exercise 2 after they hear each sentence. Make sure they understand the *spoken* letters A–G. (You may want to dictate these letters to the class as a quick review before beginning the exercise.)

ANSWERS: **1.** yes   **2.** yes   **3.** no   **4.** yes   **5.** yes   **6.** yes   **7.** no

□ **EXERCISE 4, p. 451.   Error analysis. (Chart 16-1)**

This is a short review; you may want to have students work in pairs and then correct their answers in class.

ANSWERS: **1.** A rectangle is similar <u>to</u> a square.   **2.** Pablo and Rita come from <u>the</u> same country.   **3.** Girls and boys are <u>different</u>. Girls are different <u>from</u> boys.   **4.** My cousin is the same age <u>as</u> my brother.   **5.** Dogs are similar <u>to</u> wolves.   **6.** Jim and I started to speak at <u>the</u> same time.

□ **EXERCISE 5, p. 451.   Let's talk: class activity. (Chart 16-1)**

Most students enjoy simple puzzles like these. Give them time to figure out the answers; perhaps assign them as homework.

ANSWERS: **1.** Figures 1, 4, 8, and 10 are the same. Figures 3 and 5 are the same. Figures 2, 7, and 9 are the same.   **2.** Six is different from all the rest.   **3.** (Seven.)   **4.** Nine.   **5.** Eleven.

□ **EXERCISE 6, p. 451.   Let's talk: class activity. (Chart 16-1)**

This is a teacher-led activity.

TEACHING SUGGESTIONS: Lead the class through the example so they know what to do; then, in a conversational manner, continue with the other items. Help with vocabulary as necessary and adapt the items to the situation in your classroom.

CHART 16-2: COMPARISONS: USING *LIKE* AND *ALIKE*

• Some learners want to say *★Your pen likes my pen,* which is nonsensical. Call their attention to the meaning of the verb *like* in Chart 5-11, p. 148, in the student book. The verb in Chart 16-2 (p. 452 in the student book) is *be.*

• The word *alike* is always the last word in the sentence in these exercises.

• The word *like* is similar to a preposition: It follows a verb and is itself followed by an object.

• WORKBOOK: For additional exercises based on Chart 16-2, see *Workbook* Practices 4 and 5.

☐ EXERCISE 7, p. 452. Sentence practice. (Chart 16-2)

This exercise can be assigned as homework. Of course, other words can complete these sentences correctly, but for the purpose of this exercise students should choose either *like* or *alike.*

> ANSWERS: **2.** like . . . alike **3.** alike **4.** like **5.** like **6.** alike **7.** alike
> **8.** like

☐ EXERCISE 8, p. 453. Let's talk: pairwork. (Chart 16-2)

Some imaginative students might produce unusual responses, but the expected comparisons are listed here. The interesting ideas can be in the explanations students give for their answers in the second sentence of each response.

> EXPECTED RESPONSES: **1.** A bush is like a tree. **2.** A cup is like a glass.
> **3.** A hill is like a mountain. **4.** Honey is like sugar. **5.** A monkey's hand is like a
> human hand. **6.** An orange is like a lemon. **7.** An alley is like a street.
> **8.** A sea is like an ocean. **9.** A sofa is like a chair. **10.** A sports jacket is like a
> suit coat. **11.** A butterfly is like a bird.

CHART 16-3: THE COMPARATIVE: USING *-ER* AND *MORE*

• You might have students look at the examples and the lists of adjectives to discover the rules. Ask them to explain the rules in their own words, if possible.

• NOTE about *farther* and *further:* Both are used to compare physical distance: *My house is farther/further away from school than Bob's house. Further* (but not *farther*) can also mean "additional": *I need further information.*

• WORKBOOK: For additional exercises based on Chart 16-3, see *Workbook* Practices 6–9.

☐ EXERCISE 9, p. 454. Comparative practice. (Chart 16-3)

There are three purposes to this exercise: using the word *than* with a comparison, spelling the comparisons correctly, and deciding which words use *-er* and which use *more.*

TEACHING SUGGESTION: It is recommended that students learn to add the word *than* to each comparison. You could tell them to think of *more/-er . . . than* as a complete unit.

If you decide to do this exercise in class, give students enough time to think before they respond. Ask them to spell the *-er* words aloud or write them on the board.

ANSWERS: **2.** smaller than   **3.** bigger than   **4.** more important than
5. easier than   **6.** more difficult than   **7.** longer than   **8.** heavier than
9. more expensive than   **10.** sweeter than   **11.** hotter than   **12.** better than
13. worse than   **14.** farther/further than

☐ EXERCISE 10, p. 455.   Sentence practice. (Chart 16-3)

You may want to assign this exercise as homework. Be sure to check spelling when going over the answers in class.

ANSWERS: **2.** deeper than   **3.** more important than   **4.** lazier than   **5.** taller than   **6.** heavier than   **7.** more difficult than   **8.** hotter than   **9.** thinner than   **10.** warmer . . . than   **11.** better than   **12.** longer than   **13.** more intelligent than   **14.** shorter than   **15.** worse than   **16.** farther/further . . . than   **17.** stronger than   **18.** curlier than   **19.** more nervous . . . than

☐ EXERCISE 11, p. 456.   Let's talk: pairwork. (Chart 16-3)

TEACHING SUGGESTION: Pairs that finish early can switch roles. After students have completed the exercise, ask for volunteers for some of the answers (particularly item 5 in the left column, and items 4, 5, and 6 in the right column).

☐ EXERCISE 12, p. 457.   Let's talk: class activity. (Chart 16-3)

Students can work in pairs or as a class. Have them write some of their sentences on the board.

NOTE: You will need to bring several different books to the classroom. They should be different sizes, subjects, etc.

☐ EXERCISE 13, p. 457.   Listening. (Chart 16-3)

The comparison ending *-er* can be very hard for students to hear. Many students cannot distinguish between words like *cold* and *colder* in spoken English. You will probably need to play the audio more than once. You may want to create more exercises like this one to give students additional practice.

ANSWERS: **1.** cold   **2.** colder   **3.** colder   **4.** happier   **5.** happy
6. happy   **7.** safer   **8.** safe   **9.** safer   **10.** fresh   **11.** funny
12. funnier

☐ EXERCISE 14, p. 458.   Sentence practice. (Chart 16-3)

This exercise can be done in class or assigned as homework.

ANSWERS: **2.** sweeter than   **3.** colder/warmer/hotter than   **4.** more comfortable than   **5.** cheaper than   **6.** faster than   **7.** more intelligent than   **8.** higher than   **9.** brighter than   **10.** more expensive than   **11.** easier than   **12.** more important than

☐ EXERCISE 15, p. 459. Let's talk. (Chart 16-3)

> *TEACHING SUGGESTIONS:* Whether working as a class, in groups, or in pairs, have the leader say each cue as a sentence: "*(Student's name)*, compare an elephant to a mouse." Help with new vocabulary. Be prepared for some interesting (perhaps controversial) responses that might need further discussion.

☐ EXERCISE 16, p. 459. Let's talk: small groups. (Chart 16-3)

> This is similar to Exercise 15, but now students must supply the items for comparison. Encourage students to use their imagination, but they should also be prepared to explain their opinions.

☐ EXERCISE 17, p. 460. Let's talk: pairwork. (Chart 16-3)

> *TEACHING SUGGESTION:* If your students don't want to tear up paper, they can simply write jumbled sentences for their classmates like this:
>
> heavier \ yours \ bookbag \ than \ is \ my

☐ EXERCISE 18, p. 460. Let's talk: pairwork. (Chart 16-3)

> Lead the class through the example, and remind them to switch roles after item 8. Tell them to substitute their own words for the words in parentheses.

CHART 16-4:   THE SUPERLATIVE: USING *-EST* AND *MOST*

• It is recommended that students learn the definite article *the* with the superlative as a single unit. Be sure that when you say the superlative form, you always include *the* with it.

• In everyday usage, many people use the superlative when comparing only two items, but the formal rule requires at least three items for the superlative to be used correctly.

• WORKBOOK: For additional exercises based on Chart 16-4, see *Workbook* Practices 10–13.

☐ EXERCISE 19, p. 461. Comparative and superlative practice. (Chart 16-4)

> You may want to do items 1-7 in class and assign the rest as homework. Require students to use *than* and *the* in every answer. That is the best way to help them avoid mistakes later when they use these forms in conversation or writing. Discuss irregular forms and spelling changes.

```
ANSWERS:        COMPARATIVE                SUPERLATIVE
          2.  smaller (than)           the smallest (of all)
          3.  heavier (than)           the heaviest (of all)
          4.  more comfortable (than)  the most comfortable (of all)
          5.  harder (than)            the hardest (of all)
          6.  more difficult (than)    the most difficult (of all)
          7.  easier (than)            the easiest (of all)
          8.  hotter (than)            the hottest (of all)
          9.  cheaper (than)           the cheapest (of all)
         10.  more interesting (than)  the most interesting (of all)
         11.  prettier (than)          the prettiest (of all)
         12.  stronger (than)          the strongest (of all)
         13.  better (than)            the best (of all)
         14.  worse (than)             the worst (of all)
         15.  farther/further (than)   the farthest/the furthest (of all)
```

☐ EXERCISE 20, p. 462. Sentence practice. (Chart 16-4)

You may want to work through a few of the items in class and assign the rest as homework.

ANSWERS: 2. the longest   3. the most interesting   4. the highest
5. the tallest   6. the biggest   7. the shortest   8. the farthest/the furthest
9. the most beautiful   10. the worst   11. the best   12. the most comfortable
13. fastest   14. the best   15. the largest   16. the smallest   17. the most
expensive   18. the easiest   19. the most important   20. the most famous

☐ EXERCISE 21, p. 464. Listening. (Chart 16-4)

This is a challenging exercise; students need to listen for comparative and superlative forms
while thinking about the meaning. Give them enough time to process each sentence.

    TEACHING SUGGESTION: Call students' attention to the pictures; they need to be
aware of each character's age, height, and facial expression (happy, serious, etc.).

ANSWERS: 1. no   2. yes   3. yes   4. yes   5. yes   6. no   7. yes
8. yes   9. no   10. yes

☐ EXERCISE 22, p. 464. Sentence practice. (Chart 16-4)

Remind students to use the comparative with two items and the superlative when
comparing more than two items. This exercise gives learners good practice in using
comparisons in natural situations.

ANSWERS: 4. older than   5. older than   6. younger than   7. the oldest
8. Alice   9. Linda   10. Karen . . . Linda . . . Alice

SAMPLE COMPLETIONS: 11. Mike is the weakest.   12. Joe is stronger than Mike.
13. (free response)   14. (free response)   15. A car is more expensive than a bike.
16. (free response)   17. (free response)   18. (free response)   19. Carol's test/grade
is the best/the highest.   20. Mary's test/grade is the worst/the lowest.   21. (free
response)   22. (free response)   23. Love in the Spring is more interesting than
Introduction to Psychology (to me).   24. Murder at Night is more boring than Love in the
Spring (to me).   25. (free response)   26. (free response)

□ EXERCISE 23, p. 467.   Sentence practice. (Chart 16-4)

You may want to do the first few items in class and assign the rest as homework.

NOTE: In items 9, 10, and 11, note the difference in the meaning of the prepositional phrases beginning with *in*. *In the world* is similar to *of all*, so it requires the superlative. But *in area* and *in population* indicate "some specific feature" and require the comparative.

ANSWERS: **1.** longer than   **2.** the longest   **3.** larger than   **4.** the largest   **5.** the highest   **6.** higher than   **7.** bigger than   **8.** smaller than   **9.** the largest   **10.** bigger than   **11.** larger than   **12.** better . . . than   **13.** the best   **14.** more comfortable than . . . the most comfortable   **15.** easier than . . . the easiest   **16.** worse

□ EXERCISE 24, p. 468.   Listening. (Chart 16-4)

Go slowly through this exercise. Writing the complete comparison or superlative expression can be difficult. This is the first time students have to decide if a comparative or superlative is being used and to write the expression (which may include the words *than* and *the).*

ANSWERS: **1.** more expensive   **2.** prettier   **3.** short   **4.** the nicest   **5.** small   **6.** the biggest   **7.** bigger than   **8.** longer than   **9.** long   **10.** the cheapest

---

CHART 16-5:   USING *ONE OF* + SUPERLATIVE + PLURAL NOUN

• Remind students of Chart 14-5, p. 419, in the student book, which shows that *one of* must be followed by a plural noun or pronoun.

• In example (c), remind students that the word *people* is a plural noun in English even though it does not add *-s.*

• WORKBOOK: For additional exercises based on Chart 16-5, see *Workbook* Practices 14–17.

□ EXERCISE 25, p. 469.   Sentence practice. (Chart 16-5)

Students can use their own knowledge of the world in Exercises 25 and 26. Encourage them to make interesting answers. If this exercise is done in class, have students work in pairs or small groups.

SAMPLE SENTENCES: **4.** New York is one of the biggest cities in the world.   **5.** The Grand Canyon is one of the most beautiful places in the world.   **6.** (. . .) is one of the nicest people in our class.   **7.** The Yangtze River is one of the longest rivers in the world.   **8.** (. . .) is one of the best restaurants in *(this city).*   **9.** The Taj Mahal is one of the most famous landmarks in the world.   **10.** The fall of the Roman Empire was one of the most important events in the history of the world.

□ EXERCISE 26, p. 470.   Let's talk: class interview. (Chart 16-5)

TEACHING SUGGESTION: Walk around the room to make sure students are forming their questions correctly. Listen especially for the plural *-s* ending (where applicable) in questions and answers. For items 4 and 6, remind students that *people* is more common than *persons*. (See the footnote on p. 469 in the student book.)

SAMPLE SENTENCES: **1.** Hong Kong is one of the largest cities in Asia.   **2.** Texas is one of the largest states in the United States.   **3.** Paris is one of the most beautiful cities in the world.   **4.** (. . .) is one of the tallest people in our class.   **5.** San Francisco is one of the best places to visit in the world.   **6.** (. . .) is one of the most famous people in the world.   **7.** Good health is one of the most important things in life.   **8.** (. . .) is one of the worst restaurants in *(this city)*.   **9.** (. . .) is one of the most famous landmarks in *(name of a country)*.   **10.** (. . .) is one of the tallest buildings in *(this city)*.   **11.** Boxing is one of the most dangerous sports in the world.   **12.** Famine is one of the most serious problems in the world.

☐ EXERCISE 27, p. 471.   Let's talk. (Chart 16-5)

TEACHING SUGGESTIONS: You may choose to do the first three items as a teacher-led activity; then have students complete the rest in small groups. Encourage them to have short conversations about the items. Everyone should give an answer to at least two items. Set a time limit for completing the exercise.

☐ EXERCISE 28, p. 471.   Let's talk: small groups. (Chart 16-5)

This exercise enables learners to apply their usage of comparatives and superlatives to real-life information.

TEACHING SUGGESTIONS: First, have students take this quiz quickly by themselves (in class or at home). Then divide the class into small groups to discuss the answers. Students should make their best guesses to the questions; it doesn't matter if they choose the right answers. The goal of the exercise is to get them talking in small groups as they use the Table of Statistics to figure out the correct answers. In their discussion, students will have to spontaneously use comparatives and superlatives.

ANSWERS: **1.** C   **2.** A   **3.** A   **4.** B   **5.** C   **6.** A   **7.** C   **8.** B   **9.** (1) Asia   (2) Africa   (3) North America   (4) (Antarctica)   (5) South America   (6) Europe   (7) Australia   **10.** D   **11.** A   **12.** A   **13.** A   **14.** A   **15.** A   **16.** B   **17.** A   **18.** A   **19.** A

CHART 16-6:   USING *BUT*

• *But* is a coordinating conjunction like *and;* that is, it connects two clauses or phrases that are grammatically parallel in structure.

• WORKBOOK: For additional exercises based on Chart 16-6, see *Workbook* Practice 18.

☐ EXERCISE 29, p. 475.   Sentence practice. (Chart 16-6)

In this exercise, learners must use antonyms — words with opposite meanings. If this exercise is done in class, students can help one another with difficult items; if it is done at home, students can consult a dictionary. Be sure to go over the answers and their meanings in class. Items 4 and 5 give two different meanings of the adjective *light.*

ANSWERS: **2.** cold   **3.** dirty   **4.** light   **5.** dark   **6.** comfortable   **7.** wide   **8.** hard/difficult   **9.** bad   **10.** smart/intelligent   **11.** invisible   **12.** wrong   **13.** wet   **14.** empty   **15.** clear   **16.** clean   **17.** hard

☐ EXERCISE 30, p. 476. Listening. (Chart 16-6)

This exercise is similar to Exercise 29; it simply adds a listening component.

The adjectives the students hear should be familiar, but processing each sentence and then thinking of an opposite adjective (an antonym) can be challenging. If students have trouble, you may want to create more exercises like this to provide additional practice.

ANSWERS: **1.** short   **2.** big   **3.** quiet   **4.** pretty   **5.** slow   **6.** strong
7. cheap/inexpensive   **8.** lazy

CHART 16-7: USING VERBS AFTER *BUT*

• Students are being asked to understand the grammar in this chart by studying the examples. There is no explanation given for verb usage in a clause following *but*. You might point out that a form of main verb *be* or an auxiliary verb is used after *but*.

• WORKBOOK: For additional exercises based on Chart 16-7, see *Workbook* Practices 19 and 20.

☐ EXERCISE 31, p. 476. Sentence practice. (Chart 16-7)

Students need time to think about negative/affirmative, singular/plural, and the necessary verb. After you lead the class through about eight of the items, students could continue working with partners or complete the rest as homework.

ANSWERS:

2. is	**7.** can't	**12.** didn't	**17.** can
3. aren't	**8.** won't	**13.** doesn't	**18.** will
4. was	**9.** isn't	**14.** does	**19.** won't
5. weren't	**10.** are	**15.** wasn't	**20.** will
6. do	**11.** does	**16.** didn't	**21.** were

☐ EXERCISE 32, p. 477. Listening. (Chart 16-7)

This exercise is similar to Exercise 31; it simply adds a listening component.

If students have trouble, you could repeat some sentences from Exercise 31 a few days after your students have done them, this time with their books closed. You may even want to create more exercises like this to provide additional practice.

ANSWERS: **1.** doesn't   **2.** can't   **3.** did   **4.** were   **5.** do   **6.** is
7. wasn't   **8.** didn't   **9.** won't   **10.** will

☐ EXERCISE 33, p. 478. Let's talk: class activity. (Chart 16-7)

This is a teacher-led activity. Pause after each question for one student to answer.

☐ EXERCISE 34, p. 478. Let's talk: pairwork. (Chart 16-7)

This exercise should be fun for students as they try to find all the differences between the two illustrations.

TEACHING SUGGESTION: Begin with the example; then ask your class to find a second difference. For example, the fish in Picture A is in a fish tank whereas the fish in Picture B is in a chair (reading). Since humor varies widely from country to country, some students may find this amusing whereas others find it merely puzzling. Walk around the room to answer any questions that arise while students work in pairs.

☐ EXERCISE 35, p. 479.   Writing practice. (Chart 16-7)

> *TEACHING SUGGESTION:* You might want to tell students how many sentences they should include in each response. If this exercise is done in class, set a time limit.

CHART 16-8:   MAKING COMPARISONS WITH ADVERBS

• Adverbs follow the same patterns as adjectives in the comparative and superlative. (See Chart 16-4, p. 461, in the student book.)

• Remind students to use *than* with comparatives and *the* with superlatives.

• WORKBOOK: For additional exercises based on Chart 16-8, see *Workbook* Practices 21–23.

☐ EXERCISE 36, p. 480.   Sentence practice. (Chart 16-8)

Point out that the verbs in parentheses are optional; the sentences are complete with or without them. After you lead the class through four or five items, students could continue working with partners or complete the rest as homework.

> *ANSWERS:*   **2.** more quickly than   **3.** more beautifully than   **4.** the most beautifully   **5.** harder than   **6.** the hardest   **7.** more carefully than   **8.** earlier than   **9.** the earliest   **10.** better than   **11.** the best   **12.** more clearly than   **13.** more fluently than   **14.** the most fluently

☐ EXERCISE 37, p. 481.   Sentence practice. (Chart 16-8)

You may want to work through items 1–6 in class and assign the rest as homework.

> *ANSWERS:*   **2.** more beautiful than   **3.** neater than   **4.** the neatest   **5.** more neatly than   **6.** the most neatly   **7.** more clearly than   **8.** better than   **9.** better than   **10.** the best   **11.** longer   **12.** later than   **13.** the most clearly   **14.** sharper than   **15.** more artistic than   **16.** more slowly than

☐ EXERCISE 38, p. 482.   Listening: review. (Chapter 16)

This exercise reviews comparisons using adjectives and adverbs. The words should be familiar, but they may be difficult in a listening format. You might find that your students still omit words like *the* and *than*. Also, make sure that students pay attention to spelling when you review the answers in class.

> *ANSWERS:*   **1.** faster than   **2.** the fastest   **3.** harder than   **4.** the hardest   **5.** more dangerous than   **6.** more loudly than   **7.** more slowly than   **8.** heavier than   **9.** clearer than   **10.** more clearly

□ EXERCISE 39, p. 482.   Review. (Chapter 16)

This exercise can be done as homework. Remind students to pay attention to prepositions and spelling.

ANSWERS: 2. B   3. C   4. B   5. A   6. D   7. B   8. A   9. D

□ EXERCISE 40, p. 483.   Chapter review: error analysis. (Chapter 16)

This exercise can be done in class or assigned as homework.

TEACHING SUGGESTIONS: If done in class, divide students into small groups. Assign different sentences to each group randomly. Give them time to figure out the correct answers. Ask for group members to write the correct sentences on the board. Have the other groups check their answers for accuracy.

ANSWERS: **1.** Your pen is <u>like</u> mine.   **2.** Kim's coat is similar <u>to</u> mine.   **3.** Jack's coat is <u>the</u> same <u>as</u> mine.   **4.** Soccer balls are different <u>from</u> basketballs.
5. Soccer is one of <u>the</u> most popular sports in the world.   **6.** Green sea turtles live <u>longer</u> than elephants.   **7.** My grade on the test was <u>worse than</u> yours. You got a ~~more~~ better grade.   **8.** A monkey is <u>more intelligent</u> than a turtle.   **9.** Pedro speaks English more <u>fluently</u> than Ernesto.   **10.** Professor Brown teaches full-time, but her husband <u>doesn't</u>.   **11.** Robert and Maria aren't <u>the</u> same age. Robert is <u>younger</u> than Maria.   **12.** A blue whale is <u>larger than</u> an elephant.   **13.** The exploding human population is the <u>greatest</u> threat to all forms of life on earth.
14. The Mongol Empire was the <u>biggest</u> land empire in the entire history of the world.

□ EXERCISE 41, p. 484.   Review. (Chapter 16)

TEACHING SUGGESTIONS: When pairs are finished, ask for volunteers to give answers. Some questions may have multiple answers. Give special attention to spelling and the forms studied in this chapter. Praise your students for their successes.

□ EXERCISE 42, p. 484.   Let's write or talk. (Chapter 16)

TEACHING SUGGESTION: If your class is weak in conversation skills, you could ask students to write ideas (not necessarily complete sentences) on a piece of paper. Then put them in pairs or small groups and have them discuss their comparisons.

□ EXERCISE 43, p. 485.   Writing practice. (Chapter 16)

Assign this exercise for homework so students have time to organize their writing.

TEACHING SUGGESTIONS: Set limits on length and style (e.g., four to six sentences = a paragraph; pay attention to spelling and punctuation; check your verb tenses, etc.).

Ask the class to hand in their papers. Correct the errors, but don't grade them. Before you hand them back, write some of the most common errors on the board and ask students to help you correct them.

Map of the World

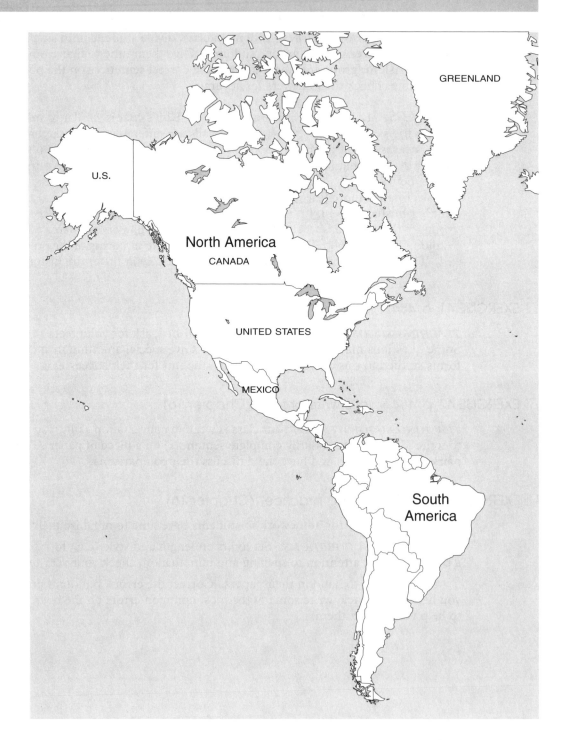

GREENLAND

U.S.

North America

CANADA

UNITED STATES

MEXICO

South America

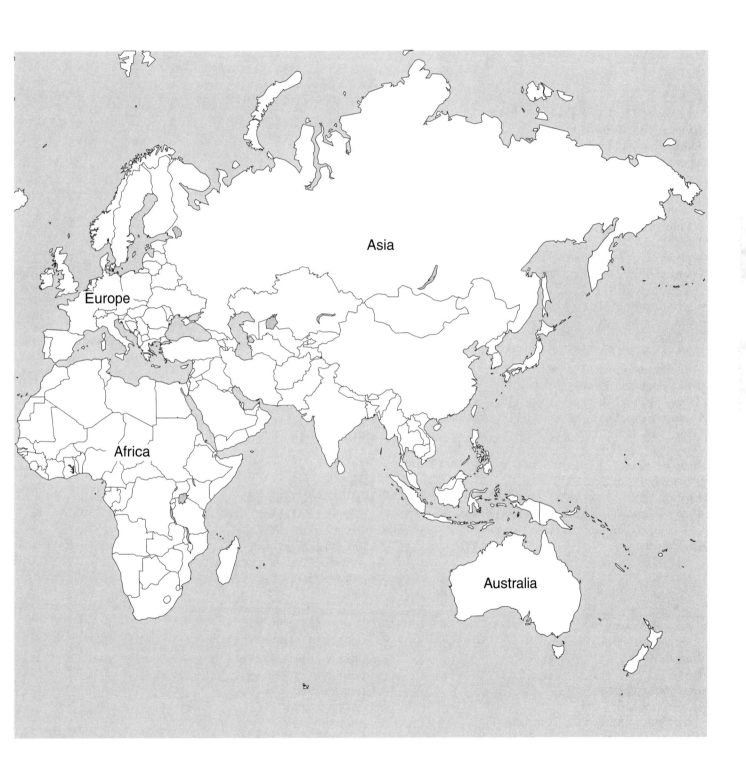

Europe

Asia

Africa

Australia

MAP **181**

Index

A

A/an, 2, 4, 70
    vs. *some,* 71
Able to, 138, 149–150
A couple of, 115
Adjectives *(good, beautiful),* defined, 8, 62, 152
    vs. adverbs, 161
    be + adjective, 8, 11, 62
    comparative *(-er/more),* 171
    following linking verbs, 160
    list of, 62
    possessive *(my, his, our),* 15, 165
    superlative, 173, 175, 178
    with *very,* 139
    word order of, 154
Adverb clause, 126
Adverbs:
    vs. adjectives, 161
    in comparisons, 178
    of frequency, 23, 25
A few, 115
A few/a little, 74
After, 103, 126
Ago, 86, 114–115
Alike vs. *like,* 171
(Almost) all of, 156
A lot of, 69
Always, usually, often, sometimes, seldom,
    rarely, never, 23, 25
Am, is, are:
    am, is, are + *-ing,* 105
    future, 111
    negative, 7, 39, 41
    in questions, 41
    simple present, 4, 7, 11–13
    verb summary of, 121
And, 4
Any, 79
Anyone/anything, 159
Apostrophe, 163–164
    defined, 6 (SEE ALSO Contractions)
Articles *(a, an, the),* 2, 4, 70, 76, 78

At:
    for place, 10, 52, 141
    for time, 47

B

Be:
    be + adjective, 8, 11, 62
    be + *-ing,* 36, 105
    be + noun, 2, 4–5, 11
    be + place, 10–11, 13, 49
    be + prepositional phrase, 10
    contractions with, 6, 12, 17–18, 49, 82
    question forms with, 12–13, 30, 33, 40–41, 83
    simple past *(was, were),* 81–82, 120–121
    simple present *(am, is, are),* 4, 7, 11–13,
        120–121
    there + *be,* 49–51
    what/who + *be,* 18
    where + *be,* 13, 33, 40
Be able to, 138, 149–150
Before, 103, 126
Be going to, 111, 120–121, 126, 128, 149–150
But, 176–177

C

Can, 149–150
    ability/possibility, 133, 138
    can vs. *can't,* pronunciation, 134
    in questions, 135, 147
Clauses, defined, 103
    adverb, 126
    future time, 126
    with *if,* 127–128
    of time, 103–104
    with *when,* 104, 107
    with *while,* 106–107
Comma, 106, 126, 176
Comparatives *(-er/more),* 171, 178
Comparisons:
    with adverbs, 178
    but, 176–177
    -er/more, 171, 178

-est/most, 173, 175, 178
like vs. alike, 171
same, similar, different, 169
Consonants, 2
Contractions, defined, 6
    negative, 29, 89, 118, 133
    with not (SEE Negatives)
    in questions, 18
    with will, 118
    with would, 55
Contractions of be:
    with not, 7, 12, 82
    with pronouns, 6, 12
    with question words, 18
    in short answers, 12, 83
    with that, 17
    with there, 49
Could, 149–150
    past of can, 137
    in polite questions, 147
Count/noncount nouns, 69, 73–74, 78

D

Did:
    in the negative, 89
    in questions, 91, 100, 129
Different (from), 169
Do/does, 27
    in the negative, 29, 41, 144
    in questions, 30–33, 41, 129

E

-Ed, 85
-Er/more, 171, 178
-Est/most, 173, 175, 178
Every, 22, 160
Everyone/everybody, 160
Expressions of quantity, 156–157

F

Feminine pronouns, 5
Frequency adverbs, 23, 25
From . . . to, 47
Future time:
    be going to, 111
    clauses, 126
        with if, 127–128
    future time words, 114–116
    summary of forms, 120–121
    using present progressive, 113
    will, 118

G

Generalizations, 78
Go/Goes, 27

Going to, with be, 111, 120–121, 126, 128, 149–150
Good vs. will, 161

H

Habitual present, 22, 41, 128
Has to/have to, 144, 149–150
Have/has, 14, 27
Hear and listen to, 43
Helping verbs, 29, 36, 149
How many, 51

I

I, you, he, she, it, we, they, 5–6, 64, 81–82, 85, 89, 143
If-clause, 127
    habitual present with, 128
Imperative sentences, 148
In:
    for future time, 115
    for place, 52, 141
    for time, 47
Indefinite pronouns, 159
Infinitives, defined, 54
    with be able, 138, 149–150
    with be going, 111, 120–121, 126, 128, 149–150
    with have/has, 144, 149–150
    following verbs, 54–55
Information questions, defined, 31
    with be, 33, 83
    with do/does/did, 30–33, 91, 100
-Ing:
    be + -ing, 36, 39
    spelling, 38
Irregular noun plurals, 67
    possessive form, 164
Irregular singular verbs (has, does, goes), 27–28
Irregular verbs:
    groups (1–7), 87, 92–94, 101–102
    introduction, 27
    list, 87
Is + noun, 2, 5, 11–12
It:
    for time, 46
    for weather, 48

K

Know how to, 136

L

Last, 86, 114
Let's, 150
Like vs. alike, 171

Like vs. *would like*, 56
Linking verbs, 160

M

Main clauses, 103
Many/much, 74
    with *how*, 51
Masculine pronouns, 5
May, 149–150
    in polite questions, 147
    possibility, 124
Maybe vs. *may be*, 125
Me, you, him, her, it, us, them, 64
Measurements with noncount nouns, 73
Might, 124, 149–150
Mine, yours, his, hers, our, theirs, 165
Modal auxiliaries, 149–150
More:
    comparative, 171
    in future time, 115
More/-er, 171
Most/-est, 173, 175, 178
Most of, 156
Must, 145, 149–150
My, your, his, her, our, their, 15, 165

N

Need, 54
Negatives:
    am/is/are + *not*, 7, 39, 111, 120–121
    can + *not*, 133
    could + *not*, 137
    did + *not*, 89
    does/do + *not*, 29, 41, 148
    may/might + *not*, 124
    should + *not*, 143
    was/were + *not*, 82
    will + *not*, 118–121
Next, 114
Nonaction verbs, 43
Noncount nouns, 69, 73–74, 78
None of, 157
No one/nothing, 159
Not (SEE Negatives)
Nouns:
    be + noun, 2, 4–5, 11–12
    count/noncount, 69, 73–74, 78
    irregular plural:
        forms, 67
        possessives, 164
    modifying other nouns, 152
    as object, 60
    possessive, 163–164
    singular/plural, 2, 4, 65, 67
    as subject, 11, 60

O

Object pronouns, 64
Objects and subjects, 60
On:
    for place, 52
    for time, 47
One of, 157, 175

P

Past time:
    with *be*, 81
    clauses, 107
    past progressive, 105–107
    past time words, 86, 114–116
    simple past, 85, 87, 89, 91, 97, 107,
        120–121
Period, 12
Please, 147–148
Plural, defined, 4
Plural nouns, 4–5, 65, 67
Polite questions, 147
Possessive:
    adjectives *(my, his, our)*, 15, 165
    nouns, 163–164
    pronouns, 165
Prepositional phrase, defined, 10
Prepositions:
    followed by an object, 10, 52, 60, 103
    in for future, 114–115
    list of, 10, 52
    place, 10–11, 13, 49, 52, 141
    time, 47, 103, 114
Present progressive, 36, 105
    negative, 39
    in questions, 40
    vs. simple present, 41
    verbs not used in, 43
Present time, 22, 29
    habitual present, 22, 41, 128
    present progressive, 36, 40–41, 43, 105,
        113, 120
    present time words, 116
    simple present, 22, 31–32, 41, 120–121
        with *be*, 4, 7, 11–13
        in *if*-clauses, 127–128
        negative, 29
        question forms, 30
        in time clauses, 126
Pronouns, defined, 5
    feminine/masculine, 5
    indefinite *(someone, anything)*, 159
    object *(me, them)*, 64
    possessive, 165
    subject *(I, they)*, 5–6, 64, 81–82, 85, 89

Pronunciation:
    can/can't, 134
    -s/-es, 26, 28
Punctuation:
    apostrophe, 6, 163
    comma, 106, 126, 176
    period, 12
    question mark, 12

Q

Quantity, expressions of, 156–157
Question mark, 12
Questions:
    with *be,* 12–13, 30, 40, 83
    with *be + going to,* 111, 120–121
    with *can,* 135
    with *could,* 137, 147
    with *did,* 91, 100
    with *do/does,* 30–33, 41, 144
    information, 31
    polite, 147
    with *there is/there are,* 50–51
    about time, 97, 104
    with *whose,* 166
    with *will,* 119–121
    yes/no, 31 (SEE ALSO Question words; Yes/no
        questions)
Question words, 18
    how many, 51
    what, 18, 33, 98, 100
    what time, 32–33, 97, 119
    when, 32–33, 97, 104, 119, 135
    where, 13, 31, 40, 97, 119, 135
    who, 18, 33, 98, 100
    who(m), 100
    why, 40, 97

S

-S/-es:
    plural nouns, 4–5, 65
    possessive nouns, 163
    simple present verbs, 22, 28
    spelling and pronunciation, 26, 28
Same, similar, different, 169
See, look at, watch, 43
Short answers, 12, 83, 91, 97–98
Should, 143, 149–150
    vs. *must,* 145
Similar (to), 169
Simple past, 81, 85
    irregular verbs, 87
    vs. past progressive, 107
    questions, 83, 91, 97
    summary of forms, 120–121

Simple present, 22, 28
    with *be,* 4, 7, 11–13
    in *if*-clauses, 127
    negative, 29
    vs. present progressive, 41
    present time words, 116
    questions, 30–32
    summary of forms, 120–121
    in time clauses, 126
Singular nouns, 65
    defined, 2
    with pronouns, 5, 22
Some, 69
    vs. *a/an,* 71
    vs. *any,* 79
Some of, 156
Someone/something, 159
Spelling:
    -ing, 38
    -s/-es, 26, 28
Subject, defined, 11
Subject pronouns, 5–6, 64, 81–82, 85, 89
Subjects and objects, 60
Subject-verb agreement, 156
Superlatives, *(most, -est),* 173, 175, 178

T

Tenses:
    future, 111, 113–116, 118, 126–128
    past progressive, 105–107
    present progressive, 36, 40–41, 105,
        113, 120
    simple past, 81, 85, 87, 89, 91, 97, 107,
        114–116, 120–121
    simple present, 22, 29, 116, 120–121
    in time clauses, 126
Than, 171
The, 76, 78
The same as, 169
There is/there are, 49
    in questions, 50–51
These/those, 17
Think about and *think that,* 44
This morning/afternoon, etc., 116
This/that, 17
Time:
    asking questions about, 97
    clauses, 103–104, 106, 126, 128
    prepositions of, 47, 103, 114
    present/past/future words, 114–116
    using *it,* 46
    ways of saying, 47
    (SEE ALSO Tenses)
Time clauses, 103–104
To, 140 (SEE ALSO Infinitives)

Today, tonight, this morning, etc., 116
Tomorrow, 114
Too, 139
Two vs. *too* vs. *to,* 140

V

Verbs:
    agreement with subject, 156
    after *but,* 177
    helping, 29, 36
    irregular, 27, 87, 92–94, 101–102
    linking, 160
    modal auxiliaries, 149–150
    not used in the present progressive, 43
    tense summary, 120
        forms of *be,* 121
    (SEE ALSO Tenses and individual items)
Very, 139
Voiced and voiceless sounds, 28

W

Want, 54
Was/were, 81–83, 105
Weather, talking about, 48
Well vs. *good,* 161
What, 18, 33, 40, 98, 100
What + a form of *do,* 33, 129
What time, 32–33, 97, 119
When, 32–33, 97, 104, 119, 126, 135
When-clause, 107
Where, 13, 31, 33, 40, 83, 97, 119, 135

While, 106
Who, 18, 98, 100
Who(m), 100
Who vs. *whose,* 166
Why, 40, 97
Will, 118–120, 149–150
    vs. *may/might,* 124
Would, 149–150
    in polite questions, 147
Would like, 55
    vs. *like,* 56

Y

-Y, words that end in, 4, 28, 65
Yes/no questions:
    with *be going to,* 111, 120–121
    with *can,* 135, 147
    with *could,* 147
    with *did,* 91, 100
    with *does/do,* 30–31
    with *is/are,* 12
        present progressive, 36, 40, 43
    with *may,* 147
    short answers to, 12
    there + *be,* 50
    with *was/were,* 83
    with *will,* 119–121
    with *would,* 147
    with *would like,* 55
Yesterday, last, ago, 86, 114